THE NATIONALIST REVIVAL IN FRANCE, 1905-1914

BY

EUGEN WEBER

UNIVERSITY OF CALIFORNIA PRESS
BERKELEY AND LOS ANGELES
1968

UNIVERSITY OF CALIFORNIA PUBLICATIONS IN HISTORY
Second Printing, 1968

UNIVERSITY OF CALIFORNIA PRESS
BERKELEY AND LOS ANGELES
CALIFORNIA

◇

CAMBRIDGE UNIVERSITY PRESS
LONDON, ENGLAND

TO

JACQUELINE

ACKNOWLEDGMENTS

I HAVE HAD THE OPPORTUNITY to discuss the events of this period with some of the men directly involved in them, and I am grateful to MM. Joseph Denais, Justin Godard, Paul Jacquier, Louis Marin, Henri Massis, J. Paul-Boncour, and Alexandre Zévaès for their opinions and memories. MM. Massis and Jacquier in particular gave me a great deal of their time: the former to discuss the atmosphere before 1914 and the position and ideas of Charles Maurras (some of whose private correspondence he allowed me to consult); the latter to clarify the policy and intentions of the Viviani cabinet of June 13, 1914, of which he is now the only surviving member. He assured me in this connection that, to his knowledge, there had been no talk of a revision of the Three-Year Law in the cabinet of which he was a member. This evidence is not final, but I have not been able to find anything conclusive on the subject. It has therefore seemed unwise to use it unsupported in the text, but necessary to mention.

My conversations with witnesses and students of events led to no new interpretations of the nationalist revival, and only in two instances to information that was in any way new or interesting. It is both possible and probable that some of my interlocutors had memories or knowledge which they preferred to keep to themselves, or hesitated to communicate to a young and unknown inquirer. It is also possible that some of them now knew the events in which they had taken part chiefly from books they had read (or written) since that time. History had taken the place of memory.

The National Archives and Records Service in Washington, D.C., whose contents are open after the lapse of twenty-five years (instead of the forty or fifty usual in European countries) yielded little to my purpose. The unfailing courtesy and helpfulness of the staff in the Army, Navy, and State Department sections could not make up for the gaps where papers were still classified, or where the local American agent had ignored certain events around him.

I have also been allowed to consult the Library and Archives of the Senate—now Conseil de la République—in which the minutes of certain committees are of some indicative interest. For this, and for all their help in my research, I must thank the Librarian, M. André Roussy, and the Assistant Librarian, Dr. J. Bécarud. I also owe my thanks to the staffs of the Bibliothèque nationale, the Cambridge University Library, and the Libraries of the University of California, Los Angeles and Berkeley, for their patient helpfulness. Most of all I am indebted to the men who, during the last few years, helped with their advice and suggestions: Professor D. W. Brogan of Peterhouse, who first suggested a subject that I have found fascinating; Dr. David Thomson of Sidney Sussex College; M. François Goguel of the Institut d'Etudes Politiques in Paris; Professor Gordon Wright of Stanford University; and the Master and Fellows of Emmanuel College, who made it possible for me to undertake this work and eventually to finish it.

CONTENTS

Introduction 1

PART ONE: THE FIRST REVIVAL

I. Mise en Scène: 1870–1904 19

II. The Reminder: 1904–1905 25

III. Algeçiras and After: 1905–1906 35

IV. The Interval 44

PART TWO: THE SMOLDERING

V. First Eddies: 1906–1908 55

VI. The Eternal Boulangism: 1908–1910 69

VII. The Intellectual Front: 1910–1911 77

VIII. Strain and Incoherence 85

PART THREE: THE SECOND REVIVAL

IX. The Turning Point: 1911–1912 93

X. Of Heroes and Hero-Worship: 1912–1913 106

XI. The Debate: 1913 120

XII. The Decision: 1913–1914 129

Conclusion 145

Notes 163

Bibliography 201

Biographical Notes 219

Index 235

INTRODUCTION

A nation is an in-group whose members coöperate to achieve certain ends. Yet the citizens compete with one another for the prizes of life. The need to cooperate is a frustrating factor in their lives. It leads inevitably to aggressions which tend to disrupt the group. Patriotism, national consciousness, group feeling (all are synonyms) is a force operating mostly at the level of the emotions to counteract the disruptive tendencies which, if unchecked, sometimes destroy group coherence. . . .

Nationalism is a sentiment. It is a thing which is less of the mind than of the emotions. It is a consciousness of the group, a feeling in the heart of the individual that his fate is inextricably bound up with those of his people. It is enhanced by external danger. (R. H. Gabriel, *The Course of American Democratic Thought.*)

IN 1939, A STUDY GROUP of the Royal Institute of International Affairs published a report on nationalism. As defined in an introductory note, the word was taken to mean a "consciousness of the distinctive character of different nations . . . and a desire to increase the strength, liberty, and prosperity of nations. Its effect is not necessarily taken as being confined to the individual's own nation . . . nor is the nationalist necessarily conceived as making the interest of his own nation supremely important."

This is not the phenomenon I am trying to capture and define; and the reason may be that the second part of the quotation ignores those undertones of chauvinism which in France were an integral part both of nationalist doctrine and of the nationalist mood. Although he frequently sought justification in principial argument, the French nationalist applied these principles only to France or French interests. If national unity was his main political objective, he remained constantly aware of the uses of a common hatred as a factor of social unanimity. But the mention of unanimity brings up the main difficulty facing an inquiry into nationalism. Even with the exclusion of such motives and circumstances as do not apply to the France of 1905–1914, almost every party nursed its own species of nationalism—Royalist, Jacobin, Bonapartist, Poincarist, and so on. It seems impossible to extract, with any coherence, that element of each which might correctly be called nationalism, and then amalgamate all these abstractions into a thing called the "nationalist revival."

Yet the thesis of the nationalist revival has become an accepted convention of French historians, who are apt to work back from this acceptance to illuminate a situation in whose existence they already believe. On such a quest, in a period whose *ambiance* is taken for granted, facts come to matter less than assumptions. I am reminded of Taine's famous question to Gabriel Monod who was going to do some research work in Italy: "And what theory are you going to verify there?"

[1]

This is a danger to beware, and one to which it is easy to succumb. It would be simple to begin by assuming nationalism, to make the study of the period a study of the nationalist atmosphere and of the nationalist state of mind: their inception, their development, and their effects. The work would not be so much one of discovery as of identification, and its results would be more interesting psychologically than historically. In doing this, the writer would presumably consider nationalism a definite state of mind, an identification of self and nation which places the nation above moral standards and accepts no higher duty than that of advancing national interest. He would certainly mention Maurras and certainly Hegel, both of whom seek to enlist the Church in the service of the state —a state whose good is not merely beyond the law, but is actually the essence of the law.

This kind of nationalism may be found together with patriotism, but has little in common with it except by accident and thus is not pertinent to this period in France. Nor do I propose to adopt the method described above, the more so since my purposes are to identify the phenomenon others take for granted and to try to understand the connection of nationalism and patriotism in its make-up. I must, in theory, distinguish between two forces that are easily confused, a threat unavoidably posed throughout the course of this work. Patriotism may be defined as love of a particular place, of a particular way of life above all others. But this love does not imply a desire to foist it on others; it is more likely to imply a reluctance to share.[1] And so, patriotism, far from being expansive or offensive, is intrinsically a defensive attitude.

This is not true of nationalism. "The abiding purpose of every nationalist," writes George Orwell, "is to secure more power and more prestige, *not* for himself but for the nation or other unit in which he has chosen to sink his own individuality." If this is so, it is clear how patriotism may become nationalism—or may be led to take up an attitude not very different outwardly from the obvious manifestations of nationalism. A defensive patriot who feels or fears a threat to the object of his affections may bristle and react the same as an offensive nationalist.

In the decade 1905–1914, little or no trace of the liberal nationalism of the nineteenth century was left in France. The term had been used by the heirs of Boulanger, and, in the elections of 1898, nationalists and anti-Semites (Drumont among the latter) had by their exertions made the country familiar with it as the title and doctrine of a political group. This group stood for *revanche*, for national unity and power based on traditional institutions (Church and army first among them), for clearing out Jews and other foreigners (at least from positions of political, economic, and social power, if not from the country itself), and for an indefinite measure of constitutional revision. It radiated an acute and often exclusive patriotism that blended well with *revanchard* aspirations and with that exaltation of the army which became one of the chief legacies of the Dreyfus Affair to the Right. These were the most obvious characteristics of what I will call the old nationalism, as distinguished from the new nationalism of the present century.

In the prewar years, after the old nationalism had had its day, a new nationalism appeared, an occurrence frequently described as a "revival." A study of this phenomenon, which in effect is largely a change in atmosphere, a change in the mood of the nation or in the temper and attitude of its politically significant minority, will tend to be a study of opinions, private and public, which may be known from recorded evidence and which affected the temper and policy of the country as a whole.

Such a study cannot hope to be exhaustive for simple reasons of time, opportunity, and availability of evidence. Fortunately, so much has been written on the political and diplomatic history of these years that there is no need for more than the barest indication of the relevant background, and the narrative can proceed without redundant passages devoted, say, to the simultaneous development of German foreign policy. Therefore, I have deliberately refrained from overelaborating the international scene, where the wealth of work already available makes such information superfluous. Just as deliberately, I have favored the *how?* at the expense of the *why?* that I could only indifferently answer here. Within these limits, however, I have tried to provide a useful, accurate picture of the changing temper of the country and, especially, of the opinions and actions of the politically significant men or groups.

This particular minority includes the leaders, militant members and parliamentary representatives of political parties, writers and journalists, bodies (like the Institut, the Université, or the unions) representative or creative of vested interests, and private individuals whose position in government service (Paléologue, Cambon) or in society (Boni de Castellane) gave weight to their opinions. It is a long time since, in his brilliant study, *French Public Opinion and Foreign Policy*, Professor Malcolm Carroll pointed out what no student of France can afford to ignore—the peculiar importance of the leaders of opinion, a social and intellectual élite, closely interconnected, often from the Grandes Ecoles–Normale, Polytechnique, or Sciences Politiques. A striking illustration of the position of the latter is that nearly 95 per cent of the men appointed to the diplomatic and consular services between 1907 and 1927 were selected from its graduates.[2] Only England might be able to offer (and it is a debatable point) a similar picture of a politically significant minority made up of intellectuals, lawyers, dons, and businessmen, all highly articulate, all rubbing elbows in the same circles, setting the tone not only of society but of a national climate of opinion and taste, focusing in their enthusiasms and their disputes the issues of national concern or policy. A study of these personalities and their activities can leave no doubt that between 1905 and 1914 a definite change had taken place in the language used and the policies advocated, and this change stood in direct relation to the phenomenon that contemporary and later historians and commentators have described as nationalism.

This change, which I have called a change of atmosphere, resembles closely what stock market operators describe as the "sentiment" of the market, a sentiment inclined to be bullish for concrete reasons of fact and also for intangible reasons of mood begotten by rumor or other mysterious causes. It is seen most clearly in the changing purposes of political activity and the changing slogans and war cries of the years. The adoption or the abandonment of a slogan or a doctrine shows the politician's awareness of its usefulness as a tool no less (and probably more) than his conviction of its intrinsic worth. Doctrines and opinions count for a great deal when they provide so much of the raw material of political dispute. There is no ignoring the constant interaction between doctrine and opinion on the one hand, between opinion and action on the other; nor the fact that doctrines insignificant in themselves may become highly significant when they arm men against each other.

If doctrines are to reach a wider public, they must be simplified. This usually means they are oversimplified to an extent that alters their original content or meaning. Thucydides warned that in civil war ideas lose their accustomed meaning and are adapted to the requirements of action. They are rendered down and turned, to paraphrase Walter Lippmann, from a vague, confused and confusing medley into a canalized, compressed force.

The making of one general will out of a multitude of general wishes . . . consists essentially in the use of symbols which assemble emotions after they have been detached from their ideas. . . . The process, therefore, by which general opinions are brought to cooperation consists in an intensification of feeling and a degradation of significance.[3]

It is this compression and canalization of a multitude of vague general wishes which explains the seeming uniformity of a phenomenon that under closer examination is seen to have consisted of a variety of doctrines and activities. These did not necessarily tend consciously to the same end, but they were gathered up by the "sentiment" of the time and channeled into apparent and temporary unity. The manifestation of this phenomenon, of the rising tide of nationalism, was as early as 1910 sufficiently impressive to make Maurras speak of it as an *idée conquérante* and Romain Rolland, looking back on these years, voices a similar impression.[4]

But if, as Thibaudet has written, *la politique, ce sont des idées,* François Goguel and G. E. Lavaud have qualified his statement by showing that politics are molded not only by ideas, not only by interests, but also by temperaments which affect men and groups in irrational and almost instinctive ways.

We cannot ignore identities of temper and prejudice influencing those attitudes that played an immense though seldom tangible part in the apparent unity of the nationalist revival. "We are not working toward the same solution," said Boni de Castellane to Déroulède, "but we both have the same hatreds and the same loathings." However, beneath the label imposed by common interest or by subsequent simplification of complex historical developments, the diversity of reactions in the country at large was striking.

To some people nationalism bespoke a challenge of principle, to others a challenge of interests. To some it was an early awareness of danger, foreign or social; to some it was intermittent outbursts of feelings that smoldered between intervals of brief, bright flaring; to others it never came at all. Such differences will be made clearer in the course of this book. But the causes underlying these differences can be appreciated only in the light of factors as varied as geography, religion, education, and, not least, the nature and traditions of political parties.

The challenge of nationalism, where and when it became apparent as a challenge, tended to take on local tones and shadings to such an extent that only with difficulty could it be considered apart from local problems. Consequently, different parts of France reacted variously and characteristically to the same issue. Some of the differences may be ascribed to long-standing attachments of regions for certain parties, such as that of the west for the Right.[5] Other traditions of more recent origin were apparently no less powerful: for instance, the patriotic and Jacobin tradition of Paris (its rebellious nature is of longer standing); the post-1871 inclination of the eastern provinces toward *revanchard* and nationalist claims;[6] and the Dreyfusist mystique that dominated the Sorbonne after the Affair.

Forms of peasant tenure have been cited by Siegfried and others as influencing the political orientation of a region; but industrialization and the consequent shifts and concentrations of population brought changes in traditional local allegiances. Thus, in the north, traditionally Catholic and Right-Wing areas were colonized by Left-voting workers. Paris, still artisan and bourgeois near the center, developed on the outskirts, especially to the north, Left-Wing electorates based on a self-conscious working-class population, destined to stay consistently on the Left to our own day. Lastly, documents published since 1917 have made very clear the important role of vested interests, such as the colonial or armaments industry, pressure groups that often influenced particular men or localities in a certain direction.[7] Were a graph traced of the fortunes of the nationalist ideas in France, the line would be a wavy one, and the graph would be incorrect unless made of a diversity of lines: personal, local, regional lines; lines representing social groups, vested interests, ideological and political tendencies, and so on.

At any rate, to begin with, the nationalists might be assumed to comprise a minority, if only because nationalism implies a positive attitude toward society and toward personal values, and might almost call for the manufacture and preservation of a crisis atmosphere; and few people are likely to maintain the intensity required. Patriotism, however, depends on acceptance of traditional manners and traditional values, and thus patriots may well be more numerous. It might even be assumed (though this is more risky) that the patriotic attitude was the norm during this period, and the nationalist as defined above was exceptional. Even if these assumptions hold good for the opening years of the decade 1905 to 1914, as the period progresses, the difference between nationalism and patriotism becomes increasingly blurred.

My aim is to discover why, by 1914, practically all French political parties had come round to supporting drastic measures of military preparedness against Germany, and to supporting Poincaré. The answer is in part the accumulated consequence of German pressure, German challenges, fear of war and press campaigns that fed, and fed on, all these things. Further, the new nationalism was the product of an interaction between these external and other internal developments, and it was specifically the events between 1905 and 1913 which gave force to the arguments of the ultranationalist writers and persuaded the patriotic mice to follow the nationalist piper.

If that be so, there is an excuse for the somewhat restricted scope of this book, which concentrates attention on Paris. In terms of political and cultural activity, Paris has long been the center of France. As Versailles under the monarchy, so Paris under the Republic was the place where things could be done, where men could get on, *la foire sur la place* where centered the strings of myriad social, economic, and cultural activities.

It would be a mistake, certainly, to think of French public opinion as united and as gradually rising against the German threat, even though broadly and superficially this is the picture. Public opinion is never wholly united, never wholly coherent, and seldom rises to a pitch of passion without being influenced by propaganda. Such propaganda came wholly from Paris—through the books and newspapers, conferences, and public speakers (even if they were not all Parisians themselves), each carrying a point of view forged in Paris.

The two or three village notables, and anybody else who read the provincial press, were the local counterpart of the national *minorité agissante* at work in Paris. But the provincial editors also read the Paris papers, maintained a Paris office if they could afford it, subscribed to a Paris agency otherwise, and the Paris Letter was a staple feature of the local newspaper. The most widespread provincial newspaper, *La Croix*, was itself little more than a copy of the Parisian *editio princeps*, and even great provincial dailies like the *Dépêche de Toulouse* or the *Progrès de Lyon* often read as echoes of the Paris papers.

No doubt parliamentarians still looked toward their constituencies with moderate apprehension and ran their constituents' errands in Paris ministries, but the movement for parliamentary emancipation was already under way, and proportional representation, designed to free the deputy from too close dependence on his electors, would be part of the platform on which a "nationalist" coalition fought and won the elections of 1919. Meanwhile, in general, provincial influence made for peace against rearmament and expense. The exceptions, in the west, in the east, and in one or two departments, occurred in regions that had long voted the same ticket for reasons that had little to do with the new nationalism.

I have said that the anxiety for French unity and power and preparedness welcomed help from any quarter.[8] And, insofar as men or movements of an earlier time influenced the new nationalism (as did the Action française), they shall be considered. The essence of this book, however, is not the more or less steadfast long-continuing patriotism of men, institutions, or regions, but the new and acute patriotism of men, institutions, and regions that had not been nationalistic or that had followed nationalism *en sourdine*. There is nothing particularly striking in the sustained patriotic affirmations of Barrès, of dignitaries of the Catholic Church, or of the Vendée, but when sound anticlerical republicans like Thomson and Messimy, and one-time Dreyfusist strongholds like the Ecole Normale, begin to get on the band wagon, something new has happened, something worth investigating.[9]

It might be well to connect this phenomenon with what seems to have been its principal cause—fear: fear of war, fear of social revolution, fear of those private opinions whose vociferousness enabled them to pass for public opinion. Of these fears the most constant, the most widespread, was that of war. Even this did not prevail at all times or in all places. From the point of view of the politically significant, most of the activity was localized around Paris. There, and even more in the country at large, the tale is one of alarms that, as in 1905, were soon forgotten by the general public. Only a few men realized and remembered the import of such alarms; and it was their activity—the activity of a minority in the streets, in the press, or in government—that furbished and used the new nationalism. Passing crises affected public opinion only fleetingly, and it was not until 1911 that a significant minority in the nation became aware of the threat of war, or that the nationalist revival came to be really recognized at home and abroad.

This minority character of nationalism cannot be sufficiently stressed. During this period self-acknowledged nationalists were few. In the streets they turned out in thousands whereas the Socialists, for instance, came out in hundreds of thousands. In the Chamber their respectable showing of 1902 shrank from 54 to 26 by 1906, and of these 26, 15 were also members of Jacques Piou's Action Libérale. The elections of 1910 again reduced their numbers. In fact, since in the new Chamber deputies could no longer adhere to more than one group, the nationalists as a group disappeared altogether. Most of them joined the group of Independents, itself only 20 strong. Henceforth the name will remain absent from the roll of parties; and this happens just when its currency in the country begins to increase.[10] No important politician, no Delcassé, Millerand, Poincaré, not even Albert de Mun, called himself a nationalist. Nationalists were the demagogues like Déroulède, the *littérateurs* like Barrès, the polemists like Drumont, and though others may borrow their formulas, they do not borrow their name. The nationalist revival was the great booming echo of a small sharp voice.

The many facets of nationalism will become apparent as the development of the movement is traced from a historical standpoint. The interest of such a development lies, on the one hand, in the details of its nature and, on the other hand, in the part it played in changing the direction and temper of French politics during these years. Because, as I shall show, from indifferent or pacifist in 1905, the temper of French opinion and the trend of French policy had by 1913 and 1914 become positive, self-assertive, and, if not warlike, at least aware of the danger of war. In an interesting study of French politics, 1898–1905,[11] Miss B. R. Leaman notes the extreme self-centeredness of French political life during those years and is moved to ask "why with a pacifistic party in control of the government did France become so nationalistic by 1914?" Part of the answer would be, of course, that the pacifistic party did not remain in control of the government for long after 1905, and it was not "France" but an important group in power which became nationalistic.

But first, since the term "nationalist revival" is to be used, what was it that revived? For nationalism to revive, it would have had to have been there before and then disappeared by 1905 or 1911, when, according to commonly accepted theories, the embers stirred and a new nationalism appeared from the ashes of the old. While a nationalism had in effect flourished shortly before 1905 and died (in terms of political effectiveness), the new nationalism that appeared after that date had little in common with the old except the name. Perhaps to say "little" is not entirely fair, for the new nationalism was deeply influenced and constantly prodded by many of the troops and the leaders of the old creed, politically defeated but still highly vocal.

Although many of the nationalists of 1898 continued active during the next twenty years, among the masses and also at the levers of power the new nationalism was different from the old, and its politically effective components were not the divisive slogans of the nationalist parties, anti-Semitic, royalist, or even particularly *revanchard*, but the patriotic reactions of frightened and resentful men seeking national union and preparedness, not for attack but for defense. That they borrowed many of the attitudes and the catchwords of the old nationalists was not surprising nor, considering the resentment of German bluster which both groups shared, was their eventual entente to wonder at.

But in this *entente tacite* the old nationalists played only a minor part. The former leaders did not inspire or direct the self-conscious national revival after 1911. In the words of anxious Belgian observers, "ce sont, en effet, MM. Poincaré, Delcassé, Millerand et leurs amis qui ont inventé et poursuivi la politique nationaliste, cocardière et chauvine dont nous avons constaté la renaissance." And Barrès admitted as early as 1910 that "we cannot do better than Millerand and Briand."[12]

The old nationalist leaders and troops rode the crest of a wave that the Germans, and perhaps also the Socialists, had set in motion. Maurras himself admitted in a later preface to *Kiel et Tanger* that the development of events had gained wider acceptance for his ideas; any other interpretation would be comparable to the mistake of the man who, happening to stamp his foot at the moment of an earthquake, takes the tremor to be the result of his impetuous force.

Thus, although the old nationalism also revived and with it activities and excesses familiar to the country in the nineties, the new nationalism that dominates the years after 1911, with beginnings as early as 1905, should not be confused with it. A division existed in spite of the similarity of much of the activity, in spite also of the apparent confusion in the minds of its votaries and observers.[13]

The difference is not easy to explain in theory. One possible touchstone would be that of constitutional respectability: the leaders of the old nationalism, journalists and demagogues like Déroulède, Habert, Maurras, used and generally advocated violence; the leaders of the new nationalism were politicians careful of the established order. Poincaré, Millerand, Barthou, or Piou would not have advocated unconstitutional action beyond the limits of ordinary political skulduggery. Such a touchstone is not foolproof. For example, Barrès, one of the great elders of the old nationalism, as a rule discouraged violence and felt himself to be a good republican. The same might be said of Charles Benoist, and few doubted the respectability of Albert Meyer in spite of his fervent royalism.

The judgment of the public at large, if not well motivated intellectually, was founded on a sound feeling for political realities and, above all, for internal peace and social order. A citizen could afford to be nationalist with a respectable politician like Poincaré, or with a respectable newspaper like *Le Gaulois* that had a solid vested interest in the established order and whose nationalism tended to defend those values. But the same phrases repeated by a Déroulède, or in the columns of *La Patrie*, might lead to an attack on that very social order. Threats to this established system aroused in the public patriotism and national self-assertiveness to the level of a national revival.

There can be little clarity about such definitions because there was little clarity about the kinds of nationalism those years witnessed. These differences will be more apparent to a reader than to the people involved in them. There is the possibility that only the memory of past nationalist activity provided the variety of defensive reactions called forth under the *passe partout* title of nationalist revival. The vagueness of this phenomenon necessarily brings about a vagueness of definition.

An analysis of the nationalist platform shows it to be simple, concrete, and not altogether unlike that of the old nationalists. The power and preëminence of France—military, economic, and cultural—with its concomitants of national unity, political and social discipline, and rearmament, appear by 1914 in all party programs right of the Socialists and the hard core of "unified" Radical-Socialists. A lowest common denominator would be some form of appeal to authority and tradition. The need felt by a portion of French society for social order, discipline, firm government, strong policies at home and abroad, made this society look to tradition for an answer to its problems. Here royalism reaped its harvests, and so did the impressive solidity of the Catholic Church. Practical men conveniently forgot the hooliganism of the Action française or the anti-republicanism of the Church, to remember only the usefulness of both as defenders of property and social order.

But social defense is not the originating factor of the new nationalism; otherwise it might well have appeared sooner and grown more steadily and in another form. The nationalist phenomenon of the prewar years cannot be understood except in connection with foreign policy and foreign threats. When Barrès reëntered the Chamber in 1908, a friend wrote to congratulate him and commiserate on his returning at the very moment when the nationalism he had created had almost entirely disappeared from the Palais Bourbon. A little less than two years later, Barrès still bewailed the fact that the idea of revenge was forgotten or dead. And yet by October, 1912, the democrat Marc Sangnier noted the obvious awakening of the national idea, and Elie Halévy related that the Viviani cabinet of 1914 "pursued no more ambitious aim than to prevent the Chamber of Deputies in its very first session from repealing the Three Year Service Bill."[14]

What had happened between 1910 and 1912? The events of 1911 persuaded many of the pacific, the hesitant, and the indifferent that the threat to France was real and that war was only a matter of time. Thus, preparedness should be the country's first concern, and preparedness required not only the improvement of existing military arrangements, but also the forging of national unity and the building of national morale. Pursuing such ends, patriotic republicans came easily enough to terms with other groups and men on the fringe of and even outside the recognized republican circles.

The Church and the Right, whose policy had remained virtually unchanged, found themselves in an agreeable position now that the swing of the pendulum, hastened by the German push, brought all good republicans back to the patriotic platform of discipline, unity, and fatherland.

Behind the *protestations de rigueur*, Poincaré's decision to adopt Jeanne d'Arc's day as a national holiday marked the new alliance, and his election to the presidency with the votes of the Right sealed it.

The nationalist idea of the superiority and strength of France was not new in the politics of the Third Republic. After 1871, nationalism in France had been associated with the Left; chauvinism had been the preserve of the uncultured, of the masses. The Jacobin tradition of the Left was not dead. Everybody remembered its latest eruption in the Commune and in the efforts and peregrinations of Gambetta.

Gambetta had been considered dangerous for fear that his *revanchard* intransigence might endanger the peace of France. But Gambetta's thought evolved as did his position, and increased power brought with it increased inclination to compromise. His heirs, first Ferry, then Méline, sought peace without forgetting that much of their moderate republican support lay in the patriotic and vengeful eastern departments. Since the danger of war lay on the Rhine, they concentrated on reconciling colonial and financial expansion with a policy of *détente* toward Germany. This gave their supporters the satisfaction of French successes without the dangers of a German war.

These were moderate men, and a positive policy along such theoretical lines as those which the nationalists advocated could not be expected from them. Thus the nationalist and *revanchard* arguments became convenient weapons in the hands of the opposition, ready to be brandished at need as a bloody shirt. Nationalism remained a radical monopoly for many years. Boulanger, for one, rose first to power, then to notoriety, with radical help. His chief enemy was Jules Ferry. But the story of Boulanger is typical of the nationalist movements that relied on a single leader, and on the enthusiasms and prejudices of individuals rather than of wider groups.

When faced with the opposition of established parties, Boulanger collapsed, and his fragile structure collapsed with him. If Boulangism lived on, it was not through some strange virtue of its teaching, but because it was itself the transient, convenient expression of a tendency that took different forms and labels, sought different support, but remained fundamentally constant in character and aim. It is worth noting that in the regions most inclined toward it, the north, the east, and Paris, Boulangism reaped some of its most interesting successes—the general's triumphant elections in the north and in Paris, the victory of young Barrès at Nancy, and the eventual defeat of Jules Ferry in his own Vosges constituency.

It has been said that the Dreyfus Affair was the last effort of the Boulangist spirit. This is, however, giving too much importance to one reflection of a tendency much longer-lived than some historians care to acknowledge, or are able to discern.

In *L'Appel au Soldat*, Maurice Barrès makes his young hero, Sturel, vow after the general's fall: "Nous retrouverons des autres boulangismes." Had he lived, Sturel would not have been too old to take an active part in the nationalist revival of 1911, and many of Sturel's old companions did. Sturel's creator carried his ideas through the years, giving them first coherence, then a name. In 1892 he first used the word "nationalism" in an article concerning the then-current debate between partisans of the classical French tradition and romantic admirers of Tolstoi, Ibsen, and Maeterlinck.[15] The transition from literary nationalism to political nationalism did not take long. But this nationalism *à la Barrès* was still republican, traditionalist, respectful of the established order even when Barrès disapproved of it.[16] Out of the Dreyfus Affair, however, inspired by Barrès but differing from him on many points, grew another nationalism. It was a rebellious nationalism, antirepublican, whose assertive traditionalism rejected a whole century of French tradition, revolutionary because royalist, and nationalist by reaction against the foreign elements in French life and culture.

Perhaps these new characteristics were due, at least in part, to the loss of electoral influence, and to the series of disastrous defeats inflicted upon the Right in general and upon nationalist candidates in particular, at all elections after 1898. André Siegfried has pointed out that the original inspiration of Boulangism had been democratic, and that only later did it become, by virtue of its alliances and electoral position, an element of the Right-Wing coalition. Nationalism, too, always tried the door until, persuaded of the inutility of such law-abiding behavior, it decided that a scullery window or even a hole in the wall would be a simpler way of obtaining access to the citadel of political power.

In the mood that prevailed in the prewar years, the propaganda of the old nationalists had its clear share; their preaching heightened the defensive tone of France, and also the aggrievedly offensive tone of Germany. Effect and cause were so closely interconnected that they are even now inseparable. Paris, too, must be granted its proper importance. The city had been revolutionary when the government was conservative, radical when the government was moderate. Boulanger had flourished to its cheers in 1889, anti-*Dreyfusard* nationalism had thrived there ten years later. Before 1914 Paris was to see the greater part of the new nationalist ferment.

This is important because, whatever its connection with some regions, the nationalism of 1905–1914 was a product of the capital, and was based on the same prejudicial emotions that had carried its predecessors to the precarious popularity of the Paris streets. Its success and its failure stem from this Parisian origin and base. It never went far beyond. While it struck up alliances, largely tacit, in regions faithful to some of the sentiments it represented, it could never aspire to electoral success based on those areas almost wholly enfeuded to the Radicals. But nationalism seeped into Paris life, thought, and society, and through them dominated and influenced the representatives of the provinces which by itself it could not impress.

From this point of view the struggle for the Three-Year Law of military service, which took place during 1913 and 1914, marked the apex of nationalist influence. The indecision of most deputies, pulled one way by their pacific and close-fisted electorate, another way by nationalist Paris and by their own growing awareness of the pressing danger, was finally settled by the coming of war in 1914.

National opinion had made itself clearly known, and the men returned in the elections of 1914 were in power with a mandate to secure peace.[17] Instead, they implemented the Three-Year Law. The French people had voted against a longer spell in uniform for their young men, against higher taxes, against the "warlike" policy of Poincaré. Patriots themselves, they did not care for chauvinsim. Prudent, they did not care for armaments. Pacific, they ignored foreign threats, feared rather their own politicians, and distrusted the army. Being provincial, they rejected Paris. This is not to say they were right or wrong. Even at this distance, it is not clear whether a different attitude on their part, or on the part of their leaders, would have brought different results, let alone better ones.

How long could the structure built during those years—founded on fear, exaggeration, idealism, hatred, great love for France, sincere desire for peace, pride, ambition, love of glory, and other such diverse materials as comprise all history—have lasted? Perhaps it was not meant to last. The events our heroes had foreseen drew them from their quandary.

That is only one aspect of the story. There is another that has greater importance in time.

The politics of the Third Republic, as those of all French régimes since 1815, were warped from the beginning by the existence of a large minority who did not accept either the Republic or the parliamentary system. Parliamentary politics is a game that cannot be played if its rules are not accepted by all the players. The existence of parties that would not play according to the rules, whose triumph implied in effect the end of the Republic, prevented a normal expression of political opinion and the free play of political tendencies. For a long time, whatever their opinions on any one issue, parties and party lines were confused by the "crisis mentality" that frequently forced all republicans to unite in opposing all antirepublicans. This prevented the clear debate of other issues: every few years, the natural antagonisms, of which politics are the expression and the spur, had to give way while the republicans rallied to the defense of the régime itself.

There could never be a conservative party in the Third Republic as long as conservative forces were divided by this fence. The natural development, after 1875, would have been for the Right to accept the régime, and, this obstacle out of the way, to coöperate increasingly with the moderate republicans whose opinions hardly differed from their own. The intransigent attitude of the Right, however, led them to choose a *politique du pire*, by which they would actively or tacitly support first Radicals, and later Socialists, against those moderate republicans with whom they could so easily have found a common ground. This policy, abandoned for only short intervals, is one explanation of the political impotence of the Third Republic.[18]

In a very few instances, though, it seemed that the Right, moving away from its habitual refusal to compromise, would loyally take part in the politics of the nation in a positive and creative way. Such an attitude could have led eventually to participation in the government and, above all, to the balancing of the political scene. It happened for the first time when Rouvier formed his cabinet in 1887. The cabinet was composed of moderates and supported by the Right.

Already in 1886, Jules Ferry, still the conscience of moderate republicanism, had called for a conservative party, to him a necessity for a well-constituted republic. When the Rouvier ministry consecrated the split between moderates and radicals, a supporter of Ferry, André Lebon, called it the greatest crisis since May 16, 1877, when President MacMahon had started his ill-fated fight against the republican majority by dismissing the government of Jules Simon. Seignobos was to call it the origin of a new party alignment, but it was not so much the origin as the suggestion, and the superior calls of republican discipline were to disintegrate the tenuous alliance again and again.

The second time such a thing happened was in the middle 'nineties when, around the cabinets of Ribot, Dupuy, and Méline, a coalition of the groups of the center had dominated the Chamber. Its bases had been religious appeasement and a common front against working-class demands for social reform.

The third occasion was when, around the person of Poincaré, a fresh moderate union, exalting the army as in 1898, opposing income tax as in 1898, inspired by the will of the moderate, patriotic center to defend France and themselves against foreign and social danger, came into being about 1912. After that date, coöperation between Right and center increased, irrespective of the Catholicism or republicanism of the parties concerned. To Albert de Mun, National Union had been sealed by the pact of January 17, 1913, the date of Poincaré's election to the presidency of the Republic. "This cannot be forgotten," he wrote, "any more than the vote of the military law. The Union shall not be made without us."[19] It was made with them. The events following the elections of 1914, far from bringing it to an end, were rather an indication of its stubborn endurance.

It is debatable whether Viviani's cabinet intended to revise the Three-Year Law. All concerned have every interest not to admit the intention of such a revision, even if it existed. What evidence there is supports the supposition that the government had accepted the *status quo*. The coming of war saved the cabinet from taking a stand that might well have proved fatal to its continued existence. After the war, the National Union of 1919 and the behavior of the "Sky-Blue" Chamber elected in that year, seemed to reflect the new confidence and will to coöperate which the parties had acquired at the beginning of the decade—the new habit of working together, confirmed by wartime experience.

If this is so, and the evidence of other studies seems to support the possibility,[20] then the nationalist revival acquires new significance. It offers the possibility of an entente of the centers, which could eventually have become a coherent conservative party. This is no mere supposition. The three years before the outbreak of war, when the atmosphere served as a catalyst, show that such coöperation was possible. The atmosphere may have proved short-lived. It would have done its work, however, could it have continuously engendered, as it did for a short time, a coherent alliance, based on common acceptance of such fundamentals as patriotism and social defense within the existing system of government. It is possible that the introduction of a form of proportional representation in 1919, by facilitating the multiplication of parties, helped to warp the development. It may not have survived long in any case. But it is worthwhile to note that, in itself, the introduction of proportional representation in 1919 was an indication that the Union, which had been one of the many objectives of the nationalists of 1911–1914, had broadened and already bred a certain amount of confidence.

Much history has already been written around *ifs*. It is not my intention to do this. But a movement, significant in itself and influential in the affairs of its time, may also have a potential importance that the historian must not forget.

I have tried in the following pages to tell the story of such a movement that, while recognized, has not hitherto been explored, but to tell it by letting men and events speak for themselves. When developments can tell their own story, it is better that, insofar as possible, the historian should remain unobtrusive.

PART ONE

THE FIRST REVIVAL

CHAPTER I

MISE EN SCÈNE: 1870–1904

My intention is rather to pursue the Method of those writers who profess to describe the revolutions of countries than to imitate the painful and voluminous historian who, to preserve the regularity of his series, thinks himself obliged to fill up as much paper with the details of months and years in which nothing remarkable happened, as he employs upon those notable eras when the great scenes have been transacted upon the human stage. Now it is our purpose in the ensuing pages to pursue a contrary method. When any extraordinary scene presents itself we shall spare no pains nor paper to open it at large to our reader, but if whole years should pass without producing anything worthy his notice we shall not be afraid of a chasm in our history, but shall hasten on to matters of consequence and leave such periods of time totally unobserved. (Henry Fielding, *Tom Jones.*)

THE THIRD REPUBLIC, founded on unwilling compromise, was never taken for granted by either its supporters or its opponents. The story of its first thirty years can be told in terms of the struggle between republicans and antirepublicans. The series of republican electoral victories, beginning in 1877 and ending with Grévy's election to the presidency in January, 1879, were never accepted as final by the antirepublican Right. On November 14, 1877, de Broglie had said in the Chamber: "The Republic means radicalism, and radicalism means social confusion; there is no middle way." The conservative republicans, of whose ascendancy Grévy was the symbol, applied themselves to prove him wrong. But their moderate regime was attacked by both the extremes.

Evidently, the Right questioned the very existence of the regime, whereas the Left questioned only its program. This explains why in moments of crisis all republicans formed square to defend the Republic that had to continue if they wanted to continue themselves. These temporary alliances, accepting lesser evils to avoid greater, did not prevent fierce political struggles, nor, for that matter, did they prevent repeated attempts to arrange the coöperation of the ends against the center.[1]

The moderate regime lasted long enough to lay the foundations of the Republic. Its first chapter ended in 1885 with the fall of Jules Ferry. It is certain that he had, during the six years in which he dominated the country's political scene, indicated the problems that were to color the following years. His education laws recognized the necessity of an educated electorate and pointed out—indeed, to some extent created—the Republic's most constant antagonist, the Church.

His colonial policy, carried on largely against the popular will, established France in Indochina and Tunis. He fell, but none of his actions were, in fact, denied by his successors, many of whom he had influenced. It should be pointed out that Ferry's first cabinet contained two future premiers, Tirard and Fallières, and two future presidents of the Republic, Fallières and Sadi Carnot. His second cabinet, improving on the first, contained five future premiers, Waldeck-Rousseau, Tirard, Rouvier, Méline, Casimir-Périer, one former premier, Fallières, and three future presidents, Fallières, Casimir-Périer, and Félix Faure: six premiers and four presidents of the Republic passed through Ferry's political nursery.

The fall of Jules Ferry opened a period of muddle and incoherence. The conservative republicans, still in power, did not know whether to be conservative or republican, and the two positions became ever more difficult to reconcile. The threat of a Royalist victory in the elections of 1885 reminded them of the importance of the Radical Left, and led to a moment of republican concentration. But the Left were divided and unreliable. Confusion was only worse confounded by the first stirrings of the Catholic *ralliement* to the republican regime, heralded by Raoul Duval in 1886.[2] A Rouvier cabinet in 1887 reflected the break between the republican center and the Left, and the growing accord between center and Right.

This was the situation when, in the autumn of 1887, the news leaked out of a nest of corruption in the Elysée itself. Daniel Wilson, Grévy's son-in-law and deputy of Indre-et-Loire, was compromised in a scandal over the sale of decorations and other favors. The scandal was taken to reveal widespread corruption in high places. Wilson was neither the only nor the worst offender, but his position made him the butt of all polemics and, involved in the storm of abuse, Grévy himself was forced to resign his office.

It was against this political background that a movement grew up around the person of the popular minister of war, General Boulanger. The general himself, cast for the part of National Savior first by the Radical Left, then by the royalist and Bonapartist Right, was not up to the part either side expected him to play. While his more idealistic followers called for constitutional revision and the clean-up of politics, and others saw in him a Monck restorer of the monarchy, his popularity in the country as a whole was due to his personifying the desire for revenge against Germany.[3] The German attitude toward France, with its repeated threats and attempted humiliations, had kept alive the hatreds of 1870–1871. Boulanger had found occasion to stand up to the Germans —Boulanger in power would be revenge on the march.

Political maneuvers apart, patriotism and patriots became identified with the cause of Boulanger, an identification still persistent when the leader himself had disappeared. The myth served the purpose better than the man. In the myth, however, diverse tendencies were to meet, which until then had had little in common. The initial strength of Boulangism had come from the patriotic and republican middle classes. It had begun, as André Siegfried tells us, "as an essentially republican movement, much more spontaneous than has been admitted, which placed in the general the hopes of a radicalism that was national, extraparliamentary, and exaltedly patriotic."[4] But in its second phase, in order to oppose the parliamentary republic, Boulangists entered into alliance with Bonapartists and royalists, on the ground that sharing the same enemies can make a friendship. Before the flight of Boulanger put paid to its hopes, the whole movement had evolved from Left to Right. More correctly, perhaps, while its popular support remained the same, the sources of financial and political support had shifted to the Right, and the inspiration of the party shifted with the sources.

The return to conservatism was not greatly affected by the financial scandals caused by the crash of the Panama Canal Company. Founded to cut a canal between Atlantic and Pacific, the company, directed by the de Lesseps, father and son, had attracted millions from small investors. The company apparently spent the greatest part thereof on publicity and some on bribes to legislators who might smooth its path.

The crash in 1892, when the company went bankrupt with 1,433 million gold francs owing and assets of only 163 million, ruined many small investors. Over a hundred parliamentarians were involved in the scandal. But the results of the elections of 1893 indicate that, however much Paris talked about it, the country as a whole refused to reflect metropolitan excitement. Wilson himself, past scandals forgotten, was reëlected by his faithful peasants of the Loire after a few years' discreet absence from the Chamber.

This long reign of the conservative republicans was to be crowned by three events: the Franco-Russian alliance of 1894, the election of Félix Faure to the presidency of the Republic in 1895, and the long-lived Méline cabinet of 1896–1898. They were the culminant points of a regime that, in spite of an unpromising beginning, had managed to live peacefully and prosperously for twenty years.

The moderate regime did not founder on the rocks of what became the Dreyfus Affair, but on dragon teeth sown during its earlier years: public education and industrialization. The end of the century saw the maturity of the generation educated in Ferry's école laique, and the ripening of social problems brought about by the growing industrial development and concentration. There was not only more industry in the country, but industrial enterprises grew bigger[5] and employed more men in one place. The tendency for industrial enterprises to spring up close to one another, whether in order to tap reservoirs of power or of labor, or to benefit from the advantage of each other's proximity, also concentrated more workers in definite areas.[6] This is the concrete background to the power struggle for which the Dreyfus case furnished first an impetus, then an excuse.

The Affair was incidental; it merely afforded an opportunity for problems to crystallize—and meet head-on. The result was not a tinkle but a dissonant row. Seignobos wrote: "The Affair itself, complicated by incidents, soon confused by maneuvers, obscured by legends, did not interest the main public which never really understood what it was about."[7] Many took their traditional sides before thinking the case out for themselves, after which they were too prejudiced to consider they might not be objective. That the case of Dreyfus himself never had more than a symbolic importance seems proved by the attitude of many of his defenders who did not care for him personally. And yet, oddly enough, not all the political alignments to which the Affair gave rise could have been predicted, say, in 1894, at the time of Dreyfus' first trial and conviction for treason. The attitude of Barrès, whom progressive youth followed as an intellectual leader, was as unpredictable and eventually as surprising as the attitude of Rochefort. The former spoke out for institutions with their roots deep in the national soil when he sided with army and Church; but he could just as well have claimed the right of an *homme libre* to judge and decide for himself. Rochefort's chauvinism pulled him into the surprising company of the mainstays of established order and, at first, of the government itself.[8]

It was natural that the Right should rally around the army; it was less obvious that the Left would oppose it. Gabriel Deville in 1893,[9] Jaurès in 1895, Millerand in 1896, had stressed that Socialists were also patriotic Frenchmen. The latter's speech at Saint-Mandé,[10] with its proud claim, "we are Frenchmen and Patriots," was accepted by all Socialist groups and imposed as part of their program to all would-be Socialist candidates at the elections of 1898.

The year 1870 was still fresh in the minds of the leaders of the Left, be they Socialists or Radicals. Jaurès was a pacifist, but he was not resigned to the loss of Alsace-Lorraine.[11] "We do not forget, we cannot forget," he said in 1895. And Marcel Sembat tells of Camille Pelletan's patriotic ardor. Yet a curious fact may explain not only the current of the following years, but also the evolution of many Left-Wing leaders: while the leaders remained old-fashioned patriots, the workers grew increasingly bored and irritated by stock references to revenge. Alsace-Lorraine or the fatherland were, they thought, irrelevant to their own problems and needs.[12] Patriotism followed clericalism on the road of popular disfavor.

This change in the attitude and temper of the working class might be due in part to the doctrines of revolutionary syndicalism, just beginning to take shape. There is a correspondence in time between the evolution of working-class attitudes and the spread of more intransigent doctrines stressing class consciousness and class action. The Fédération des Bourses du Travail and the Confédération du Travail were set up in 1892 and 1895.

Eventually, the Left moved against the army to fight the army's allies. The Socialists, for a long time consistent with their doctrine, kept out of this bourgeois fray until the advantages of participation became too obvious to be ignored. Then they joined what was for them the logical side to be on. The exigencies of the campaign forced one side into chauvinistic nationalism, the other into violent antimilitarism. Tendencies that had lain dormant, and that may not have manifested themselves but for the heat of battle, became apparently relevant and eventually dominant.

The same extremism affected all persons and parties involved. The supporters of Dreyfus perforce became antimilitaristic, antipatriotic, anticlerical. Their eventual conquest of power was also the triumph of their extreme ideas. This led to the reconstitution of the Right, generally accepting the republican label, socially conservative, and opposed to the anticlericalism and antimilitarism of the Left. The understanding between the monarchist, clerical, and nationalist Right and the moderate republicans had been steeled in the fires of the Dreyfus Affair. The moderates were not scared by the militaristic and antiparliamentary agitation of their more extreme allies. They had learned to discount the phraseology, and soon the two groups would become practically indistinguishable.[13]

On the other hand, antimilitarism and anticlericalism became official government policy. The culmination of the first came with the "republicanization" of the army, carried out by Combes and General André, and with a reduction of the period of military service from three to two years in 1905. The culmination of the other came in the separation of Church and state, achieved that same year. Antipatriotism was largely a reaction, as the other two had been, against the exaggerations of the opposing side. It was also a defensive reaction of the intellectual pacifists.

It would seem that by 1903 antipatriotism had become the rule among schoolteachers, especially in primary schools. The brief of a case against them is given in the works of a patriotic schoolteacher, Emile Bocquillon, who raised a very loud cry of alarm.[14] When allowance has been made for exaggerations, it seems certain that a great deal of the self-conscious antipatriotism existent among schoolteachers led to excesses just as silly and harmful in their way as those of their opponents. The widow of Paul Bert, Ferry's great collaborator in the creation of the école laïque, a man who had always conceived the school as a center of moral and patriotic education, was told that a biography of her husband would be dropped from a collection entitled *Les Grands Français* "because of his chauvinism."[15]

Such a trend led to a few protests and to some incidents. But it had to be admitted by critics as patriotic as Maurice Paléologue, that it seemed to be what the country wanted.[16] Paris, as was its wont, remained *anti*. With Waldeck-Rousseau in power and the Right routed, the municipal elections of 1900 saw the nationalists triumph in Paris. Galliffet, writing to Caillaux in May of that year, commented:

Étant par habitude contractée toujours optimiste, je ne suis pas autrement attristé par les élections de hier. La province n'a pas été nationaliste, et Paris n'a fait que ce qu'il fait d'habitude: des bêtises.[17]

But the general trend was better expressed by an article in *L'Européen* of December, 1901: "Peace in Europe, neutrality in European affairs, no conquests, the least possible campaigns outside Europe, protection, such is the policy of the parties, essentially a negative and passive one."

The tumult and the shouting were dying. France was at peace. But not for long.

Chapter II

THE REMINDER: 1904–1905

Your vicious things shall melt in air . . .
. . . But for the Virtuous Things you do,
The Righteous Work, the Public Care,
It shall not be forgiven you.
(G. K. Chesterton, "Ballade d'une Grande Dame.")

Thus, at the beginning of the century, nationalism in France was the preserve of relatively unimportant groups on the Right. It was an opposition movement and a literary school. "Its program," commented Seignobos,[1] "resolves itself in upsetting the government. Nationalism is above all a Parisian phenomenon." Electorally speaking, the next twelve years were to see this judgment endorsed at one general election after another.

The Action française had been founded in July, 1899, by Henri Vaugeois, who had left the committee of the nationalist and anti-*Dreyfusard* Ligue de la Patrie française to join with the royalist Maurras in founding a more intransigent and, they anticipated, more effective organization. Their hopes were not crowned with immediate success; their importance and their reach remained for a long time very restricted. The newspaper of the same name was to write reminiscently:

Qui alors nous a offert une doctrine pour soutenir de raison les sentiments que nous éprouvions devant le chambardment de la France. ... Qui? Maurice Barrès. Maurras n'avait pas encore atteint le grand public.[2]

The nationalism of Barrès was then, as later, focused on Alsace-Lorraine. He had made this cause his own to such an extent that, when in 1918 the two provinces were returned to France, Cocteau was moved to remark: "Il faudra qu'il se fasse naturaliser allemand, pour qu'il puisse continuer à réclamer l'Alsace-Lorraine." It would be fair to say that most of this activity did not go far nor deep outside Paris.[3] Even there, intellectual circles were never for the greater part dominated by Barrès or by kindred minds.

In the provinces, intellectual leadership went to the republican, anti-militarist teachers, whose syndicates had long discarded the ideas of Paul Bert and whose opinions had been informed by the arduousness of their own military service, *sac au dos*. Seignobos, well aware of the political isolation of Paris, wrote in his *Etudes de Politique et Histoire*:

The nationalist, militarist, and anti-Semitic tendency springs from the Parisian lower-middle class of radical origins, but, above all, of rebellious tradition, whose lack of political experience leads it to manifest against all and every government. It is traditionally xenophobic and anti-Semitic because of its hatred against capital. It has been reinforced during the Dreyfus Affair by its absorption of the remains of the old royalist and Catholic parties.[4]

All this movement, this ferment of thought, might have remained merely that, had it not been for circumstances quite outside the control of its professors.

The foreign policy of Hanotaux, concerned to avoid friction with Germany, had led to a clash with England, the fall of Hanotaux, and the coming to the Quai d'Orsay of Théophile Delcassé on June 28, 1898. There he was destined to remain seven years, and in this time to lay the lines along which French foreign policy would continue after his fall.

It is easily forgotten that the surrender of Fachoda was as great a humiliation to the French as any in the history of the Third Republic;[5] and French resentment against England was the greater because the crisis occurred in the midst of the xenophobic currents of the Dreyfus controversy. England could be as hated as Germany, as Clemenceau had discovered to his cost, and the historical justification of Anglophobia was rather better than anything that could be worked out against another country. The nationalists spent much of their fury on perfidious Albion and its (to them) rather ludicrous queen. Resentment ran so high that even an understanding with Germany seemed almost possible in the spring of 1899. But Bülow, though ready to throw a little sand in the mechanism of Anglo-French relations, was not sufficiently interested, nor was Foreign Minister Delcassé sufficiently convinced.

The new foreign minister sought rather to avoid a clash with England and was brought, with suitable British assistance, to establish unusually cordial relations with England. This *rapprochement* worried Germany. It drove her to actions that succeeded only in increasing French dislike, and pushed France and England gradually closer together. It would be interesting to know when Delcassé made up his mind on the lines of his words to Paléologue in 1904: "I am deeply convinced that in a near future the arrogance and charlatanism of William II will bring him to try the hazards of force, and declare war upon us. That day, I want us to be able to defend ourselves."[6] All we hear is that he had expressed similar views as early as 1898.

It was in 1902 that two diplomatic maneuvers were carried out, which profoundly altered the relative quiet of the diplomatic scene. In April, a German diplomat overheard Joseph Chamberlain and Paul Cambon using the words "Morocco" and "Egypt" so often that he guessed the coming change in British foreign policy. The first steps were being taken toward the Entente Cordiale. A little later, Italy secretly promised France a strict neutrality should France, as the result of a direct provocation and in defense of her honor and security, find herself compelled to take the initiative of a declaration of war. Even ignorant of such terms, the Germans were well aware that Camille Barrère, the French ambassador in Rome, was working hard and not unsuccessfully to detach the third member of the Triple Alliance and to secure France's Mediterranean interests.

Further developments are familiar. Closer relations between France and England were viewed with alarm and dislike from Berlin. Taking advantage of the fact that Russia, engaged in a disastrous war in the Far East, coping with social revolution at home, was in no position to help her ally, Germany attempted the *Coup de Tanger*, hoping for three results: the dismissal of Delcassé, a dangerous and open enemy; the break of the young and untried Entente Cordiale; the prevention of a French "Tunisification" of Morocco, and the staking out and protection of German claims to strategic and commercial advantages there or elsewhere in Africa.

Of these three aims, only the first was fully realized. The British stood stoutly by their 1904 agreement with France, and the Algeçiras conference brought out the close relationship between the new friends. The inconclusive results of the conference left the seed of future complications rather than a possible foundation for international coöperation, or even for advantageous German action in Morocco.

The effect of the crisis on French public opinion was remarkable. In April, 1905, an old-fashioned and patriotic Republican politician, René Goblet, had complained of a great change: "Not only there is no more talk of revenge," he had written, "but I strongly doubt whether there is still thought of it. . . . These last few years there has been no talk but of peace."[7]

In spite of a certain activity, Goblet's impression was correct. The country was indifferent; the politicians were concerned with things other than revenge. The Chamber, as a royalist deputy described it, was republican, Radical, and Socialist.[8] The Republic seemed generally accepted. Harduin could write in *Le Matin*: "There are no royalists left in France—at least, there are only three or four which, considering the size of the population, is not very much."[9] The Combes cabinet had united the Left in the antinationalist and anticlerical fight.[10]

To republicanize the army, Combes' minister of war, General André, had introduced a check on all officers carried out by, or in collaboration with, Freemasons, some civilians among them. The discovery of this system, and of the personal files in which officers' religious and political ideas were carefully noted navigating between the war office and the Masonic *Grand Orient*, caused a public scandal and encouraged the nationalists, always ready to enlarge on questions of honor. A nationalist deputy, treasurer of the Ligue des Patriotes, Gabriel Syveton, who with another deputy, Guyot de Villeneuve, had opposed the system, was forced by a private scandal to commit suicide before he was able to make the most of his material. The nationalists used the somewhat obscure circumstances of his death as more grist to their mill.

The scandal of the files, to translate *l'affaire des fiches*, led to the resignation of several officers, among them the minister of war. The scandal furnished plausible reasons to deputies of the erstwhile Combist majority to justify their voting against Combes. But it is worth remembering that the files of André and of Vadécard, secretary of the *Grand Orient*, were not an innovation, nor were they out of line with previous practice. They were at worst an improvement or extension of the system that had existed long before. What shocked the Right was that civilians had been used as informers and, above all, that the system had been used against themselves.[11]

Whatever the rights and wrongs of it, the scandal served its purpose and Combes had to go. He went, but not without warning against the movement of nationalist and clerical reaction he saw taking shape. He was replaced by Rouvier.

Rouvier appears in the early part of the history of the Third Republic much as Poincaré does in the latter part, a stabilizing, reassuring personality. There was a difference: Rouvier was a businessman of doubtful reputation in financial matters, whereas Poincaré with all his faults was absolutely honest in money matters. Yet both men had the confidence of the great banks and the middle classes. The new prime minister belonged to the Alliance Démocratique, a powerful group of generals without troops whose adhesion to the bloc had carried with it the support of important social and business interests. Christophle, the sometime governor of the Crédit Foncier had been one of its founding members, as had been Raynal, out of Ferry's nursery, notorious in railroad affairs, Etienne, Siegfried, and Hennessy of the Charente. Among its younger members were such men as Ribot's protégé Jonnart, Barthou, Poincaré, and Chautemps.

Five powerful newspapers were, to say the least, sympathetic to the interests of the Alliance. Prévet, senator and iron-master, owned the *Petit Journal*; another senator, Jean Dupuy, owned the *Petit Parisien*, a paper whose sales, past the million mark in 1905, would stand by 1913

at 1,550,000. Two families whose fortune was not unconnected with the
Panama swindle, the Letelliers and the Bunau-Varillas, directed two
other great popular newspapers, *Le Journal* and *Le Matin*. These four
together with the nationalist *Echo de Paris* shared between them five- of
the six-million circulation reached by the forty-one political dailies of
the capital by the end of 1914. But they could not always be relied on to
reflect the "party line," and the sedate and influential *Temps* was normally taken to be the mouthpiece of the group.

Divided from *Progressistes* and *Pioutistes* by the important line between adherents of the bloc and its opponents, the Alliance Démocratique was yet in close touch with these circles of similar social and indeed
economic background and interests. Jonnart was the son-in-law of the
great Catholic banker Aynard, one of the Progressist leaders; Adolphe
Carnot's son, François, stood as Progressist candidate as did senator
Dupuy's son-in-law, Arago; and Hennessy, heir to the great Orléanist
distilling fortune, had married the daughter of Albert de Mun. Jacques
Piou himself was related to the great sugar baron, Lebaudy, of the old
Centre Gauche; Léon Say was related to Lannes de Montebello who had
acted as his *chef de cabinet* and whose election in 1893 had been made
under the old man's auspices. As for the rich Edmond Blanc, one of the
founders of the Alliance, his sister was the Princess Radziwill and his
daughter had married a la Rochefoucauld. Even so had Swann been the
friend of the Guermantes, and Gabriel-Louis Pringué frequented the
Rohans and the Broglies.

In this little world social connections often counted for more than
party ties. In like reference, Byron had written,

> Lord Henry was a great electioneerer
> Burrowing for boroughs like a rat or rabbit. . . .
> His son, the hon. Dick Dicedrabbit
> Was member for the "other interest" (meaning
> The same self-interest, with a different leaning).

Soon the similarity of interests would begin to assert itself over the different leanings; for the moment a man from this quarter was a reassuring
sign.

The reassurance needed was against the excesses of the victorious
Dreyfusards who had held the levers of power far too long; but the reaction against them in 1905 was as yet slight and uncertain.

It came, as from René Goblet, in the form of indignation at antipatriotic excesses. It also appeared in art and literature. In Louis
Dimier's amusing memoirs, this schoolmaster-member of the Action
française tells the story of a campaign during the early years of the

twentieth century to "nationalize" certain periods and schools. He cites as an example the 1904 Exhibition of French Primitive Paintings in which, among others, Van Eyck's reredos of Ghent was claimed a product of French art.[12]

But the trend was not solely concerned with painting, nor did it pass unperceived. Camille Mauclair devoted a long article to the "nationalist reaction in art," in which he traced the new mood in large part to politics.[13] But concern was not widespread and no notice was taken of any warnings. When in March a "small group of neo-monarchists founded a league, called Ligue d'Action française," *L'Humanité* commented: "The name, which has nothing of monarchism, already reveals the extreme weakness of that forgotten party. . . . It is evident that nationalism has been decisively defeated."[14]

Ten days later, on March 23, *L'Aurore* uneasily noted the announcement of the Kaiser's forthcoming visit to Tangier. The next day, Clemenceau commented on the relationship between the virtual elimination of the Russian army from the European balance of power and the new strain in Franco-German relations. But Clemenceau was the only one to worry.[15] *Le Petit Parisien* qualified press comments on the significance of the visit as "much ado about nothing." Delcassé's explanations seemed to satisfy the Senate; there was no disquiet or opposition there, in spite of a bitter attack by Clemenceau in *La Dépêche de Toulouse.*[16]

The first of April brought news of the Tangier visit. The Paris newspapers showed more interest in the mid-Lent festivities, in the discussion of the *affaire des fiches* in the Senate, and of separation in the Chamber. Alone in the *Dépêche*, Clemenceau warned of the importance this event might have for the future and for peace. But the impression he gave was one of bitterness not caring what was grist to its mill, and he was therefore easily written off.

Even newspapers, like *L'Echo de Paris*, that had warned their readers of the gravity of the event and had commented upon it pessimistically, became more cheerful as the Kaiser's words seemed to lose their ominous significance.[17] Reassured by the visit of King Edward VII and by the Kaiser's warm condolences on the occasion of Jules Verne's death, press and public expected an easing of the tension. Tension in fact soon disappeared, except backstage, until the beginning of June. Then, as the visit of the King of Spain, Alphonse XIII, and the news of the Russian naval disaster at Tsushima held the headlines, there came news of a sudden German stiffening, coupled with the diplomatic victory of the German agent over the French and British envoys at Fez. Delcassé's resignation followed at once.[18]

The sudden crisis came as a surprise to almost everyone. Parliament had been no better informed than the public, and it reflected emotions sometimes close to panic. Demands for information on the part of Socialists and nationalists after the brief flurry of the Tangier visit had remained unanswered.[19] That this was not due to pressure of work is shown by the fact that in a similar case of "urgency" of discussion concerning certain troubles in Limoges, the government was ready to talk over the matter at once.[20] When the Moroccan question was at last, and incompletely, discussed, the general consensus saw in the weakening of France's Russian ally the real cause of the German attitude.[21] Neither this nor anything else could yet prevent attention centering on the question of separation, which took precedence over everything in the debates of the Chamber and the Senate.[22]

Thus all sections of the public were ill-prepared for the crisis when it came, *par ce demi-clair matin*, on June 6. At first it did not appear as a crisis but, on the contrary, as the removal of an obstacle to better understanding with Germany. The *Progrès de Lyon* was relieved: "With Delcassé it was difficult to come to terms with Germany. That is what everybody said in parliamentary circles yesterday. Now that Delcassé has gone, tension has relaxed."

The Radicals were to change their sentiments in time, but this was their first reaction. However, although the press remained calm, its pages showed clearly the anxiety and alarm everybody felt.[23] The clearest expression of the general emotion can be found in the pages of Charles Péguy. It is in them that we can henceforth feel the mounting stress, the ever-greater strain of waiting for the clash that will soon appear inevitable, and the increasing need for moral and material preparedness. This growing concern informed all Péguy's thought and writing from then on, and not only that of Péguy.[24]

Certainly, on that sixth of June, many men, even Péguy himself, went to buy boots and thick woollen socks to prepare for the mobilization which they thought near.[25] The son and the nephew of d'Estournelles de Constant, the pacifistic senator, made ready to rejoin their units. On June 8, Flotow noted a general tone of fear and panic in one of Paris' most brilliant political salons. The panic was encouraged by certain articles of Professor Schiemann in the *Kreuzzeitung*; the view was put forward that, in a war between Germany and England, France would be the battlefield and the "hostage." This view was widely quoted together with rumors of uneasy negotiations, and widely resented.[26]

The brief panic[27] was soon followed by a more confident mood when the German game was seen more clearly as one of bluff. On June 19 Maurice Paléologue, then a high official at the Quai d'Orsay, was impressed by a decided awakening of the national spirit. A week later, although the diplomatic situation had not improved, he noted again:

> The mood this evening is altogether different from that which had so painfully impressed me on the fifteenth of June, *chez Boni de Castellane*. There has been a recovery: no more fear, no more cowardice, no more bending to the German will; the idea of war is accepted.[28]

It was accepted even by pacifists like Jules Renard who, on June 24, noted in his *Journal*:

> Oui, la guerre est odieuse! Oui, je veux la paix, et je lâcherais tous les Maroc pour vivre en paix. Si, tout de même, les Allemands prenaient cette soif de paix pour de la peur, s'ils s'imaginaient qu'ils vont nous avaler d'une bouchée, ah! non. ... On marcherait, et bien, je vous le jure!

The sense of national humiliation over the dismissal of Delcassé under orders from Berlin[29] and Germany's clumsy handling of the negotiations, had results that Germany certainly never expected. Paléologue quotes a conversation with Paul Revoil who was to represent France at Algeçiras: the two men met and talked on July 12, only four days after the signature of an accord agreeing to an international conference, as Germany demanded.

> —In fact, said I [Paléologue], the accord of July 8 resolves nothing. One of the two parties is humiliated, the other is disappointed. The future remains as black as before.
> —I think so too. The accord of July 8 is no settlement. The dangerous crisis through which we have just passed will start again. Germany will continue her game of alternating sweet words and threatening gestures.
> —The game has served her too well: why should she give it up? But our national pride which is obviously waking may rear up, may revolt at any moment. If that happens nothing could prevent a war.
> —What you say, Rouvier was saying to me only this morning: "If Germany wanted to make war inevitable, she would not act otherwise."
> —He has come a long way. Soon, you will see, he will think like Delcassé.
> —He is not far from that point now, and it is German diplomacy and German methods that have brought him there.[30]

Supplementing German diplomacy and German methods, the atmosphere of the Quai d'Orsay had played its part in Rouvier's change of mind. Delcassé had gone, but his principal collaborators remained as did Revoil and Paléologue, in Paris, and in the great embassies held by the Cambons, Barrère, Bompard, and Jusserand. Paul Cambon, who had been one of Ferry's young men and who represented a certain republican *haute-bourgeoisie* linked with high industrial and banking circles as well as with the Catholic *ralliés*, had especially come over from London (June 17–20) to insure a firmer tone. Revoil was one of his friends, and

Revoil's assistant, Regnault (later French minister in Tangier) had been Cambon's assistant in Tunis. So, incidentally, had Maurice Bompard (who before that had been his general secretary in the Préfecture du Nord.)

The influence of such a team, small but united and powerful by its position and command of current affairs, continued to make itself felt whoever should be the political head of the ministry. But if Rouvier was the first to show how great were their powers of persuasion when combined with those of the Germans, in the political world he was not alone in his revulsion. The Chamber, which had shown some hesitation in approving the Senate's Political Amnesty Bill, voted in its favor 541 to 3 in October, and enabled Déroulède to make a triumphal return to Paris the same month. The vote, and the welcome the returning leader of the Ligue de la Patrie française received in Paris, can be taken in part as acts of defiance toward Germany.[31] Certainly they appeared so to the Germans. Bülow wrote from Baden-Baden, attributing much of the trouble to Delcassé who, he thought, had joined the ranks of the nationalists. A closer observer, the Belgian minister in Paris, gave his view in a dispatch of October 24:

Une immense désillusion a envahi ceux qui someillaient dans des rêves pacifiques, le chauvinisme nationaliste s'est reveillé, on discute l'efficacité de la défense comparée à l'organisation formidable de nos voisins de l'Est, et on se montre disposé à faire de nouveaux sacrifices pour que la flotte et l'armée soient prêtes à toute éventualité.[32]

There was another and quite unexpected result. We have seen that, in the mood following the humiliation of Fachoda, England had been classed with Germany as the national enemy. On the French side the Entente Cordiale had been the doing of a small group of men, around Delcassé at the Quai d'Orsay, around Etienne, leader of the colonial interest, in certain business circles touched by the activities of enthusiasts like Thomas Barclay or Roper Parkington.[33] It had been greeted with moderate enthusiasm and Charles Benoist spoke for many of his colleagues when he explained that he would vote for a *détente cordiale*. While the moderate Right (to the left of *Le Gaulois* and *L'Echo*) had smiled upon it, the attitude of the more distinctively nationalist circles remained unfriendly

Between 1904 and 1905, Paul Cassagnac in *L'Autorité*, Edouard Drumont in *La Libre Parole*, and Millevoye in *La Patrie* persisted in the Anglophobia they had indulged during the Boer War.[34] They could not bring themselves to trust perfidious Albion nor to forgive its past offenses. By the end of the summer their tone seems to have changed, if only because their wrath was now clearly and definitely turned solely against

Germany. The organs of the moderate Right had held fast to the English alliance;[35] now the purely nationalist sheets began to accept it. The crisis had shown clearly where the enemy lay, provided some assurance of the reliability of English friendship, and identified to some extent the English connection with the cause of a Delcassé who would soon return brighter than ever to stand for a strongly and astutely anti-German policy. Without giving up their objections to England,[36] even the old nationalists no longer attacked her. Those circles whose intervention would soon play an important part in the new nationalism of the prewar years, and whose press would be its most powerful instrument, now looked upon the Entente as an indispensable and indeed indisputable part of the structure of French foreign policy.

There is no reason to suppose that the Germans had envisaged all the consequences of a pompous Wilhelmian speech. G. P. Gooch tells us that the fall of Delcassé had moved Barrère, in Rome, to exclaim: "Henceforth war is unavoidable. There are certain stains which only blood can wash out." Others expressed themselves less melodramatically, but on much the same lines.[37] The pattern of future developments had been laid down.

CHAPTER III

ALGEÇIRAS AND AFTER: 1905–1906

I sent a message to the fish:
I told them "This is what I wish."
The little fishes of the sea
They sent an answer back to me.
The little fishes' answer was
"We cannot do it, Sir, because—"
(Lewis Carroll, "Humpty Dumpty's Song.")

THE CONFERENCE OF ALGEÇIRAS, designed to settle the Moroccan differences, lasted from January 12 to April 2, 1906, and its results benefited no one eventually. Algeçiras was a diplomatic defeat for Germany, and a passage in the memoirs of Tirpitz which refers to a somewhat similar situation in 1911 shows us how German leaders reacted in such cases. For Tirpitz, Agadir too was a diplomatic check. To make up for this, more money should go into armaments. It was a reasonable point of view, and one he pressed consistently.[1]

France, Spain, England, and Russia seemed to draw closer together. Visconti-Venosta's attitude had shown the weakness of Italy's attachment to the Triple Alliance. Above all, the Anglo-French Entente had assumed a new character. From that moment, Germany had to seek a diplomatic victory elsewhere to recover lost face. Tardieu, in his book on the conference, *La conférence d'Algeçiras*, comments: "If one wishes to define the change that took place, one could say that at Algeçiras the Entente passed from a static to a dynamic state. Its force increased from the speed thereby acquired."

As early as the beginning of 1906, however, fresh impulses were communicated to the Entente from other quarters. In his historic speech of August 3, 1914, Sir Edward Grey informed the House of Commons that, as early as January, 1906, the French government had drawn his attention to the international situation. It had informed him that it considered the danger of an attack on France by Germany to be a real one, and intimated it was in the government's opinion desirable that conversations should take place between the French general staff and the newly-created general staff of Great Britain regarding the form most advantageous for military coöperation in resisting invasion of the northern parts of France. M. Pierre Renouvin points out[2] that it was Rouvier who confidentially informed Cambon of his desire to see a beginning of such talks.

In agreeing to the talks, which assumed gradually more and still more ample terms of reference, the British government did not feel it was committing itself to anything. This was not, however, the impression of its partners, nor of the Germans when they learned of the talks. To cast a brief look ahead, however negligently these and further talks were treated from the British side, they were continually being pressed forward by the French. For the latter, by the time of the exchange of the Grey-Cambon letters in October, 1912, they had assumed great importance.[3]

Outside official spheres, also, German flat-footedness had awakened old rancors. On October 18, 1906, a German dispatch from Paris described the militarist revival in the middle class, the renewal in the popularity of the army, and concluded that tempers might flare dangerously at any moment. This was hardly true. The general public did not think of war—at least not seriously or for long once the alert of 1905 had been forgotten, and then with only little zest.[4] But in certain circles, however partial or superficial this may have been, there was a strong reaction to what was considered a national humiliation. Students, intellectuals, and politicians were affected more, and more deeply, than others. Seventeen years later, the self-conscious patriots of the prewar years were to date their awareness from July, 1905.[5] Perhaps they over-simplified and remembered the emotions of that month in the light of later events. But the general greement justified Agathon, who characterized the Kaiser's visit to Tangier as a fact of the first importance. For Agathon it was, as he put it, the wound inflicted to national pride, which fermented secretly before breaking at the time of Agadir. When this happened, the transformation in public temper was so complete that it came as a surprise to leaders who had not foreseen it.

The change made itself felt even at the time. Newspapermen were the first to perceive it. In *Le Matin*,[6] Jean d'Orsay saw that nationalism had got out of the doldrums. It was the end of one nationalist crisis—the flood tide of another. Equally sensitive barometers, public figures, slowly turned their faces toward the sun shining from a new direction. Mid-September of 1905 was to hear official orations of a tone that had become unusual during the past few years. Ministers and other dignitaries of the Republic pleaded for patriotism in their week-end speeches. Already, August had heard *la religion de la patrie* exalted by Paul Doumer in a prize-giving speech at Tergnier and, ten days later, the great Lavisse himself, following suit on a similar occasion at Nouvion-en-Thiérache. This brought approving, if slightly ironical, comments from the Right-Wing press. For *L'Echo de Paris* the general impression was comforting. Love of the fatherland stressed in public, generals once more allowed to wave the flag, prize-giving speeches bringing patriotism back into the schools—all very different from customary expectations. It seemed clear that a complete reaction toward nationalism was on its way. Growing awareness of past dangers, growing acceptance of the possibility of war, growing emphasis on material and moral readiness, were clearly marked in all quarters,[7] especially among the young.

That the possibility of war was generally accepted in the second half of 1905 and the first quarter of 1906 is made quite clear by the matter-of-factness of incidental remarks on the subject. Thus, *Le Gaulois*,[8] the newspaper of Paris society, published an imaginary conversation to show how little danger soldiers really ran in war. It began: "As we were drinking a cup of tea between two games of bridge, Mrs. X said 'So there is still talk of war?' " and went on to speak of anxious times and troubled morrows. Over a cup of tea, between two games of bridge, the gentle readers of *Le Gaulois* could be assumed to talk of war and its dangers as easily, as naturally, as they talked of their servants. The prospect of war had entered the women's page.

The *Vossische Zeitung* printed a letter from Paris to a Berlin export firm, relating that Paris was convinced that the Kaiser and his people wanted war. It is impossible, complained the writer, for Germans to do business with the French who, certain that a war is imminent, turn to Belgium or Britain for their orders.[9]

Accepted with resignation and little thought by most, such ideas could not fail to exasperate those who concerned themselves more actively with current affairs. Our own experience should help us to understand that of another generation. "Rather than this continuous tension, better have a war and get it over," was not an uncommon attitude in certain circles. These circles were restricted as yet, but growing steadily larger. Henri Massis[10] tells us that most of his friends at the Lycée and Sorbonne, neither nationalists nor militarists, felt this way. It was not a follower of Maurras but a Jewish fellow-student, Julien Cain, the future administrator of the Bibliothèque nationale, who said to him in the court of the Sorbonne one afternoon in 1906, "War is the only remedy." Massis comments:

> It was in these circles, which yesterday were still for Dreyfus, it was among these intellectuals who ten years earlier would have expressed their anarchist sympathies by collaborating with the *Revue Blanche*, that I saw for my part the first signs of the national revival which affected our youth: "Yes," they would calmly say, "rather a war than this endless waiting."

Undoubtedly there was a good measure of ignorance and affectation, and a great deal of thoughtlessness, behind such words and attitudes. This does not make them any less real or less important. Seldom is it known why people say or do something. What they say or do must be assessed for significance in relation to their time and circumstances. Thus, fear and anger mingled in expressed opinions until the German menace began to be forgotten once more in the excitement of the coming general election, and in the awareness of a new menace, an internal menace this time.

In his study, *Democracy in France*, David Thomson sees the social, no less than the ideological, content of the alignment of Left and Right changing between 1905 and 1914.[11] On February 7, 1905, the national council of the French Socialist party (P.S.F.) had voted a motion of Jaurès ending collaboration with other parties. On the tenth and thirteenth of the same month, *L'Humanité* had predicted that the P.S.F. would unite with the Guesdist group. Six weeks later, the Socialist Congress at Rouen voted unanimously for the reunion of French Socialist parties into one Socialist party, which would be the French section of the Workers' International (S.F.I.O.).[12]

The consequent split between Socialists and Radicals was not really understood by the latter. The bloc of the Left in which the parties had collaborated during the days of Combes continued in fact for several years, and elections saw its regular renewal. But, if collaboration continued in practice, the Socialists accepted it on their own terms and denied it in theory. The Socialist and especially the Syndicalist electorate had left their official leaders far behind. The Socialist party had to move steadily toward the extreme Left to avoid losing the mass of its followers, whom the extreme antimilitarism and antipatriotism of men like Gustave Hervé seemed to inspire. There was thus a progressive Hervéization of the Socialist party, while Radicals, largely as a reaction to this, moved further toward the Right.

It must be explained that the S.F.I.O. had obtained outward unity and discipline at the cost of great concessions to the different tendencies within it. As the most extreme tendencies were also the most aggressive, recognized leaders like Jaurès, Guesde, or Vaillant had to accept the presence of a man like Hervé for the sake of unity, while they disapproved of him and his ideas. But although Jaurès himself hoped that free discussion would prove the weakness of Hervé's arguments, other observers saw in him, perhaps more justly, merely the expression of an unreasoning conviction that no coherent argument could affect.

One of these, Marcel Braunschwig, tried to dissociate intellectual pacifists like himself from the mass of dissatisfied workers who reacted against social injustice by antipatriotic demonstrations. He merely succeeded in pointing out the uncomfortable gap between the more moderate, reasonable minority and those masses that welcomed the violence of men like Hervé. It was not a handful of agitators who bore the responsibility of the workers' antipatriotism. Such an idea exaggerated the importance of a few individuals who led only in their interpretation, in their voicing of a mood. Hervé, Braunschwig had to admit, "has simply expressed the opinions of the Syndicalist groups on the burning issue of patriotism."[13]

Thus, not only did antipatriotic excesses breed similarly excessive reactions for purely theoretical or emotional reasons, they also soon appeared as a symbol of social discontent and eventually of social danger. To face this danger, many moderate republicans and even Radicals moved ever further to the Right.

Such a growing fear of social revolution led the Radical majority to accept ever more "moderate" government and, increasingly, to adopt nationalist symbols. For that matter, as Seignobos pointed out, many deputies who personally were moderates had adopted the Radical label in order to belong to the dominant party.[14] Daniel Halévy stresses: "There are hundreds of Radicals, but radicalism is a mere word, empty of all meaning."[15] As Vaillant pointed out in the name of the Socialist party: "The Right begins for us much further Left than you would think."[16]

The spring of 1906 brought increasing awareness of the social threat, and increasing publicity for it in the Right-Wing press. Henri de Jouvenel, the most clear-sighted of critics, wrote of the rival candidatures of Fallières and Paul Doumer to the presidency of the Republic: "There is little difference between them. The character of the one is slightly more conservative, which will insure him the Socialist vote; the other is more inclined to novelty—the moderates support him. Ten years ago this would have been unbelievable; in ten years' time it will be incomprehensible."[17] Ten years before the "novelty" had been on the Left; now it was on the Right. Democracy with its Radical or *Dreyfusard* implications was becoming old-fashioned, at any rate for the time being. The trend toward increasing authority and greater national pride was just beginning. This was the novelty toward which Paul Doumer inclined.

The approach of elections saw the fever rising. During March and April, 1906, *L'Echo de Paris* published daily as its chief feature a series of articles on the coming revolution. The articles dwelt at first on Syndicalist hopes, and then on the concrete expression of these hopes in the miners' and postmen's strikes. The strikes outlasted the articles and soon replaced them as central features illustrating the newspaper's cherished theme of a threatening class warfare. *Le Gaulois* felt the revolution was getting under way. The partisans of order would be forced to fight for its preservation. Significantly enough, the enemies of order were branded as internationalists, freemasons, and antimilitarists.[18]

In this way the Right-Wing press constantly associated strikers, hooligans, terrorists, revolutionaries, and anarchists with antimilitarists, freemasons, Socialists, and anticlericals. Lumped together, terms such as these soon became interchangeable to the minds of both these newspapers and their readers. The fallacious and facile association insistently repeated influenced the middle class. Fearing for their lives and for their property, they began to seek defenders on the Right for themselves and for the menaced social order.

The strikes in the north of France were headlined "Revolution in the North," and were followed by a description of "The Terror at Denain."[19] *La Libre Parole* featured "The Insurrection" and carried tales of "Bloody Riots." It asked—*La Révolution est-elle pour mardi?*[20] The Tuesday in question was May Day.

Fear of a May Day uprising was widespread: housewives laid in stores sufficient to withstand a long siege, and then had to serve the accumulated macaroni and ham for weeks to protesting families.[21] But though apparently persuasive in this respect, the campaign failed in its immediate end. The elections were disastrous for the Right. In an editorial entitled "Toward Social Revolution," *Le Gaulois* told its faithful and disappointed readers that the hooligan triumph and the reactionary defeat of the elections meant the victory of the coming social revolution.[22]

Confused thinking of this type in the minds first of Right-Wing agitators and publicists, then of a growing section of property-owners, was often perfectly honest. To them, very naturally, the principles held by their political opponents seemed to lead as a matter of course toward social dissolution and chaos. Drumont believed in his darkest prophecies. So did many of his readers. An investigation in *La Libre Parole*[23] revealed the most pessimistic expectations among solid citizens. There were gloomy or defiant letters from real-estate men, doctors, and lawyers, among the latter the chairman of the Foix Bar. A Dr. Abeille of Nantes wrote darkly: "As for myself, I have no illusions. On the day of the Götterdämmerung, if God will allow, I shall see my wife and children safely abroad. Then I shall barricade myself in the house which my forebears built and where so many generations have happily lived, and there await expropriation, rifle in hand. I shall die on my feet, *pro aris et focis*. And there are many small property owners quite resolved to do the same."

The dialogue of novels on this period reflects the generally accepted idea of class warfare and the widespread fear of social revolution. The great industrialists in *Les Hommes de Bonne Volonté* look at their workers, wondering when these will try to string them to a lamppost. Like the intellectuals in *Les Thibault,* such men took the class war and the coming revolution for granted. Lavisse himself told Drumont in 1909 that he had expected the revolution for a long time: the movement appeared to him to be the logical development of French evolution.[24] At the other extreme, the old nationalist deputy, Gauthier de Clagny, expressed a sense of helpless despair at the prospect:

> On se sent glisser sur une pente au bout de laquelle on prévoit des abîmes. ... Tout se désagrège, tout se dissout; toutes les bases de l'édifice social sont ébranlées; une secousse nouvelle suffirait à nous ensevelir sous les ruines.[25]

The same feeling, the same fear of the coming Götterdämmerung can be found in the letters of a more worldly figure, the cosmopolitan Princess Radziwill.

The reaction to such a dreadful prospect could not but be useful to the nationalist movement. Its opponents knew this. In 1905, the Socialist deputy Dejeante had said in the Chamber: "Nationalism is nothing but the exploitation of fear. Capitalists are told—Socialism, there is the danger! and this is how fear is exploited."[26]

Some observers feared war as offering a convenient opportunity for social revolution. D'Estournelles de Constant and Bülow agreed in this view, which was also shared by some Socialists, and were pleased to think that by trying to avoid an armed conflict they also helped to avoid the social one.[27] On the other hand, some had come to envisage the possibility of a war as an antidote to the revolution they feared, and to the insubordinate and rebellious tendencies of the masses. Anatole France understood this when he spoke of the Right's enthusiastic support of the Franco-Russian alliance as well justified by their knowledge that it would help the cause of counterrevolution in France.[28]

Those who thought they discerned such motives behind certain policies would have felt justified had they known Paul Doumer's words to the German ambassador, Prince Radolin:

> I consider France in a desperate state. We must get out of it at any price by a violent crisis. The war between Germany and England has become unavoidable. Germany does not want war, but England does, and cannot admit that the German fleet should pass a certain limit. Thus it will be England who will lead, and France will follow.[29]

Doumer seems to have spoken freely to Radolin. Three weeks before this, Radolin reported that Doumer, disappointed in his hopes of the presidency, fearing the progress of Socialism and national demoralization, was for early war. This was the only way, in his opinion, of uniting the people of France once more in the right feelings.

In the meantime, as far as could be seen, the clearest result of the elections was the utter defeat, the almost total annihilation, of the nationalist party that had appeared in the elections of 1898. The press on Left and Right agreed on this one point,[30] but perhaps only Drumont saw what the future was to make clear when he suggested that nationalism was not dead just because a number of men calling themselves nationalists had failed to secure reëlection.[31]

It is true that, as Drumont had said, nationalism was not dead. Its troops were staying at home, or else they were voting for moderates, or even for Radicals, when the label counted for less than the man himself. Nationalism was in search of a new shape and a new framework, shortly to be forged outside the circles traditionally connected with it. New men, new war cries, new methods, were being evolved out of the challenge of changed circumstances.

To begin with, the difference between patriotism and nationalism tended henceforth to grow less. Not only had antipatriotism been banished from its brief hold on power but, after 1905, as before 1898, patriotism became once more an honored ingredient of the politician's vocabulary. To understand the magnitude of this change, one must read through the political debates of the previous years and see how ready government circles had been between 1898 and 1905 to equate interventions in support of the army and its prerogatives, pleas against antimilitarism and patriotic formulae, with nationalism and the nationalist party. But after the shock of 1905 when, as *Le Matin* had put it on July 21, 1905, *l'impérial coup de tête de Tanger* had awakened France, and after the elections of 1906, patriotism became to an increasing extent a plank in the platform of all parties, from the extreme Right, beyond the Radical-Socialists to the ranks of the republican Socialists and of such doubtful "Socialist patriots" as Paul Adam.[32]

Only the Socialists, although some of their leaders claimed a patriotism as exalted as that of their opponents, had to leave it out of their party program. The Radicals, whose program was on the whole similar to that of the Socialists, were not under the cloud of antimilitarism and antipatriotism. They could benefit from the general desire for reform, and also from the general distaste for antipatriotic excesses. "Patriotisme et réformisme, l'un portant l'autre, c'est désormais la formule qui s'impose," wrote *La Dépêche de Toulouse*.[33]

From the nationalist party there was nothing more to fear: "Ses fameux 'défenseurs de l'armée' restent sur le carreau et mordent la poussière [*sic*]. Leur passage incohérent à travers la politique française sera un incident énigmatique pour les futurs historiens. ... C'en est fait: le nationalisme arrive à son heure dernière." But the conclusion was a happy one: "Le nationalisme a perdu presque tous ses sièges à la Chambre," wrote Bouglé in *La Dépêche de Toulouse*: "autant de gagné pour le patriotisme."[34]

Patriotism, after all, was nothing to be afraid of and, once freed of its nationalist associations, was a very good thing. Good republicans rediscovered it with pleasure, and affirmed it against Hervé, against Germany, and against the nationalists' arrogant claim to monopolize it. Most of them were glad of an opportunity to do so: "Au demeurant, il n'est peut-être pas mauvais que la réaction nous ait mis dans l'obligation de nous expliquer et de renouveler les affirmations d'un patriotisme qui, depuis 1793. ... est la vraie tradition républicaine."[35]

Henceforth, patriotism would furnish an almost unquestioned guarantee of political respectability, the differences between republican and antirepublican or arepublican patriotism would become increasingly blurred, and the old nationalism cast out through the electoral door would reappear as a new nationalism through the patriotic window. Thus admitted and encouraged, its nature would be affected by the fact that patriotism, no longer the private preserve of one party, could not henceforth be used as an effective party weapon except against the Socialists.

This being so, any party for which patriotism was the reason of its being, the essence of its ideology, and the basis of its program, had to be more patriotic than other patriots, had constantly to overbid, to win those elements for whom patriotism rather than social reform would count. This constant overbidding would be the essence of the new nationalism.

Chapter IV

THE INTERVAL

Le Nationalisme est dirigé contre quelqu'un; non seulement
contre quelqu'un à l'étranger, mais contre quelqu'un à
l'intérieur de nos propres frontières. (J. Madaule, *Le Nationalisme de Barrès.*)

The period beginning in 1906 was to be one of great social stress and
struggle. The rift, opened in 1905 between Socialists on the one hand and
Radicals and Radical-Socialists on the other, widened in spite of feverish
attempts on both sides to mend it. Generally, some kind of common
action was periodically arranged, usually at election times. This worked
well enough, though it gave rise to the usual crop of recriminations. But
recriminations should not obscure the tacit, largely effective coöperation
that gave rise to no comment at all.

This last warning is particularly relevant to these pages, for what is
significant may well be an isolated occasion, indicative of mood or trend.
I have found it necessary to dwell on those instances when one of the
parties, rising counter to the general rule, attacked its former partner
or refused it aid when aid could be reasonably expected.

I hope to show that the Radicals distrusted the Socialists increasingly
because, in spite of the repeated protests of its leaders, the Socialist party
moved ever toward antimilitarism and other similar extremes; because
Socialist and Syndicalist action appeared more and more a threat to
established social order; and because the Socialist party attracted too
many of the more advanced among the Radicals. In their turn, Socialists
distrusted Radicals more and more because these latter seemed too
inclined to compromise with moderates, and to accept moderate leadership against Socialist challenges and claims.

This trend, with cause and effect inextricably mixed, began unwillingly
in 1905, became clearer in 1906, and went on until the concrete challenge
of the Three-Year Law forced all to take sides. With brief interruptions,
1906 marked the beginning of a fifty years' struggle between Radicals
and Socialists.

Misunderstanding between the two parties was encouraged by the
Right-Wing press, which devoted many headlines to the threat of the
coming social revolution, to antimilitarism, and, to please both sides, to
the incompetence of Radical politicians. Police then were fewer than
today, and not yet armed; the period was much troubled with lawlessness; Right-Wing commentators lost no opportunity deliberately to con-

[44]

fuse hooligans with Socialists. Their equation was simple: lawbreakers were anarchists, anarchists were Socialists, therefore, lawbreakers were Socialists.[1] To proceed from that, conversely, Socialists were lawbreakers. At any rate, once the connection or confusion, not unfamiliar in our own day, had been established in the reader's mind, mention of one would implicitly be mention of the other, and all crimes could be connected with the more-than-regrettable spread of noxious doctrines.

Campaigns against lawlessness, campaigns against antipatriotic teachers, all became part of the anti-Socialist campaign. Once the existence of a social danger was proved, the need for social defense was more strongly felt. In filling this need, some nationalists found the reason of their being. Bouglé thought as much when writing in the *Dépêche de Toulouse* of the nationalist campaign against antipatriotic teachers: "Their job is the exploitation of the patriotic idea. Public fear is the reason of their being; alarm is their element; in order not to fall flat, they need the perpetual ringing of an alarm."[2] In keeping society on the alert, such men were plentifully supplied with material by Gustave Hervé who, in his new paper, *La Guerre Sociale*, somewhat oddly named for a pacifist sheet, headed those Socialist and Syndicalist circles that pressed for direct action and called for insurrection in case of mobilization.

While Hervé's influence grew constantly, Socialist leaders were doing their best to persuade themselves and the public that it was on the wane. In an interview he gave to *Le Matin*, Jaurès stated: "No one is Hervéist any longer, except perhaps Hervé himself."[3] He explained that Socialists were internationalists, but not antipatriotic, and that there was a great difference between the two positions. A month later he went further. In a great speech in the Chamber he explained and justified the facts: the superficial and excessive language of some workers and their leaders was not directed against the fatherland, but rather against the too-frequent abuse of the idea and the word.[4]

Right and Left accused each other of antipatriotism, each interpreting facts and definitions as it suited them best.[5] The significant fact remains that at no time was antipatriotism accepted in an official Socialist statement, while Hervé and his doctrines were reproved and denied throughout. The word "antimilitarist," which, like the word "antipatriot," had begun by having a very special meaning, that of being against militarism, not against the military, was now in disgrace.[6] No republican still dared to use what only two years before had been a proud challenge. Only men like Paul Lafargue, the only contributor of *L'Humanité* fit for the *Libre Parole*, would still write outside a Syndicalist paper that patriotism and militarism are the two means of exploiting the working class.[7]

This point of view was out of favor at the Socialist Party Congress held at Nancy in August, 1907. The congress, faced with the choice among three antimilitarist motions, voted for the motion presented by the Federation of the Seine, similar to the one voted at Limoges the previous year. This was a moderate victory and marked a defeat for Hervé, whose more extreme motion had now been defeated for a second time. The impression was making itself felt that these questions were being given too much time and too much attention.

A few men on both sides realized that the eventual value of such indoctrination was slight indeed. To the great majority, it became clear only at the outbreak of war that a man's opinions count for little when faced by a firm order backed by power. Briand knew the strength of his former Socialist comrades' opinions. That he held them to be of little account is shown by his attitude in October, 1910, when he broke the railwaymen's strike by calling up the strikers.

Much of the fear of antimilitarism was based on ignorance of antimilitarists. Those who observed them more closely—an experience that the time's social barriers rendered more difficult than would be imagined —were less worried. Thus a young writer, René Benjamin, who took part in the autumn maneuvers of 1908 in the ranks of the reserve, paid homage both to the power of antimilitarism and to the power of discipline to neutralize it. His fellow-soldiers, he wrote, all expressed themselves in similar terms, reciting the Hervéist manuals with surprising precision. Antimilitarism and antipatriotism were the current, established ideas of Paris working people. "But," he added, "on the day of mobilization they would be so scared of the gendarmes, that they would be the first to leave for the front. Antimilitarism is almost popular, a part of our workers' make-up; but antimilitarists are just poor chaps who will behave very well, provided they are marched up to the line of fire well in step."[8]

Jules Guesde felt the danger to the party that lay in the eventual success of antipatriotic doctrines. He took the first opportunity to state publicly that, in his opinion, antipatriotism was also antisocialism."However internationalist we may be, it is on the national plane that the organized proletariat of each nation has to work for the emancipation of all humanity." And he quoted Karl Liebknecht's phrase: "Those who try to establish an opposition between nationalism and internationalism are either insane or conscious liars."[9]

The minutes and reports of the International Socialist Congress, which met at Stuttgart only a few days after the Congress of Nancy had ended, give the clear impression that there, too, the votes merely confirmed the most moderate line possible in the circumstances.

Unfortunately, not many people read the minutes. Those who merely saw the text of the motions that had been passed, without being able to compare them to those that had been defeated, were not at all impressed by their relative moderation. Unrelated to the debates and circumstances of their passing, the motions seemed anything but moderate. This was the more so since all sides had promptly claimed a victory for their idea, and Hervé as loudly as the others. Those Radicals still working for an understanding with the Socialists, noted with distress the strong reaction in Radical ranks to what appeared a Hervéist triumph—if only half of one—at Stuttgart as well as at Nancy, and a surrender on the part of Jaurès.[10]

At this point, the *Echo de Paris* began a series of articles intended to show the reactions of a number of public figures to the burning question of antimilitarism. It was the beginning of a campaign designed to influence the coming Radical Congress toward an overt split with the Socialists. *L'Aurore* and *La Dépêche* worked hard to avert this. The anti-Socialist campaign scored when the *Echo* published a letter of Senator Delpech, vice-president of the Radical and Radical-Socialist Party Committee, calling for the exclusion of Socialists from the republican community.[11]

Delpech thought that the republicans were now strong enough to hold their own without such compromising auxiliaries as the Socialists. Three days later, on September 23, 1907, the Radical and Radical-Socialist Federation of the Seine adopted this motion to be presented to the Radical Congress: ". . . placing the Fatherland and the Republic above all discussion; resolves that its candidates may not in any circumstances stand down in favor of others who have not clearly, publicly, and in writing, repudiated the General Strike, and insurrection in case of war." As no Socialist candidate, whatever his private opinions, could have afforded to take such a stand, the passing of this resolution in Congress would have sealed the separation between the two parties.

In the event, the resolution of the Seine was by-passed in favor of another, supported by Camille Pelletan, which declared the Radical and Radical-Socialist party to be resolutely hostile both to nationalism and to antipatriotism, ardently patriotic, and which affirmed the uncontestable primacy of the military duty. This was enthusiastically carried. The party's leaders made clear that if they disliked certain Socialist slogans, they still wanted Socialist coöperation.[12] And Delpech had to explain, less intransigently than before, that it had been thought necessary after all to treat circumspectly such political groups whose help might still be needed.[13]

The reaction against antipatriotism did not stem solely from partisan reasons. Patriotism was increasingly exalted, both in public and in private. This was striking to observers in all quarters who remembered the different attitude that had prevailed not long before.[14] The growing popularity of flag and fatherland was not without inconvenience for some of those who, during the past few years, had been left the monopoly of their use. "Oh, la tête des nationalistes," wrote Marcel Sembat, "alléchés de nos ruptures, mais très embêtés qu'on leur chipe leur drapeau! Et le patriotisme de tous ces patriotes retapés de frais!"[15]

The debate between Socialists and Radicals continued. The beginning of winter saw the defection from the Socialist party of a number of deputies and local councilors who wanted to dissociate themselves from the partisans of Hervé.[16]

The spring of 1908 brought bitter recriminations in Parliament and press over the "reactionary" policy of the Clemenceau government. Obeying that law by which the responsibilities of power modify and dominate the man or the party regardless of ideology, Clemenceau had ruled with a firm hand, putting down all attempts to question his authority or the established order of things. He had tolerated no challenge, either from the Right or from the Left. When in 1907 the south of France was troubled by widespread riots caused by the crisis in the wine industry and the resultant misery of wine-growing districts, Clemenceau had been inclined to see in the growing dissatisfaction the hidden hand of Right-Wing reaction.

In fact, the widespread misery and disaffection had been ably exploited by the nationalists. In the Gironde the local organization of the Action française, led by the Comte de Lur-Saluces, had taken a hand in organizing the local resistance. Similarly, in Saintonge, Lannes de Montebello had helped to foment trouble. The Archbishop of Montpellier, Monsignor de Cabrières, had opened the churches of his town to shelter the malcontent manifestants. That his action was not solely motivated by Christian charity may be suspected from his open allegiance to the king and the Action française.[17]

Such, at least, was the government's impression: "These gentlemen of the Right," grumbled Clemenceau, "have managed to get into all the viticultural committees. Under the formula 'No politics' it is they who direct at this moment the insurrectional movement in the *Midi*."[18]

But an authoritarian policy remains authoritarian in content and methods, no matter against which side it is temporarily directed; and those were not mistaken who remarked on the rightward drift of the government's policy.[19] If Clemenceau had not sacrificed any of his own ideas, he had acquired new ones, and those the Right recognized as their own. Not only the Right either.

Attacking the government for having carried out none of their program, Jaurès suggested that Clemenceau had simply taken over and interpreted the ideas against which he had pretended to struggle before coming to power.

"As a justification of your policy," said Jaurès, "you have been brought to rehash against us the clumsy interpretations that melinist reaction gave to Socialist thought. Thus, in you, social reaction finds its tradition and its continuity."

Pelletan, too, was moved to rueful comment. The elections had returned to the Chamber a real majority for the forward march. Now, it seemed all the Chamber could think of was retreat.[20]

Whatever the labels of its members, the Chamber was essentially moderate. Its chief interest was the preservation of peace, order, and the deputy's mandate. The tone had been given in its first session by the rushed vote raising deputies' pay from 9,000 to 15,000 francs a year. Ready enough to raise their own pay, they were less ready—whatever their patriotic protests—to spend money on national defense, or to endanger their electoral success by maintaining burdens of national service when these could be lightened.

Against the advice of the government, the deputies voted for the release of the 1903 contingent in July and of the 1904 contingent in September, 1907. The deputies had looked toward their constituencies, as old Combes had once advised them to do. Military leaders were distressed, the chief of staff, General Hagron, resigned, and *Le Temps* commented: "The parliamentarians who govern us have shown themselves more ready than ever to sacrifice the national to their electoral interest."[21] This was nothing new. No sooner had the reverberations of the Tangier crisis died down than the Radicals, not to mention the Socialists, had begun to protest against the undue growth of the army budget.[22] With only a limited amount of money available, were armaments to eat up what was needed for social reform? A great deal of the opposition to the army and to rearmament may be traced to resentment at the cost in effort and money wanted elsewhere. Such material objections pulled far more weight than any moral argument ever did.[23]

Clemenceau believed that a government should govern and never, on any account, give in to threats. Use of, even reference to, violence in support of any claims or demands only exasperated him and moved him to increasingly heavy-handed repression. But Clemenceau also believed in the reality of the German menace, and in the urgent need for France to be strong, united, and prepared to face an attack that he considered imminent.[24] That was his chief concern; that, and his own political power. As J. M. Keynes described him,

He felt about France what Pericles felt about Athens—unique value in her, nothing
else mattering; but his theory of politics was Bismarck's. He had one illusion—
France; and one disillusion—mankind, including Frenchmen, and his colleagues not
the least.[25]

By the summer of 1908, he had come to envisage war with Germany as
both certain and near.[26] To have the Congress of the C.G.T. vote a
Hervéist and violently antipatriotic motion would hardly improve his
mood.[27] Drawn apart by their most active and extreme elements, Socialists and Radicals saw their friendship cool ever further.

The local organizations in particular, whatever the efforts made at the
top to maintain republican discipline, mirrored increasing awareness of
different interests. In the Limousin where the Socialists successfully
challenged Radical strongholds, at Bobigny on the outskirts of Paris
where the Radical committee supported moderate candidates after 1906,
republican discipline was sacrificed to more pressing economic interests.[28]
The senatorial elections of March, 1909, marked more strongly than
before the split between Radicals and Socialists. The election of a
Radical-Socialist on a second ballot in Toulon, in Clemenceau's own department of the Var, was indicative of the new relations between the
two parties. Although the Socialist candidate had obtained a majority
in the first ballot, the Radicals united against him and carried the
election.

A year later, the Radical Committee of Valenciennes decided to uphold
its two Radical candidates against two Socialists who had obtained a
majority in the first ballot, though not the absolute majority necessary
for election.[29] The Radicals' motive was to oppose a revolutionary policy
that, they felt, had become a danger to the country. A radical speaker
put the case thus:

M. Mélin [one of the Socialist candidates] stands for the expropriation without
indemnity of industrial property. We should be cowards if we did not react to this,
if we stretch out our hands to such opponents. We must show that there is an abyss
between radicalism and socialism, and that the Radicals of Valenciennes will not be
the ones to fill it.

The Socialists were successful, but that did not alter Radical sentiments
or avoid the clash of party doctrines.

These general elections of April–May, 1910, left no clear majority in
the Chamber. The Socialists had gained; the Radicals and Radical-
Socialists had lost. Henceforth, the problem of the latter would be
whether to seek their complement of votes on Left or Right. Tradition
inclined to the Left. But a further complication arose: the Socialists were
ardent supporters of proportional representation, which the Radical
party, relying on a parish pump policy for its main support, opposed as

ardently. The over-all character of Radical membership was even more obviously inclined to moderation in 1910 than in 1906. All this goes a long way to explain why, during the following years, although Radicals and Radical-Socialists remained the strongest party in power, five out of eight prime ministers belonged to other groups.[30]

If the electorate gave no clear indication of the political temper of the country, it did express a general feeling of dissatisfaction by failing to return 207 of the 507 deputies who had stood for reëlection. Thus, in the Loire five constituencies out of eight, in the Isère five of seven, changed representatives. But if the person of the representative changed, the party allegiance seldom did. It is worth noting that, with two-fifths of the seats in the Chamber changing hands, the party alignment hardly changed at all. Official figures show the "Progressive Liberals" (a label Pelletan and others translated more simply as "reactionaries") losing nine seats, Radicals and Radical-Socialists losing seventeen. On the other hand, nationalists won one seat, moderates (*Républicains de Gauche*) nine, Independent Socialists one, and the S.F.I.O. nineteen.[31]

The Right-Left proportion in the Chamber remained much the same, but the proportions within the Left changed significantly: the Radicals became weaker. More than ever they had to consider those other groups of the Left without whom no government could secure a majority. On the basis of figures, they could have obtained such a majority by an alliance with the S.F.I.O. They were, however, much closer to their neighbors on the Right, the moderate republicans, be they *Républicains de Gauche* or *Gauche Démocratique*. In any case, party figures did not mean that a party could marhsal its voters as a British party can. Far from it. The S.F.I.O. apart, there was no party in our sense of the word, and no party discipline. Until 1910, when administrative necessity led to the setting-up of official and exclusive parliamentary groups, a deputy could belong to more than one group at the same time, and usually did. A "unified" Radical-Socialist party, which hoped to imitate the discipline of the S.F.I.O., was founded in 1911 and excited much comment. It was not followed by brilliant results and did not lead to emulation.

But these, however important, were problems for connoisseurs. Although parliamentary talk turned around them, the country was not particularly interested. Poincaré commented on this indifference in a letter to *Le Temps*.[32] He judged that the general calm of the election campaign bordered on torpor, and attributed it to a disquieting slowdown of political life.

PART TWO

THE SMOLDERING

CHAPTER V

FIRST EDDIES: 1906–1908

Mais Paris est un véritable océan. Jetez-y la sonde, vous
n'en connaîtrez jamais la profondeur. (Honoré de Balzac,
Le Père Goriot.)

CERTAINLY THE EXCITEMENT of the Dreyfus Affair had died away. But
one may wonder whether popular interest in politics had ever been very
widespread or very deep, particularly as no woman had any concrete
interest in them as yet. The carnival queen of 1910, a dressmaker living
in the center of Paris, had never heard of Aristide Briand, who was prime
minister at the time. Apart from the president of the Republic, Fallières,
the young woman had heard of only one political figure: Pataud, that
leader of the Electrical Workers' Union who had risen to fame by plung-
ing Paris into darkness on two occasions to stress the urgency of his
claims. "The electrician," she smiled.[1] This was in an election year.

But in better informed circles, opinions on politics and parliament, if
ampler, were no better. The sad incoherence of political life, devoid now
of any great Cause, disgusted many observers. Some, like Henri Fournier,
were unpleasantly struck by the sordid character of the game the men in
Parliament seemed to play.[2] Others, like Barrès, failed to find clarity or
purpose in the game they themselves were playing.[3] Still others saw Parliament as a stage on which the actors had to be treated as such, and not
as if they were in earnest. By 1914, Robert de Jouvenel could write that
there was less difference between two deputies of whom one was a revolutionary and the other not, than between two revolutionaries of whom
one was a deputy and the other not.[4] More important still, many found
reason to agree with this view.

The decrease of confidence in the efficacy of the parliamentary system
of government and the ability of elected representatives to solve the
problems facing France, facilitated the acceptance of ever stronger,
more authoritarian government. It brought growing sympathy to just
those antiparliamentary movements that were doing their best to diminish the power and effectiveness of parliamentary government.[5]

The most active of these movements was the Action française. Born
of the Dreyfus Affair in 1899, it was never very important until after the
war of 1914–1918. But importance is relative: the Action française made
a lot of noise. If it counted for little in the political and electoral balance
of our period, its tireless activity and its violent campaigns brought it a
notoriety that could not fail to touch the politically minded public. Its

influence did not go beyond the metaphorical walls of Paris,[6] but its activity was great, and growing. Fertile in expedients for publicizing its ideas, it reached deeply into intellectual and student circles, and was much appreciated in military and Catholic society.

In 1905 was founded the group known as Etudiants d'Action française, and in February, 1906, the Institut d'Action française opened its doors. This Institute was destined to play the part of a *Sorbonne Royaliste*.[7] One of its professorial chairs was that of the Syllabus, for the teaching of Church history. Its name was meant to point and seal the alliance between renascent nationalism and the intransigent wing of the Catholic Church.

The gospel of the Action française went through the country on the lips of a few score enthusiasts, but reverberations were few and too often limited to such marks of appreciation as met the Marquise de Mac-Mahon, one of its most enthusiastic propagandists and president of the Society of Royalist Ladies, who was elected Honorary Butcher of the city of Limoges. Butchers seem to have had a weakness for nationalism: they appear again and again in its annals, but never, I feel, in a more pleasing light. *L'Illustration* informed its eager readers that the Marquise "shows herself very flattered and touched by this unusual and unexpected tribute," acquired while propagating "ideas she holds dear."[8] The Marquise was the daughter of Eugène-Melchior de Vogué of the Académie française, himself president of the managerial committee of the great Catholic weekly, *Le Correspondant*.

Until 1908, the new organization published a fortnightly bulletin,[9] replaced in that year by a daily newspaper of the same name. The new daily was to be the chief organ of the party's propaganda and, by its brilliant virulence, its violent polemics, and the clear, hard-hitting criticism of Maurras, would become in a short time the mouthpiece of the nationalist Right.

The newspaper was fortunate to have in Leon Daudet a polemicist dreaded by all, and in Jacques Bainville a political analyst and historian whose judgments were to be vindicated by future events more often than is given to most. Maurras himself, philosopher and uncontested leader of the party, would influence many who did not share his political opinions, but admired his brilliance.

The philosophy of Maurras, a system that Maurras himself considered positive, and that critics might place in the Machiavellian school without any pejorative connotation, started by taking note of the decadence of France. This decadence, the necessary basis for all future development of his doctrine, was proved by the French defeat in the war of 1870, by the consequent loss of Alsace-Lorraine, and by the falling numbers of the population. All these were both causes and effects of the country's general decay, and the moral and social upheaval that was only too obvious (as it nearly always is) was cited as additional evidence.

Only a decadent nation could be so brutally split over issues like the Dreyfus Affair, and later, the separation of Church and state. And this was stressed by the growing number of foreigners to be found in public life and public affairs, *metics* who, Maurras said, could not react to French problems in a French way, because they had no roots in French soil, and carried within them none of that intuitive understanding that would belong to men who, by their descent, share a long common heritage.

The trouble resulting from this general unsettlement was obvious to all. It could be traced back to the lack of a common, and commonly accepted, principle of unity; that common principle, embodiment of the common purpose that alone had made the greatness and the power of France in the past, was the monarchy. Around its kings, the French people had acquired a consciousness of peculiar unity. Slowly, perseveringly, the nation had been forged, its territory assembled, its self-consciousness hammered out by a long line of men who identified themselves with the nation, who devoted themselves to the nation, which they ruled and led—so much so, that even natural human selfishness operated in favor of national interests.

At best, this made France greater, more powerful, more prosperous. At worst, the hereditary principle insured at least some continuity of purpose, and prevented national energy being squandered in disputes over the succession to power. The monarchy also insured that no dispute and no divergency should shatter national unity. In the last resort, all parties would be one in their loyalty to France, a France embodied in the person of the king, and no one party could "own" France to the exclusion of all others. A party out of power could—and would—still consider itself "His Majesty's Opposition."

As long as this state of affairs lasted, France prospered. It may not have been perfect, but it worked, and for a long time, for the greater glory and the greater good of France. But then, theorists, men who thought they could perfect that which needed no perfecting, interfered. The revolutions of 1789 and after were the result of their violent meddling. The murder of Louis XVI broke the great contract between France and her kings, and left her at the mercy of adventurers and of parties, all of whom tried to capture power in order to further their own ideas or interests. Except for the short interlude of the Restoration, the story of France since 1793 could be told in terms of a struggle for power between diverse groups, all eager to run the country in their own interests. But these interests coincided only by chance with the interests of France. This had to be, for no faction or party could identify itself with the whole nation, as the king had done, who belonged to no party but stood for the country as a whole.

Thus, present disruption must be traced back to the unfortunate moment when, having made the helmsman walk the plank, the French let the ship of state wander every which way, at the mercy of winds, tides, and drunken members of the crew. But if the cause of present ills was clear, so was their solution: the monarchy must be restored; the rival factions must submit once more to nonparty rule; the rival interests must be ordered by the one figure whose interest is vested in the good of the nation as a whole. With the return of the king, the process of purging the nation of the evil habits it acquired during its errant century-and-a-quarter could begin. But can the monarchy be restored unless, to begin with, the nation has been purged at least sufficiently to see its need of a king? To advance the restoration, to help the work of persuasion, all means are good. All means—even legal ones. And the end will justify the means.

The hard logic of such arguments seemed impressive. Even more provocative were the circumstances of their formulation. Arguments drawn from history can be twisted every way to prove a desired point, but arguments based on present circumstances, even misinterpreted, are otherwise impressive. Certainly the mood and the internal disorder of France after the strain of the Dreyfus Affair and during the struggles of the *Inventaires* (the taking of Church inventories which was part of the administrative aspect of the separation of Church and state) weighed heavily on the side of Maurras. Intellectually, often spiritually, many resented the general impression of disorder and disunity, sought for a force that would heal social and intellectual rifts, and discipline those national energies wasted on religious struggles and the switchback of parliamentary politics.

The movement toward the Catholic Church, almost a movement of Catholic revival, seems very much a reflection of this same spirit. As Henri Massis has suggested,[10] it was part of a trend in favor of authority, hierarchy, and discipline, rather than a search for ultimate truth which did not seem nearly so interesting. Even as serious a convert to Catholicism as Ernest Psichari was eager and happy to find in it, as his biographer tells us, "clear duties, well-defined dogmas, an internal and external rule." And Mlle Goichon adds significantly: "Dès le début de sa vie chrétienne, il se voua au catholicisme intégral."[11] There is a highly relevant point in these words, which refer to a sympathizer of the Action française. The young Georges Bernanos, soon to become a *camelot du Roi*, clarifies the point when he writes to a friendly priest of his feelings for Action française: "Comme c'est clair! Comme c'est à l'emporte-pièce!"

Action française was something to believe in, and it was so clear and convincing that one could discover in it a revelation of obvious truth, and be carried away by it, elated and excited. But I do not intend to exaggerate the importance of the intellectual appeal, however great. Even an old *camelot* admits that this was not all that held him in the ranks of the Action française. As strong or stronger than the dialectic of the movement were the opportunities for action which it offered. Ernest de Malibran confides:

Nous lui avons dû de connaître surtout les charmes de la rude et saine camaraderie de combat. Georges [Bernanos] qui voyait bien ses défauts n'était pas insensible à cet entrainement.[12]

Bernanos, in time, came to realize the drawbacks of both the doctrine and the means. As he said, the kernel of a doctrine, the stuff of it, "is not the definition or the distinction which can always be brought up so easily, but the current—the movement—which the doctrine creates." By the time Bernanos sat down to write *Le Scandale de la Vérité*, in 1938, it seemed clear that

The current of Maurras' thought, pursuing its way through the deep layers of the conservative *bourgeoisie*, has ended by moving toward the dictatorships. Nationalist doctrine may well conclude in favor of the monarchy, the mystique of integral nationalism ends in dictatorship for the public good.[13]

Here Bernanos touches on a great weakness of the doctrine of Maurras, a doctrine that claims to be above factions and above factional interests: by ignoring the developments since 1789 except to condemn them, Maurras succeeded in effect in merely adding one more faction to the French political spectrum.

His was not the only party that had claimed to speak for the nation. The party's language and its disregard for the will of the people, while professing to represent their best interests, were reminiscent of the approach of those disciples of Rousseau who made the Terror obedient to a General Will that they alone could perceive or interpret. A party to which all means seemed good, but that by disregard of current historical realities could only be a minority party, was self-condemned to seek notoriety, success, eventually power, by violent means. It could, in fact, hope to win only by reviving the revolution it professed to loathe.

But if, in order to fight the results of the revolution, the party fell back on revolution, it would be a counterrevolutionary revolution. Hence, it easily conceived itself as defending the people with whom it became identified through its evolution as a political faction—the property-owning middle class.

Thus, the party of Maurras by its stand on present realities became a revolutionary party, but revolutionary professedly in a counterrevolutionary sense. This could not fail to endear it to those sections of society which had most to fear from a possible revolution. Feeling themselves ill-guarded by the state they did not control, or control sufficiently to trust, the middle classes welcomed a movement whose violence, dedicated to a counterrevolutionary cause, reassured them when they needed reassurance. The excessive nationalism of the Action française seemed an antidote against the excessive internationalism of the Socialists. One violence could be countered by another; one excess by another. Suddenly, from being the heroic challengers of the rotten established order, the Action française found themselves its heroic defenders. This nonplussed some of its members,[14] and caused the movement to miss in 1914 its best chance of upsetting the Republic.

Had the Machiavellian ideas of Maurras inclined him toward consistency rather than toward the Académie française, the upheaval of war would have presented the ideal and obvious occasion for revolution and restoration. Julien Benda has pointed out very reasonably that, had the Action française been true to their principles, they would have worked for the defeat of the Republic as Louis XVI and Louis XVIII had done in their time.[15] By placing the interests of their land above their political ideal, they showed themselves to be mere materialists.

Emile Faguet has compared the Action française to a gentleman of 1760, *royaliste, voltairien, et athée.*[16] Replace *voltairien* by *positiviste* and the description would apply better to Maurras. His royalism was a result of his analysis of the basic purpose of nationalism. "He has obliged us all," a Socialist wrote,[17] "by taking nationalist tendencies to their logical conclusion, by uniting them, filtering them, and distilling therefrom the essential. He has integrated nationalism and proved that integral nationalism means a monarchy."

Maurras had come to nationalism by way of his hatred and fear of the Germans. Watching a German motorized column roll through his home town of Martigues in 1943, he told Massis that this had been the nightmare of his life. Ever since as a three-year-old child in 1871 he had watched the National Guard drilling on the Promenade, he had carried with him the fear of seeing the Germans there in the far south. "These memories have never ceased to haunt me . . . ever since, I have always thought of the possible attack, of the possible invasion. . . . On this fear that I felt since my earliest youth my political thought has fed: everything . . . stems from that."[18]

This recalls the very similar experience of Barrès, although in his case the Prussian danger had been closer. He too carried through life a memory of 1870 that made the possibility of war, invasion, even defeat, seem more actual than it did to many of his followers. Barrès it had been who, with Déroulède, had led the nationalist troops at the beginning of the century. With returning normalcy, the Patrie française, founded on a crisis, had begun to lose in numbers and effectiveness. By 1902, the results of the electoral failure of the Ligue went together with a failure of Barrès within his own party.[19] From then on, Barrès would be a respected elder, considered increasingly out of date. Leadership passed to less spiritual-minded men, and to men who thought less and less of the Republic.

The position of Barrès in the nationalist camp was determined by his choice at the moment of the Dreyfus Affair. The step he took then could never be retraced. After being a leader during the heroic years, Barrès, whatever his own subsequent development, could never be anything but a nationalist. Nor could nationalists, however far from their positions they should find him, ever forget his services to the common cause or his place in their mythology. Thus Barrès went his way, and the new nationalists went theirs, without admitting the growing distance between them.

When Henri Massis told him that a daily *Action française* was to be published, Barrès was not pleased. The enterprise seemed absurd. Worse still, these people claimed the support of his name and might well compromise him. He seriously considered an open break that would save him from becoming involved in their affairs.[20] He was no more sympathetic to Agathon's campaign of 1910 against the Sorbonne and the university authorities: "If I understand rightly, you are not satisfied with your teachers. We were all like this at your age," was his reaction. And in a letter written during the campaign: "You see the faults of your teachers. Ah! if you could have seen ours!" Such an attitude somewhat naturally exasperated his young admirers, who sought not objectivity but enthusiasm. What they ignored was that his growing religious preoccupation was already overshadowing his nationalism.[21]

Maurras saw the danger of the doctrinal slackness of Barrès.[22] Nationalism in his opinion needed a theory, not a song. This he set out to provide.

The positivist doctrine of Maurras was based on the idea that the life and survival of a society are subject to natural laws outside which there can be only anarchy and disorder. This postulates a traditionalist policy, condemning 1789 and all its consequences—the Revolution, democracy, parliamentarianism, individualism—in the name of reason and science. Democracy is a negation of the real needs of social life, to which only a monarchy can bring the necessary stability and continuity. The revolutionary spirit is that of a vague ideology, ignorant of facts, anarchistic, far from the exigencies and nature of France.

To this point of view, Maurras and his disciples brooked no contradiction, yet here, as elsewhere, theory and analysis remained inaccessible to the masses. Quite likely the theory seemed irrelevant to their immediate problems, or perhaps the masses remained impervious to theorizing. Men continued to support the side they had always supported. The troops of the Action française were the same as those who had followed Boulanger and the anti-*Dreyfusards*. Such followers apart, Maurrasian influence was restricted to the students and young intellectuals accessible to the Master's hard-bitten logic.

While official nationalist forces were routed, the Action française continued its activity. The autumn of 1906 saw a number of angry, disdainful articles in the Radical press, concerning the subscription opened by the Action française to buy a gold medal for that General Mercier who had played such a great part in the trial and conviction of Dreyfus. But the anger of the tone belied the disdain.[23] The Action française never admitted the validity of the decision of July 12, 1906, which cleared Dreyfus and annulled the judgment of the Rennes court-martial.[24] By dint of obstinate repetition and unrelenting offensive action, it succeeded in persuading a section of the public, and particularly its own adherents, that Dreyfus had been guilty and the judicial revision of his case illegal.

However, a review published monthly and an agitation centered on a matter everyone wanted to forget were not sufficient to insure success. A daily paper was necessary for sustained action and for the diffusion of ideas that, by 1908 at the latest, had taken coherent shape in a series of articles and conferences. Negotiations with a view to buying *La Libre Parole* failed, owing probably to the opposition of Drumont's collaborators, Devos and Gaston Méry, both of whom hoped to take over the direction when the old man should vacate.[25]

When the first number of the new, daily *Action française* did appear, on March 21, 1908, nobody thought it could last,[26] least of all Barrès, who gave it less than six months. The nationalist reading public was limited and the newspaper had to fall back on endless subscription lists.[27] In the event, it took away subscribers from other Right-Wing papers to such an extent that, to face their new competitor, a project of fusion was mooted between *La Libre Parole*, *L'Autorité*, and *Le Soleil*.[28] Nothing came of it.

The beginning of 1908 found the Radicals assuring themselves—as they had been doing for the past few years—that the nationalist menace had disappeared. They were whistling in the dark. Had the menace not existed, they would not have thought to deny it. But, on February 13, while asserting the death of nationalism, *Le Progrès de Lyon* warned that beneath the calm surface the enemies of the Republic were at work: soon they would appear under some new pretext, the same men in a new disguise. It did not know how right it was. Three weeks later, the same newspaper had to note: "We are facing, not a moderate awakening—they have never dozed off on their repeated and sometimes resounding failures—but a rising in arms."[29]

The government having decided to transfer the ashes of Emile Zola from their previous resting place to the Panthéon, the debate in the Chamber over the grant of credits for the ceremony was rather an opportunity for renascent nationalist forces to count themselves, than an indication to the country of a "rising in arms." That would come later. In the Chamber, Barrès bitterly attacked the government's plan.[30] The debate was the first for some years in which nationalism was remarked and accepted by both sides as a political and parliamentary position. The credits were voted, but the government, frightened by the violence of the emotions released over this issue, put off the ceremony as long as it could.

The nationalists triumphed, and *La Libre Parole* voiced the general impression when it claimed: "Everybody understands that the government is afraid."[31] By the end of March, the agitation and the nationalist meetings over Zola's right to a place in the Panthéon led the *Action française* to comment: "At the very moment when our newspaper enters the scene, nationalist agitation flares up, and Paris stirs." But they preached chiefly to the converted. Those stirred who had stirred before. By the newpaper's own testimony, it took the anti-Semitic and nationalist crowds and converted them to royalism.[32] Perhaps even this assertion was too sanguine. In any case, there was not a shift in public opinion, but merely a shift within one section of public opinion; and there it was more a change of symbols than of opinion.

If the sections of public opinion already predisposed to nationalism might be described as idolatrous—some chiefly royalist, some chiefly anti-Semitic, some chiefly antirevolutionary or patriotically anti-German —then it can be seen that the Action française merely stressed the importance of one of the divinities in the nationalist Panthéon. Its importance came from the fact that, in a world of loose associations based on loose arguments, it insisted upon discipline, organization, and made of a coherent system of philosophy a respectable basis for its activity. This activity mobilized the traditional nationalist forces, and produced in a very literal sense a nationalist revival.

Action française nationalism was for the Action française the only real, the only possible, nationalism. Maurras insistently stressed this exclusive character of his doctrine:

> There is no true and false nationalist doctrine. There is a superficial and inconsequent nationalism—it is republican nationalism. There is a coherent and complete nationalism—it is integral nationalism.[33]

Integral nationalism was royalism, but royalism on the terms of the Action française. To defend these terms and to persuade their king, the Action française would fight bitterly to destroy, as far as it was in their power, those in the royalist ranks whom they failed to convert to their views.

In spite of this insistence on the importance of the crown, the influence of the Action française increased rather despite than because of their royalism. As a politician and publicist important in nationalist ranks, the Paris deputy Joseph Denais said afterwards: "Royalism, no one took it seriously."[34] The Action française provided a rallying point, it kept the flag of nationalism flying, it inspired many a student disgusted by the vagueness of democratic theory and practice.[35] It did not go much further.

There is no doubt that Jules Lemaître was right when he claimed in 1908 that the influence of the Action française was growing in the University and in intellectual circles.[36] Jules Renard, who in 1904 had still been antinationalist and anticlerical, approved of the Action française by 1908, though with his usual scepticism.[37] The Radicals in power had been no different from any other government in power. This disappointed their more idealistic supporters, and confirmed those already inclined to dislike them.

Charles Péguy, who had been laboring in relative silence over the production of his *Cahiers*, wrote in angry and discouraged terms proclaiming the defeat of those of his generation who had fought for justice in *Dreyfusard* ranks.[38] "When would the awakening come?" he asked. What work would justify the lives of his generation, a "sacrificed generation, defeated sons of the defeated"? He did not know that even as he wrote the reaction was under way, the awakening had already come, and his work would stand as one of its firmest bases and inspirations.

About the same time a young man in Bordeaux was writing to his friend, Henri Fournier, in Paris:

> I take sides for reasons unconnected with clear, reasonable thought; I take sides by my childhood, by all my Catholic, reactionary upbringing. I still prefer the Action

française, none of whose stupidities escape me, to the Radical-Socialist league for which I feel a truly physical repugnance. In spite of everything, when I hear talk about Radicals and Socialists I feel the same slightly superstitious horror that I had as a child for the *Dreyfusards*. I always imagined these latter as more or less deformed, with something of the devil about them. This sentiment has remained, even after my mind sloughed off its misconceptions. Naturally, I do nothing to rid myself of it. . . .[39]

This throws a light not only on the scars left behind by the Dreyfus Affair, but also on the kind of prejudices and sympathies on which nationalism in general, and the Action française in particular as the most active of its battalions, could count.

The revived agitation led to a reaction in radical and governmental circles, which felt that they must answer the new nationalist challenge. "Nationalist and Reactionary polemics," wrote Ranc in *L'Aurore*,[40] "have taken on such a tone, such a manner, that we cannot hesitate any longer. . . . We cannot draw back before the raging cries of the Mercier gang." *La Lanterne* also noted the nationalist revival.[41] Soon it was declaring Paris to be affected by a fresh fit of the nationalist madness. *Le Progrès de Lyon*, which only six weeks earlier had asked triumphantly where nationalist gangs had got to, was shocked by the revival of nationalist demonstrations.[42] Barrès had claimed a nationalist triumph in the battle over Zola's ashes:[43] *Le Progrès* blamed the government's weakness and its feeble pretexts for putting off the ceremony.[44]

But before the government should decide to move, another issue offered the nationalists an opportunity to renew their tactics of the time of the Affair. An eminent Germanist, Charles Andler, professor at the Sorbonne, had been asked to lead a group of thirty students on a visit to Germany during the Easter vacation. The visit had been arranged with a view to fostering better understanding and improved relations between the two countries, and was in fact given a semiofficial aspect by the German hosts of the visiting party.

The idea of such officially—or even officiously—sanctioned visits, led by a Sorbonne professor who also happened to be a leading Socialist, exasperated the nationalists. A press campaign was only the prelude to more active campaigning in the streets of Paris. The *Dépêche de Toulouse* commented ruefully: "One could have thought nationalism dead and buried. But here it is again . . . and on the Boulevard St. Michel cudgels are selling like hot cakes once more."[45]

It is possible that the campaign, begun just before the municipal elections, had been envisaged as useful election material.[46] It is improbable that it did much to affect results influenced by a general trend toward the Right.[47] But this trend itself was not unconnected with the reaction against Socialist antimilitarism. "One excess breeds another," wrote *La*

Dépêche.[48] "It is the weight of Hervé, this ball and chain of which you cannot rid yourselves, that makes Barrès go up." On the same day, *Le Progrès*, commenting on the election results, saw reaction, as yet only an agent of disorder, well on its way to becoming mistress of the hour.

In the beginning of the summer term at the Sorbonne, organized rioting flared in the Latin Quarter, professedly in protest against Andler and his group. The visit to Germany had been taken up by the Action française on April 24. It had called a meeting, *Contre l'oubli de '71*, on May 4, as a prelude to demonstrations in and around the Sorbonne. The object was to prevent the continuation of Andler's lectures there. Andler explained in a letter to *Le Temps* on May 10 that the trip had been organized chiefly to allow the students to travel at half-fare as members of a group led by a professor, as regulations required. The demonstrations only grew worse. On May 16, the *Action française* commented: "One thing stands out . . . nationalism, our sentiment of 1898 . . . that is what we find again, identical, intact, in these young men."

The comparison with 1898, significant enough, was not unjustified. Serious clashes took place in the streets, in the courts of the Sorbonne, even in its lecture halls. The days of Andler's lectures became days of overflow at the police station in the Place du Panthéon. This agitation rose to its highest point on June 4 when, on the occasion of Zola's reburial in the Panthéon, a journalist, Grégori, fired two shots at Dreyfus, one of which hit him in the shoulder. Tried before the Court of Assizes, Grégori was acquitted three months later. The fourth of June did not see great riots, but it convinced the Action française as well as its opponents that the nationalists now dominated the Latin Quarter.

Summer came, and the Action française had to turn to new fields because there were no students left in the old ones. Maurras had realized that his movement could get nowhere without more troops and more widespread support than intellectual prestige alone could command. The obvious reservoir to tap was the working class, but this he had to dispute with the Socialists, who were already well established, and who disposed of an organized network of local sections.

The summer of 1908 marked very clearly the attempt by the Action française to establish a bridgehead on the working-class shore, and its failure to achieve this. For, as suggested already, the logic of the *Nationalisme intégral* was not easily accessible to the layman who was not already inclined toward it for other, nonlogical reasons. In addition, the Socialists themselves disposed of a highly coherent and integrated doctrine, and they retained their grip on the masses by concrete and reiterated calls for immediate reforms, couched in terms of realities the

workers could understand. On this ground they were almost unchallenge-
able by integral, i.e., Royalist, nationalism. True, the Royalists had
found with Syndicalists some common terrain—violence—and the Socialists had brief alerts from time to time, when for an instant the nightmare of a Nationalist-Syndicalist alliance appeared to be taking shape.
But it did not happen. The alerts never materialized.[49]

In the autumn, the newspaper returned to its old public. The switch
spring–summer–autumn is obvious, and was not repeated any year before
1914. Although the *Action française* may have given up the hope of
winning over the workers, it never ceased to hope for an understanding.
Maurras reserved his broadsides for the "disintegrating" intelligentsia.
Working-class organizations were always treated rather as erring sheep,
not to be cut up—not at once, at any rate—but to be persuaded back
to the fold.[50]

This sympathy was so apparent that the Action française was attacked
for supporting revolutionary syndicalism. Paul Deschanel thought he
saw growing between them the "eternal alliance of demagogy and reaction."[51] But though his theory was right, by the time his words were
spoken, the movement in that direction had proved vain, and his warning
was out of date.

While they had been checked at a point that the future would show to
have been crucial, the nationalists were nevertheless riding the crest of
an incoming tide. Not as obvious as it would be three or four years later,
it was nonetheless sufficient to excite comment from sources that had
refused it any attention before. *Le Matin* had made no mention of the
Action française or of nationalist agitation. It had not commented on the
incidents of the fourth of June beyond a mention of Grégori's attempted
crime. In July, however, it gave half its front page to an interview with
the Duc d'Orléans. In summer news is rather short, but *Le Matin* gave
as the reason for its departure the awakening that it discerned of monarchist ideas. When a "brilliant elite of writers and orators daringly con-
fesses its royalist faith and its firm intention of 'subverting' the Republic," it was time for *Le Matin* to take notice.[52]

L'Humanité commented sadly: "All the effort of the last few years has
been in vain. We find ourselves once again full in the midst of reaction."[53]

On September 12, Grégori was acquitted after an extremely agitated
trial before the Court of Assizes. Showing complete contempt of court,
a contempt that went directly counter to their assertions of 1898 now
conveniently forgotten, divers members of the public, followers of Maurras, had interfered with the proceedings. One of these, André Gaucher,
was arrested for his violent criticism of the Court of Appeal's verdict of

1906. This, based on Article 445 of the Code of Criminal Instruction, had annulled without appeal the judgment by which the Rennes court-martial of 1898 had once again convicted Dreyfus. Now, around this same article, the Action française was conducting a violent campaign. André Gaucher was not the only *camelot* to carry its echoes into the court-room where Grégori was being tried. To nationalists, *l'Article 445* became the "talisman" that proved the injustice of the judgment of 1906, and the "talisman campaign" was probably not unrelated to Grégori's acquittal by a jury of his peers.

"And who was it that claimed nationalism was no longer anything but a bad dream?" plaintively inquired *Le Progrès de Lyon*.[54]

The agitation led to interpellations in the Chamber concerning the Action française and also Article 445. It is the first time that we find the Action française mentioned in the debates of the Chamber, its importance acknowledged, and the disturbances it instigated examined. The situation was seen, and rightly, as a fresh stage in the evolution of nationalism.[55]

The nationalist revival was by now obvious enough to worry the Left-Wing leaders and the Left-Wing press. Their comments show the new awareness of the growing danger, a danger perhaps exaggerated by the concentration of almost all nationalist agitation in a relatively narrow sector of Paris. Whether this was a considered tactic or merely, and much more likely, a course of action forced upon them by their own numerical weakness, the method served the nationalists well. Paris could not help taking notice of the propaganda. Political chroniclers writing from Paris spread this notoriety to the provinces, among the politically minded.

And yet, it may be doubted, if only because of the lack of any indication to the contrary, whether nationalist agitation throughout the rest of the country ever reached important proportions, or whether it was as yet widely regarded as much more than schoolboy pranks and hooliganism.[56]

Chapter VI

THE ETERNAL BOULANGISM: 1908–1910

Exécrer un même homme! Ah! la raison puissante de s'aimer!
(Maurice Barrès, *Du Sang, de la Volupté, et de la Mort.*)

Worried heart-searching on the part of some observers had led them to the conclusion that too much fuss had been made about antipatriotism. The general agreement on the dangers of antipatriotism had played into the hands of the extreme patriots, always ready to save the Republic from itself. There was nothing new about the agitation. Republicans recognized their traditional antagonists—clericals, monarchists, and nationalists—behind the mounting tension. "Boulangism in 1889, nationalism in 1899, nationalism again in 1909," wrote *Le Progrès*, "but integral nationalism—that is to say, monarchism. The Republic is undergoing its decennial crisis."[1]

Republicans may have remembered the words of the deputy abbé Gayraud, who had warned the Chamber during the debate on the separation: "We have centuries to take our revenge, and history shows that we always do."[2] Certainly the Church was not unsympathetic to the new trend, and the nationalist Right had always counted on its staunch patriotism. But Republicans were misjudging their opponents if they thought they were merely, and only, the old ones warmed up.

The "troops," as I have endeavored to suggest, were in fact much the same. The new leaders knew perfectly well that their strength lay in the same nationalist crowds that had followed their predecessors at previous moments of national agitation. The cheering public of the *camelots du Roi*—the young storm troops of the Action française, so-named because they began by selling the newspaper in the streets—and of their leaders, Maurice Pujo and Maxime Real del Sarte, was the same that had cheered Mercier in 1906 at the time of the final revision of the Dreyfus case. The nationalist emotion was the same in 1909 as it had been ten or twenty years before.[3]

The winter of 1908–1909 saw a renewal of nationalist violence in the Sorbonne, directed chiefly against the public course of M. Thalamas. While teaching history at the Lycée Condorcet in 1904, M. Thalamas had expressed opinions on Jeanne d'Arc which had caused a minor scandal and led to his being transferred to another lycée.[4] As the new lycée was also in Paris, and its standing was as good or better than the last, the professor did not suffer. But he remained from that day one of the nationalists' pet aversions. The announcement that he had been permitted to give a series of public lectures in the Sorbonne moved them to transports of rage.[5] The subject of the lectures, which were concerned with pedagogical method, was irrelevant to the symbolic importance attached to the presence of a detractor of Jeanne d'Arc in the halls of the Sorbonne.

The nationalists were not altogether mistaken in treating the appearance of Thalamas in the Sorbonne as a personal affront. Authorization for his lectures had been given less to fill a need than to spite the nationalist attacks. In the summer of 1908, the Faculty Council of the Sorbonne, faced with Thalamas' application for permission to lecture, had considered that a refusal would seem like a confirmation of nationalist attack on him. Its decision was a reaction against, almost a defiance of, nationalist threats.[6]

From then on, the *camelots du Roi* played an active part in disrupting the courses of the academic year 1908–09, in riots which involved large forces of police and led to pitched battles within and outside the Sorbonne between *Thalamistes* and anti-*Thalamistes*. On one occasion, the lecturer himself was tracked down and attacked by *camelots* who had managed to enter the heavily guarded amphitheater by a forgotten side entrance. Other incidents followed: Jewish lecturers, as well as the dean of the faculty, the eminent Hellenist Croizet, were the victims of *camelot*-staged campaigns. Those arrested in the riots were in their large majority below twenty years of age, hardly ever over thirty. The power of the Action française in this milieu of Left Bank university students would henceforth be their chief—almost their only—asset. The fact that the campaign of 1908–1909 remained typical of all their disturbances until 1914 shows how well they themselves realized this.

The Republican press, shocked and scared by these disturbances, repeated its warnings of the danger behind their continuation, a continuation which alone seemed to stress the growing success and power of the forces of reaction.[7] But those forces of Republican defense which had been ready to oppose reaction at the turn of the century were now lacking. The nationalist gangs of 1899 had found *Dreyfusards* ready to fight them in the streets and in the schools. Whether these were groups like those which Péguy and Lucien Herr led down from the *rue d'Ulm*, or else militant workers, their cudgels had been as ready, their fists as heavy, as those of their opponents.

But those cudgels and fists had belonged mostly to Socialists or to men of Socialist inspiration and now, in 1909, the Socialists no longer wanted any part in a fight between two sides they disliked equally. The political struggles of the past three years had convinced them that most Republicans were as reactionary as their opponents. The Right, for the Socialists, kept moving toward the Left.[8]

The government could expect no support from the Socialists, but it is doubtful whether it wanted help from such a quarter or, in fact, whether it wanted help at all. A Russian observer suggested that the nationalist agitation suited the government because it proved the absurdity of royalist claims.[9] This was probably too subtle an explanation, but it is not impossible that by that date the moderate Republican government in power did not look askance at the increasing propaganda in favor of strong government and patriotic duty. Such sentiments could do no harm, particularly as their royalist accompaniment was not taken seriously.

The beatification of Jeanne d'Arc, on April 18, 1909, was a gratifying occasion for the Right in general, and for nationalists in particular. For a long time Jeanne of Lorraine had been the symbol of French patriotism. Her origin usefully stressed the revendicatory nature of the movement, and no attaint was tolerated against the myth of Jeanne d'Arc as promulgated by nationalist and Catholic authorities. Whoever, like Thalamas, permitted himself doubts of her holiness, virginity, or military genius (not to mention her authenticity), was an enemy of the nation. Timid Republican voices observing that it was unreasonable to take for symbol of a royalist and Catholic movement a heroine abandoned by her king and condemned by her Church, were treated with the indifference and contempt they obviously deserved.

Writing on the ceremonies marking the beatification, Albert de Mun felt that the breath of national awakening had passed over the public in Notre Dame.[10] By the end of 1909, the Action française could look with satisfaction on the progress made by its doctrines.[11] But was it the doctrines that made for its success, or was it its activities and the prejudices of its followers? Thus anti-Semitism, which raised its head even in Parliament, often went hand in hand with the new nationalism[12] and fed on prophecies of social disintegration, social revolution, anarchy, *Götterdämmerung*, as well as on pure envy, honest dislike, or ignorance. Nationalist agitators knew this, and relied on such factors for much of their success.[13]

But the *nationalisme intégral* was not without competitors who, while admitting that the opponents of the Left must stay united under the nationalist banner, proposed another banner, another brand of nationalism than that of the Action française. Ernest Judet, for instance, editor of the *Eclair*, thought that only the Bonapartist formula of national imperialism could succeed, where mere nationalism had failed.[14]

If nationalists struggled for popular favor under their diverse banners, all stressing the greatness and the security of the fatherland and the integrity of French culture, these did not go unnoticed by a government highly interested in social cohesion and stability. The parliamentary recess of 1909 brought the usual spate of official speech-making, and the press was moved once more to remark how constantly the patriotic note had been sounded in all official statements.

Ministers continued to hold the language that the Tangier crisis and the reign of Clemenceau had reintroduced. Since 1905 reminders had been frequent that France should keep her powder dry. In the event, the problem was found not to be one of humidity, but of insufficient powder or its equivalents. *Si vis pacem, para bellum* had become the favorite dictum of all politicians—even of those who understood Latin. It was natural that concern for the nation's armed strength should go hand in hand with concern for its moral strength, for its pride and confidence in itself. Chéron, undersecretary for the navy, recommended valiantly:

> The minds of young people must be obstinately directed toward their country and all things relating to it. Let them take pride in its traditions, be moved by its past sorrows: they will be the security of its hopes. Let them ardently love the flag.[15]

The Republicans were getting away with the nationalists' flag.

The moderates now proclaimed themselves antinationalist, although greatly caring about the honor and the power of the fatherland. The moderates had always been thus concerned, and no nationalist could grudge them a share of the flag,[16] but the growing official interest in such things seemed an unfair way of cutting the ground from under nationalist feet.

Maurras proclaimed the success of the Action française and the conquering forward march of its ideas. Even as he spoke, the dynamic part of the party's ideology was no longer its own.[17] As Paul Bourget had pointed out, nationalism was not a party but a doctrine.[18] Barrès had stressed the fact in the title of one of his books, *Scènes et Doctrines du Nationalisme*. The Action française never accepted this. Yet in fact, far from being even one doctrine, nationalism became increasingly (partly through the work of those parties that claimed it as their own, partly through the influence of circumstances outside their control) a series of impressions and manifestations of reflexes and impulses, in fact an atmosphere.

This atmosphere became apparent in many ways. One example of its workings was that in his speech receiving the popular novelist Marcel Prévost into the Académie française, on April 21, 1910, Anatole France thought it necessary to introduce a panegyric of the fatherland, somewhat unusual in his case.

Maurras himself might concede that there could be patriots, even nationalists, holding, however misguidedly, views other than his own. But he would not allow himself to be challenged on his own territory of royalism. It seemed obvious that the best confirmation of a royalist's good faith was the confidence of his king. This confidence Maurras was not prepared to share with any other man or group whom he could not control and who might contest his authority.

In two stages, the years 1910 and 1911 were to see the defeat of those who competed with Maurras or, more correctly, against whom Maurras competed, for royal favor and royalist support. By the early summer of 1911, Maurras had established his uncontested supremacy as the representative of his king in France, and this is how it came about.

Le Gaulois was the newspaper most widely read in Paris society. Its editor, Arthur Meyer, a royalist and Catholic of Jewish birth, had been one of the most faithful supporters of the Orléans family. Deeply involved in the later stages of the Boulangist conspiracy, he had given warm support to the antirevisionist forces during the Affair. When the death of Syveton, its champion and treasurer, had endangered the good name of the Ligue de la Patrie française, Meyer had not hesitated to blame those who wavered in their faith. He attacked even Jules Lemaître for his feeble admission of the likely truth that Syveton had committed suicide, an admission that risked staining the nationalist escutcheon. Léon Daudet had been one of his regular contributors, and the two men had parted on the best of terms when Daudet left the *Gaulois* in 1908 to join the new *Action française*.

But the *Action française* could not stomach the caution of its older fellow-traveler, nor its inclination to temporize. *Le Gaulois* was too firmly established in society, it had too great a vested interest in the existing state of things and the preservation of order, to sympathize with the younger publication's revolutionary talk. It is probable that Meyer's Jewish origins, if they were not at the bottom of the rift, at least helped the *Action française* to persuade itself of the justice of its cause against him and the foundation of its distrust. All Jews were potential traitors. All Jews were cowards. The royalist camp should no longer be dominated by Meyer.

The *Action française* produced its filthiest language[19] and succeeded in frightening the princely patron from his old, but ineffective, supporters. But this first triumph only led to another obstacle to be surmounted, another battle to be won.

The second part of the struggle, which had begun with the elimination of Meyer from the royalist general staff, concerned the make-up of the king's political bureau. Maurras' young king, Philippe, Duc d'Orléans, made his headquarters near London. By a law that kept out of French territory all pretenders to the throne, he was refused entrance to France but he was allowed to keep in touch with his loyal subjects through the men whom he chose to direct his political bureau, and whom his confidence, as well as their abilities, designed to keep the king's party in touch with their king. It was their duty to advise him and to transmit his instructions to those who still heeded them.

Such arrangements, made necessary by the peculiar circumstances, gave great power to those in charge of the political bureau, and jealousies were rife. All went well, however, and there was loyal coöperation between the bureau and the *Action française* until two of the king's advisers fell foul of Maurras. Their nefarious influence had to be eliminated, and better counsel substituted. Thus, in December, 1910, the transgressors, their publication *La Correspondance Nationale*, and for good measure the hapless *Gaulois*, were all subjected to a barrage of insults. At the same time, the *Action française* mobilized all its royalist sympathizers in an effort to prove that the real strength, both numerical and material, within royalist ranks, lay on its side.

A subscription was opened for a "fighting fund," and both *Le Gaulois* and the *Correspondance Nationale* began to lose "disgusted subscribers" to the rival *Action française*. This time the prince was harder to persuade: the two advisers whom Maurras was trying to remove were old and trusted friends, in particular the Comte de Larègle. The hullabaloo tended rather to predispose Philippe against the detractors. He issued an official statement of blame for the *Action française*, and called them to heel. The *Action française* ignored him and continued the fight. If it could only defeat its rivals, it could persuade its king, victim of his wicked advisers, of the justice of its cause and the reality of its devotion. Etienne Marcel had wanted nothing more.

The fighting fund grew daily: by the end of 1910 it had reached nearly 150,000 francs. Philippe had to forgive his loyal servants of the Action française on May 19, 1911. They returned to the fold, receiving appropriate expressions of good will on his part and offering submission on theirs. But the struggle was not over nor victory assured for another month, when, on June 15, a royal letter excommunicated the *Correspondance Nationale*, and accepted Larègle's resignation from the political bureau. Henceforth, and for fifteen years at least, the bureau would be dominated by the *Action française*, speaking as the official mouthpiece of the king.[20]

These divisions in the royalist camp did not particularly affect the results of the 1910 elections.[21] The royalists counted for too little outside the particular regions where no internal dissensions could affect a foreknown vote. The general tendency was still moderate. The dissatisfaction of the electorate expressed itself in refusal to return a sitting member, but usually spared the party he had represented. Although the Right sustained losses, it was its moderate wing that suffered. On the other hand, there was reason for thought in the fact that three old Boulangists were returned to the Chamber—one of them, Castelin, having beaten Paul Doumer at Laon (Aisne) on the nationalist ticket. *Le Gaulois* was moved to inquire: "Would they be looking for a new Boulanger?"[22]

If the Right came out of the elections weakened in its more moderate elements, moderate elements predominated in the new Left. This situation would dominate the political scene during the coming years. It was not then clear at first to commentators, who looked at returns and at official labels rather than at the men who had been elected, but it became obvious by the midsummer.[23]

The annual celebrations on July 14 showed a great revival of the old enthusiasm for army and flag. Judet, a relatively objective witness in spite of his Bonapartist prejudices, noted with satisfaction: "Le mouvement de retour aux idées nationales, aux sympathies militaires, aux tendances que j'appellerai tricolores."[24] Maurras, sanguine as usual, saw a renaissance not only of nationalist, but also of royalist, feelings. In this appreciation he was probably overconfident.[25] He tended to confuse his personal position with that of his party, and the mistake was understandable enough. Maurras was aware that his personal influence affected men well outside his own circle.[26] His books were widely read, his arguments seemed convincing to many. Even Marcel Sembat was moved to write him an appreciative and sympathetic note on the newly published *Kiel et Tanger*, where he found the criticism of Maurras to be vigorous and true. As for Maurras' analysis that France was faced with the choice between monarchy and disintegration, Sembat did not think this choice inevitable. Certainly there was a gap at the top of the national structure, but why fill it with a king? The Socialist answer would be a new collective organ, which would coördinate and direct national activity. "It has not yet been invented, it is true, and this lack is dangerous."

One vague panacea affronted another. The *Action française* published the letter, which had been written on September 25, 1910; but the identity of the writer was not made public until January 15, 1912, when Sembat had shown his growing consideration for the power of integral nationalism by arguing that it stood as the only possible alternative to Socialism and peace.[27]

As competitors became ever fewer, the *Action française* began to be regarded as the chief representative of nationalism, as the nationalist party *par excellence*. *La Libre Parole*, sold to Joseph Denais and Henri Bazire, appeared on October 1, 1910, with an article by Edouard Drumont announcing the "transformation of the *Libre Parole*." Although Drumont referred to a physical change—more pages, better news service, new features—the tone of the newspaper was also more moderate. Denais and Bazire were Pioutistes, friends of Jacques Piou, and his Catholic "Liberals." They were not averse to supporting the government and, above all, established order.[28] Drumont stayed on to write the leading articles, at a salary of 1,000 francs a month. Yet, far from reducing their influence, the fact that certain nationalists were moving away from the lunatic fringe toward more conservative positions, ensured a wider circulation for their views.

Oppositional nationalism had become once again an enemy worthy of the government's steel. Briand and his supporters were beginning to see it as the counterpart (on the Right) of revolutionary syndicalism, and a danger to the continued existence of the Republic. *Le Temps* called for republican union against it, as had been formed in previous moments of crisis.[29] The parallel between nationalism and Boulangism had become obvious to all. The *Action française* itself saw all patriots, nationalists and anti-*Dreyfusards*, united in an eternal Boulangism.[30]

Chapter VII

THE INTELLECTUAL FRONT: 1910–1911

La littérature d'un temps ne paraît jamais chaotique qu'en son temps même. Trente ans après elle paraît harmonieuse, et l'on voit parfaitement les lignes générales, et même l'unité, et même le principe d'unité. C'est d'abord parce qu'on les y met après coup ... c'est ensuite qu'il y a réellement un esprit général du temps, lequel n'est sensible qu'à un suffisant recul. (Émile Faguet, preface to Gaston Riou, *Aux Ecoutes de la France Qui Vient.*)

THE YEAR 1911 OPENED with patriotism high in fashion. Like all current fads, it was put to every possible use—not to the same extent as in 1913, but to a degree that would have been unbelievable in the not so far off days when its use still carried reactionary implications.

When the budget came before the Chamber, the debate on the foreign ministry's estimates produced heated recriminations against the foreign minister, Stephen Pichon.[1] He had allowed the publication of the first volume of documents relating to the origins of the war of 1870 by an editor called Ficker, an only-recently-naturalized German Jew. The question became one of confidence. Party limits ceased to count when Independents like Paul Painlevé and Radical-Socialists like Albert Sarraut joined Socialists and the Right, to vote 157-strong against the government.[2]

A decision of the foreign minister settled the scandal—for it had become one, though in a parliamentary teacup—by deciding that in future all the ministry's publications would be printed by the Imprimerie Nationale.[3] A deputy commented in the Chamber: "This will show what no one ignored, that on all sides of the Chamber, from extreme Right to farthest Left, there is only one thing in question—patriotism."[4] What it did show in fact was that "patriotism" had been recognized once more as a useful handle for parliamentary politicians.

The bloody shirt could be waved in all directions. One of its earliest uses was in the economic field, where French capacity for producing loan capital was constantly used to support her diplomacy. But at home, too, there was room for economic patriotism. Marc Reville, deputy of the Doubs, pointed out in *L'Aurore* the danger of a German economic invasion: "It is above all in the economic field that France must belong to the French."[5] As in the case of a highly vocal, highly patriotic press campaign in favor of French trade abroad, Jaurès was right in his advice not to take too seriously certain patriotic claims whose purpose was to shield the fruitful operations of a publicity campaign.[6] Investment in patriotism was a good thing once again.

Publicity campaigns could be of various kinds. That which the *Action française* provided for Bernstein's play, *Après Moi*, was in no way helpful to the author. Henri Bernstein had been something of a playboy in his youth. Disgusted with the rigors of military service, he had deserted after seven months and had, from Brussels, written the kind of letter to the press that foolish young men tend to regret when they are no longer so foolish or so young. This was to be his case when, in 1911, already a successful playwright, his youthful misbehavior officially forgiven and, it could have been hoped, forgotten, the Comédie française accepted his play, *Après Moi*. The announcement, however, brought prompt reactions from the nationalists, who determined to prevent this desecration of France's national theater.[7]

The play was put on, but to the accompaniment of such disturbances both in the theater and outside that the author withdrew it after a fortnight. The keynote of the campaign had been anti-Semitism. The first night had found Paris and the theater itself plastered with *Action française* stickers denouncing *Le Juif Déserteur* on top of all the posters advertising the play.[8] The voices of the actors at all performances had repeatedly been covered by disturbances and altercations from the body of the hall. Cartoons showed the interior of the theater with every other seat occupied by a policeman. Those who had been able to ignore the student riots because they had taken place on the Left Bank, could not remain unconscious of the disturbances that now took place in the very heart of Paris.

The *Paris Daily Mail* itself was moved to publish a study of anti-Semitism in France, motivated by what it called the "recent Bernstein incident."

All the latest disturbances prove that anti-Semitism is a political weapon wielded by two minorities . . . the Action française . . . and a few revolutionaries like Urbain Gohier. . . . The only lesson taught by the events is the eternal fact that patriotism and militarism are still predominant characteristics of the people of France.[9]

One may wonder whether it was patriotism and militarism that expressed themselves in anti-Semitism, or whether it was the other way round.

The nationalists were once more triumphant: "Yesterday the Latin Quarter carried Paris with it," wrote Xavier de Magallon in the *Libre Parole*.[10] "Youth is with us. The future is ours." They exulted. No one had expected to find nationalist anti-Semitism so lively—and kicking—after all these years.

Radicals were disquieted, nor could they be cheered by any encouraging connections between the nationalist blackmail and the patriotic revival. *L'Aurore* was frankly worried. It renewed its calls for Republican unity, warning of possible nationalist plots and urging that a stern eye be kept on the army, whose loyalty past memories made *L'Aurore* doubt.[11] To Bouglé, writing in the *Dépêche de Toulouse*, the anti-Semitic victory seemed ominous. He suspected a hidden danger: "Around it," he wrote, "the neo-royalists, frantic with joy, are sounding their call. And there are revolutionary Syndicalists who echo their words."[12]

The Socialists were not unaware of this threat. One of their veteran publicists, Eugène Fournière, followed Bouglé with an article that tried to wean away those who might have been affected by the anti-Semitic campaign.[13] Maurras, still trying to win a hold on the working-class reservoir, had come very near to success, thought Fournière somewhat too generously. Who knows whether, but for his indigestible royalism, a national-socialism d'Action française would not have preceded all others?[14]

The battle of the *Palais Royal* won, the Action française turned to other tasks, and continued to use violence in the service of (its) reason.[15] The equanimity of the organization was troubled in passing by the scandal of M. d'Abbadie d'Arrast, organizer and president of the Action française at Evreux, son-in-law of Henri Lasserre, the well-known Catholic writer and historian of Lourdes. M. d'Arrast had left his wife and seven children, and sailed for Canada under a false name with a young schoolteacher half his age, after having tried to make his disappearance seem to be murder. The story was to the public's taste, but the beginning of summer was not devoid of news, and only political spite can have led the Radical press to give the affair so much attention. Having been brought back to France, the crestfallen seducer returned to his forgiving wife and seven children.[16]

Small diversions such as these could not draw off the nationalist fire concentrated on the Sorbonne. The nationalists of 1899 had tended, often justly, to look upon every intellectual as a *Dreyfusard*. This had made intellectuals as a group close their ranks and, with notable exceptions, such as Brunetière, Barrès, Lemaître, not to speak of Maurras himself, adopt a *Dreyfusard* point of view. There were no means of remaining neutral. The nationalists of 1899 were as ready to assume an intellectual to be a *Dreyfusard* as they were to assume a Jew to be a traitor.

This left the Sorbonne with an antinationalist tendency, which was only enforced by the natural aversion of reason for excess and of intellect for the use of violence as a means of persuasion. The *Dreyfusard* victory led to the rise of *Dreyfusards* to leading functions in an institution whose appointments were as politically motivated as those of any ministry.

The nationalists were right in concentrating their fire on one of the chief enemy strongholds, and one can see from the Sorbonne's reaction to the Thalamas riots the reaction they evoked. The scepticism and critical spirit of the scholars, who directed the chief teaching institutions of the country, made it easy for their critics to reproach them for lack of patriotism or, indeed, of any faith at all.[17]

On July 23, 1910, *L'Opinion* published an article criticizing the spirit in which the Sorbonne was administered. It was signed Agathon, a pseudonym representing two young men, Henri Massis and Alfred de Tarde. Neither of them was nationalist in the sense of the Action française; both were republican. Massis tells us that the "patriotism of Agathon and his friends was liberal, basically emotional, and one which, military duty apart, obeyed neither policy nor discipline."[18]

Agathon, like many of his contemporaries, had been greatly influenced by the philosophy of Bergson, and he is one of our best witnesses to the great role the philosopher played in the change of mood, in the birth of hope, among some of the intelligentsia. Bergson's lectures at the Collège de France were attended side by side by ladies of Paris society who sent their footmen ahead to keep their seats, and by ardent disciples and students who found a new freedom in Bergson's moving picture of space and time. "He has broken our chains," Péguy would say.[19]

With Péguy, with Joseph Lotte who was Péguy's great friend, with Jacques and Raïssa Maritain, Emile Clermont, Jacques Rivière, Charles Demange, Ernest Psichari, Massis attended the lectures of Bergson. He brought away not only a new freedom of intellectual movement, but a great contempt for the rival establishment across the road, the Sorbonne, whose teaching openly asserted its scorn of general speculations, and whose faculty, dazzled by Teutonic science, had as he saw it lost all sense of French culture and tradition.[20]

For over a generation now, the Sorbonne had taught the relative and fragmentary nature of truth. The jigsaw puzzle of their new-found knowledge became the despair of young people in search of a model of reality, a picture of the whole, to which they could relate the fragments in their possession. But their masters' doubt had removed the prototype, the whole, and the ultimate from vocabulary and from thought. It left the young generation, those of them who thought about such matters, victims of a scepticism that failed to satisfy them and that they became increasingly ready to shed for a coherent, forward-looking faith.

Agathon protested on behalf of his fellow-students (whom he did not, in fact, represent) against methods and attitudes that were out of tune with the times. He blamed particularly the Germanic influence, which, according to him, had insidiously contaminated everything, lowered the standard of the teaching of French language and literature, and diminished the importance accorded to the classics, both French and ancient. The article produced a commotion beyond the hopes of the young authors. However, they readily grasped their opportunity and, from a single article, they made first a campaign, then a book, then another book, and a reputation.

In an open letter to the dean of the Faculty of Arts, Agathon put his case: "An ever-growing section of your students," he wrote, "is hostile to the teaching it receives. . . . One can feel in them something like a refusal to undergo much longer the restraint of a few masters dazzled by Germanic science. It is a rising, a reaction, of French minds."[21] The exact phrase used in this connection, *un redressement, un sursaut des esprits français*, would often be repeated in the coming years.

The articles, the books, and the press-polemic to which they gave birth, caused a great stir. Marcel Habert saw an awakening of patriotism, and wrote: "It cannot be denied that a deep current in favor of patriotic ideas has recently been running through our youth."[22] A less prejudiced observer than Déroulède's best friend was moved to comment on a patriotic demonstration which brought together all the student organizations of Paris: "We can congratulate ourselves on the great patriotic movement that has made the hearts of all French students beat as one."[23]

Less lyrically, Aulard cast a sceptical look on the polemical battlefield and went right to the point:

The real grief against the Sorbonne, that which united against her so many different passions, is not in fact, whatever may be said, either literary or pedagogical. It is political. It is religious. She has against her conservatives and clericals of every shade. . . . She is an alarming center for those who want to subject youth to the old political and religious dogmas.[24]

As if to stress these words, *Le Figaro* had just printed the manifesto put out by Jean Richepin on behalf of the newly founded League for French Culture, presided over by himself, aiming at the restoration of the principle of authority and the preservation of the churches. Its membership included Barrès, Lemaître, and the bicephalic Agathon.[25]

The simultaneous "Catholic revival" has sometimes been connected with the general nationalist revival. No doubt the new interest in religion apparent among young people stemmed, as did much nationalist activity, from their desire to find something in which they could believe and on which they could base their actions. But, from the Catholic point of view, the prewar revival was not a whole but a number of fragments, sometimes more contradictory than complementary, and expressing not one but a number of tendencies.

Thus it is important from the point of view of this particular study to distinguish between the officially fostered Catholic revival, whose interest was peculiarly Catholic, and those political tendencies or parties, which, whether by interest or conviction, sought the support of the Catholic masses and the approval of the Catholic hierarchy. The former has its place in the story of Church politics, both general and French. The latter is more pertinent here.

The death of Leo XIII on July 20, 1903, the more uncompromising nature of his successor, Pius X, and the increased influence at Rome of more intransigent prelates, led by gradual stages to the abandonment of the *ralliement*, of the policy of recognizing the established order. The new policy was not made clear until the summer of 1909. Then, it encouraged those political groups that had retained or revived their implacable hatred of and opposition to the Republic. But the aim had been to encourage and facilitate the formation, if not of a Catholic party, at least of a Catholic policy. This aim was not achieved.

The years following separation, and the break of relations with Rome, were years of ferment in Catholic ranks; the ferment found expression chiefly in internal warfare. There was no Catholic party, but there were, both on the Right (where we would expect to find them) and on the Left, parties and groups either chiefly or exclusively of Catholic membership and inspiration. It would be difficult, however, to present their development and their struggles, which were directed so often against each other, as instances or results of a nationalist sentiment.

The members and leaders of such movements were deeply patriotic, but patriotic *because* Catholic, and also because one traditional faith so often implied the other. One party alone, largely supported by Catholics, primarily nationalist in aim and inspiration, the Action française was Catholic because nationalist. And it was the most fierce in its campaigns to destroy such rival Catholic movements or politicians as threatened to draw too deeply from the common pool of Catholic support.[26] Its bitter campaigns against the Sillon and against such liberal Catholic leaders as Henri Bazire, during which it did not hesitate to league itself with the Masons and the anticlericals whom it professed to detest in order to eliminate any offending Catholic competitor, were vicious. But the Action française apart, other Catholic movements, such as the A.C.J.F. or the Sillon, appear irrelevant to this study. Whereas they and their leaders reflected the preoccupations of their time, their motives and purpose were religious and only incidentally connected with national politics.

There is, however, another way of seeing the history of Catholicism in

France during this period: its intellectual history shows an impressive spate of individual conversions, which began at the turn of the nineteenth and continued into the twentieth century. This is nothing new, but it appears new at this time, considering how long Renan had dominated French thought, and it appears significant as one more reaction to the discovery that apparently science could not explain everything after all, that there was a need to fill the gap reason had failed to fill.

In 1892, Huysmans; in 1895, François Coppée; in 1898, Paul Bourget; in 1900, Brunetière; in 1905, Francis Jammes: the road had been staked out. But the years that followed were even richer in spiritual crises. Psichari and Massis, like Péguy, found in their faith in God a confirmation and a complement of their faith in France. The first two saw in the Church, as did Henri Bazire, not a convert himself, the basis of social order and almost a staff for the flag. Joseph Lotte, Péguy's friend, found in the Catholic faith the peace of acceptance after the struggles of ceaseless questioning; Raïssa and Jacques Maritain, a hope that the sceptical philosophy of the Sorbonne had denied them; Paul Claudel, the freedom he had sought so long. Even Barrès, though he died "unconvinced," had been moving ever nearer to acceptance.

But if a great deal of serious thought, and many interior struggles, led to a number of isolated, if significant, conversions, the "Catholic revival" among most young men was the expression of their search for order. They had grown out of childhood under the full blast of the corruption and incoherence of current politics. Now they wanted an authority they could accept and obey, they wanted a promise of order (which they felt threatened) and of discipline (from which the past generation had struggled so hard to free itself).

Tired of the analytical criticism of their masters, they were certainly not seeking to discover ultimate truth. Inevitably, such superficial groping led some of them to the Church, by a road the very opposite to that followed by a Paul Claudel, a Jacques Maritain, or an André Gide (who never got there). "They did not enjoy voluptuous heart-searchings," wrote Henri Massis. "What they wanted was the stability of the Church."[27] It was a Church they wanted, and not a faith. A Church . . . or a party.

At the same time, if Catholicism was on the upswing, the effects were limited and opinions differed. Louis Gillet in the *Eclair* thought he saw a revival of Christian literature, but another correspondent, inquiring into the reading habits of contemporary youth, had found a slackening of religious interest.[28] In 1911, answering an investigation of the *Mercure de France*, a school inspector, Payot, had affirmed that before long the map of Catholic France would coincide with the map of illiterate France.[29] Daniel Halévy, visiting a family of very literate and Catholic peasants, had found the Bible (bought from a Protestant hawker) standing next to the work of Drumont.[30]

But Halévy's host was a member of the Sillon, and two years later the Sillon was to be condemned by the Pope; much of the fine enthusiasm it had mobilized in the cause of living, social Christianity would be lost.[31] Another farmer, also a Catholic, was bitterly anticlerical: "They have kept the people in ignorance," he told Halévy. The hard logic of the French peasant worked only too often against his Catholicism: "I have tried everything. I have had a Mass said, and it did not pay. I bought artificial manure, and it paid. I am sticking to the better bargain."[32]

Chapter VIII

STRAIN AND INCOHERENCE

Nos amis les Allemands pèsent lourd sur l'Europe... On souhaiterait un coup de tonnerre pour détendre l'atmosphère, car
vraiment ce n'est pas vivre que d'être écrasés ainsi par ce poids
de plus en plus lourd de canons et de cartouches qui ne servent à
rien. Il y a même de la bouffonerie à s'intimider mutuellement en
mourant de peur chacun chez soi et à s'armer jusqu'aux dents
pour ne jamais se battre. Cela ne peut pas durer. (Louis Gillet to
Romain Rolland, June 1, 1913, *Correspondance*.)

As Barrère had told the British ambassador in Rome, the fall of
Delcassé had not made much difference in the policy of the Quai d'Orsay.
"The leaders of French diplomacy, the Cambons, Jusserand, and himself,
were firmly united in sympathy for the policy of their late chief and considered that there was no call for alarm." Rouvier had come under the
influence of the "house" to such an extent that outsiders attributed some
of his acts to "Delcassé men" like Revoil, Georges Louis, and Paul
Cambon.[1]

The Delcassé spirit had won a fall when in the autumn of 1905 it broke
the treaty of Björkö, snubbed Bülow's advances, and stirred up public
indignation against Germany to heights not reached since the Schnaebele
incident of 1887.[2] Soon these "heights" were to be left behind: Stéphane
Lauzanne in *Le Matin* and André Mévil in *L'Echo* began to shape the
myth of the national humiliation inflicted by a brutal Germany which
had forced Delcassé's resignation.[3] The press, that extraordinarily effective tool of democratic politics, had been fed with stories now known
to be untrue and used to sway a relatively peaceful public opinion, until
even German correspondents in Paris were impressed by the bitterness of
the new anti-German sentiment.[4] Once the diplomatic object of an international conference had been achieved and agreement reached at Algeçiras, passions and language became calmer, popular indifference resumed
its sway. But the bitterness smoldered during the years, and could be
stirred to life by press campaigns raking through the ashes.

Nor did the conference of Algeçiras efface the reminder of armed threat
on the eastern border.[5] The newspapers continued to publish warnings
that France must be strong and show no fear, a concern that also appears
in the electoral manifestoes of 1906.[6] Interest in the army grew, as it did
in the armies of friends and allies, especially in the Russian. It began to
be taken for granted that the Moroccan crisis of 1905 had been due to
the Russian defeats at Mukden and Tsushima. It followed that France

and her allies must not be unprepared. Henri Michel apostrophized the Chamber: "You no longer think of anything but the possibility of a war with Germany."[7] Clemenceau thought of it too. In an interview to a Berlin paper, he admitted his impression that the Moroccan affair had destroyed whatever understanding had been built up in the previous years.[8]

Clemenceau's public speeches during his period of office were the most chauvinistic a prime minister had yet made. A speech of his in the Vendée, early in 1906 when he was still only minister of the interior in Sarrien's cabinet, was compared by some critics to Barrèsiana. When prime minister, in 1908, he unveiled a bust of Scheurer-Kestner and made the senator's origin an excuse for significant mention of the Alsatian question. On July 28, 1908, Georges Louis quotes him as saying: "I expect the war, I consider it inevitable and I have even said so in writing. . . . We shall do nothing, we need do nothing, to provoke it, but we must be ready to fight it."[9]

Yet under Clemenceau, whom German dispatches accused of nationalist sympathies and underhand pacts with Déroulède,[10] the foreign minister, Stephen Pichon, had sought to bring about improvement in Franco-German relations, and a better understanding between the two countries. In June, 1907, the ceremonies at Kiel furnished an occasion for cautious unofficial overtures: Etienne, Bourgeois, the Prince of Monaco, good friends of the Republic and substantial men, all lent a hand.[11] In the Reichstag the Prince von Bülow joined in. He appealed to public opinion and goodwill to clear away those mutual misunderstandings which, he said, alone stood in the way of an enduring peace.

Public opinion was swayed perhaps more readily by such judicious articles as, for instance, Paul von Gontard caused to appear in the Paris press toward the end of 1907. Herr von Gontard was managing director of the Deutsche Waffen und Munitions-Fabrik of Berlin and Karlsruhe. The articles, printed in *Le Figaro, Le Matin,* and *L'Echo de Paris,* described great advances in the structure of French machine guns. Through a friend of Gontard's in the Reichstag, these articles were used to secure increased appropriations for machine guns, most of the money being spent with von Gontard's firm. However that may be, with the Reichstag spending large sums of money on machine guns, the French could not afford to lag behind. They might have invested heavily in machine guns even without the German example, although we have no evidence of such intentions. But the von Gontard campaign made quite certain that a profitable competition in machine guns would start between France and Germany.[12]

The method of urging increased armament by pointing to the activities of military rivals seems to have produced results: Philip Noel-Baker in his work on *The Private Manufacture of Armaments* states that in the five years from 1909 to the World War the cost of British armaments increased by more than 30 per cent, of Russian by 53 per cent, of German by 69 per cent, and of French by 86 per cent.[13] But, that between 1908 and 1913 France almost doubled her defense expenditure, may also be explained, at least in part, by the relatively small sums she had allotted to it before, and by certain peculiarities of her artillery and naval building programs.

The soldiers, of course, who reaped the benefits of the new orientation, had clung steadfastly to the hope of a revenge whose chief instruments they were to be. On March 19, 1907, at a farewell dinner offered by the officers of the 26th Infantry Regiment to their retiring colonel, General Bailloud who commanded the 20th Army Corps at Nancy was heard to say: "We were on the brink of war in 1905. The same causes or new pretexts may lead us to the same situation. There will be war. Let us hope that the 26th will contribute with the others to the recovery of our lost provinces." These words, reproduced in a Paris paper,[14] led to the general's displacement from Nancy to the command of the 16th Army Corps at Montpellier. News of the action taken against him caused widespread indignation and led to a parliamentary debate that permitted the first open discussion of the possibility and danger of war which the Chamber had heard.[15]

General Bailloud had the sympathy of the public. *Le Gaulois* commented: "At Nancy, any officer suspected of not wanting war would be the object of general contempt."[16] The government itself did not disapprove of the general's words, but it did not on any account want to endanger the state of Franco-German relations. Its work to better these relations resulted in a brief improvement,[17] which was seized upon as an opportunity to decrease the annual service period in the army reserve from 28 to 21 days.[18] This constituted one more instance of the readiness of deputies to avail themselves of every possibility to cut down the defense budget.[19]

In spite of this, the general tone remained different from what it had been before June, 1905. Clemenceau's references to Alsace-Lorraine brought echoes from every corner: "For the first time since Frankfurt," wrote *Le Matin*, "the head of our government has pronounced words that go straight to every Frenchman's heart."[20] Confidence was maintained during the short period of tension at the end of 1908 over the Casablanca deserters' affair, though not without anxiety about the possibility of a conflict.[21]

The brief *détente* following the settlement of this affair was soon troubled by the Bosnian crisis, which developed at a bad time from the viewpoint of both the Franco-Russian alliance and public opinion in France. M. Nintchitch in his work on the Bosnian crisis has made much of the pro-Austrian influence of the French ambassador in Vienna, Crozier. This must not be underrated, but it cannot certainly have counted for more with Clemenceau than that of Barrère did with Poincaré three years later. The fact is that the Quai d'Orsay did not want to endanger negotiations that, on February 9, led to the accord on Morocco and, the accord concluded, did not want to abandon its implications and its hopes. Nor was public opinion prepared for a firm stand on an issue it ill understood, and Pichon admitted as much when he informed Izvolsky on February 25, 1909, that opinion in the country "would not understand" a more active intervention of the government in this dispute.

How much such preparation might have counted became clear when in March the crisis became acute, the attitude of the government firmer, and the tone of the press began to rise. By mid-March an Austrian dispatch from Paris noted the newly aggressive tone of the press and its vigorous insistence on the duties of France toward the Russian ally.[22] This excitement was not meant to last and relief greeted the settlement of the dispute. Before the month was past, the German ambassador could report that papers like *Le Figaro*, *Le Gaulois*, and *La Petite République* welcomed Bülow's "golden words." Only *L'Echo* and, significantly, *Le Temps* cavilled at Germany's diplomatic victory over the Entente.[23] Yet it was true that the settlement had been a diplomatic defeat, and it appears that the conclusion was drawn in Paris that the "Western powers together with Russia must now pay attention to the systematic development of their armed forces in order to be able . . . to set up on their part demands that would restore the political balance that has now been displaced in favor of Germany and Austria."[24]

Few among those who were politically awake still thought that France could stay out of an increasingly inevitable war. Some thought it would come as an Anglo-German clash,[25] others believed the real antagonism to be between France and Germany. *Le Temps* wrote: "If Europe knows dangers of war other than a Franco-German conflict, it is yet the menace of this conflict which has, during the last five years, troubled the peace."[26]

It was felt that there could be no lasting Franco-German understanding as long as the question of Alsace-Lorraine continued to stick out like a sore thumb. Debates on foreign policy showed the impossibility of any lasting settlement before this problem was solved.[27] The tension, however, should not be ascribed to such feelings but rather to an awareness of the concrete and ever-growing threat of the German armament policy, which was still, in spite of press campaigns, localized and hardly touched the wider public.[28]

The report of the parliamentary commission of 1910, which edited the usual collection of election addresses, shows no tendency to harp on, or even to mention, patriotism, foreign danger, the army, or related subjects.[29] In this it differed significantly from the report of 1906, when the nearness of danger and the problems of antipatriotism and antimilitarism had figured prominently in candidates' declarations, and from the report of 1914, when the Three-Year Law dominated all other issues.

Thus by 1910 the mass of Frenchmen had reverted to its normally parochial outlook, and candidates who sensed this wisely adhered to home affairs in their declarations. But nearer the center of political power everyone felt the strain in foreign affairs, and even Jaurès was moved to point out how dangerous the equivocal state of Franco-German relations was, and how closely it was connected with chauvinistic manifestations in both countries.[30]

Jacques Bainville found the dominant sentiment of public opinion to be a wish for peace and tranquillity at any price; he feared that the weakening of conservative forces in Germany might bring a German diversionary movement that could well threaten this state. He did not, apparently, apprehend a similar reaction to a similar weakening of, or threat to, conservative interests in France. Soon he saw the horizon to be darker in 1911 than even in 1905.[31] Jaurès was not more cheerful; the state of armed peace, thought by some to be essential to national security,[32] seemed to him an impossible situation: "Neither fair nor foul, but the miserable and persistent fog of an armed peace, more ruinous, more disastrous in some ways, than war itself."[33] But when protests were raised against the growing expenditure on armaments, the answer came readily: "Have you read the speech of the German Chancellor?"[34]

Military issues began to figure more prominently in political debate, and the military point of view to make itself heard in the Chamber through men like Maitrôt, Driant, Rousset, and Guyot de Villeneuve. Politics, for their part, were not absent from feuds in high military circles, which focused on the clash between the offensive and the defensive conception of warfare. The practical issue was between a greater use of reserve troops favored by the Left as a step toward the ideal of a *nation armée*, and subordinating or ignoring the reserves in favor of a highly-trained body of long-service troops alone considered capable of speedy, effective action.

A brilliant group, including Foch, Lanrezac, Bourderiat, had for some years advocated the latter point of view in their teaching at the École supérieure de Guerre. In two famous lectures delivered in the spring of 1911, Lieutenant Colonel de Grandmaison publicized the offensive theory and its implications, presenting it to a public vaster than the general staff. The struggle for power within the army was to come to a head in July, but would pass almost unnoticed because of a greater crisis.[35]

Before that, in June, the staggering government of Monis, decapitated by an accident in which its leading personality, Berteaux, had lost his life and Monis himself had been severely wounded, fell before an interpellation concerning the make-up of the high command. The moderate Republicans voted with the Right, against the government.[36] The Right claimed a victory in this proof of general concern for and pride in the army.[37] Camille Pelletan, more sceptical, attributed it to a kind of absent-minded incompetence.[38] It was, at any rate, an indication that the union of the center and the Right, reminiscent of 1887 and 1896, a union that common economic interests suggested but failed to forge, could best be made on issues of national interest, not least the military.

The new prime minister, Joseph Caillaux, declared: "Il faut un gouvernement qui gouverne." There was applause from the near Left and the center, noise on the extreme Left and the Right.[39] Caillaux was going to need all his ability and strength to face the crisis already in the making.

PART THREE

THE SECOND REVIVAL

CHAPTER IX

THE TURNING POINT: 1911–1912

Maintenant, après la liquidation de la crise marocaine, la
question de savoir qui remplacera MM. Caillaux et de Selves
n'a pas, au fond, beaucoup d'importance. Plus ça change,
plus c'est la même chose. (Izvolsky, *Livre Noir*, I, 174.)

IN AN ARTICLE IN THE *Deutsche Revue*, September, 1921, Conrad von
Weizsäcker states that as early as April, 1911, Kiderlen-Wächter had
made up his mind to send a warship to a Moroccan port. The failure of
long-drawn-out negotiations for a joint Franco-German exploitation of
Morocco led to the sending of the *Panther* to Agadir on July 1, 1911.
It was thought that this would persuade the French government to offer
Germany compensation elsewhere for the "loss" suffered in Morocco.

If the German action was both rash and stupid, the French were not
without responsibility for the situation in which they found themselves.[1]
In 1905, *Le Matin* had written: "No one will ever know how easy it
would have been not to go into Morocco." Now this was wishful thinking. It may have been so even in 1905. It is not pertinent here to discuss
whether the "peaceful penetration" could have been avoided, which, by
1914, kept in North Africa some thirty thousand or more troops of the
Metropolitan defense force. Powerful interests wanted the acquisition
of that land. Morocco took over France, as Tunisia and Indochina had
done at an earlier date, against the expressed will of the majority.

The official explanation was that the Algerian frontier on the one hand,
and the security of European trading establishments on the other, required military protection inside Morocco. There was some truth in this,
but the accepted explanation was given by a senator as early as 1907,
and very much in public:

> *M. de Lamarzelle*: Alors, que voulons-nous au Maroc?
> *Un sénateur, à droite*: C'est ce qu'on se demande!
> *Un autre sénateur, à droite*: Faire des affaires![2]

As Daniel Halévy has justly remarked, the story of French colonial
expansion in modern times is not explicable only in terms of material
interests and economic expansion.[3] There was a romantic side to it
which is too often forgotten, but which the public of the time knew well.
The French elector was hostile to colonial adventures; but the French
newspaper-reader followed them with interest and sympathy. They were
exciting, they were romantic, they intercalated flashes of glory and high

adventure in the dusty, sometimes dirty, chronicles of Republican politics. As Lyautey said: "North Africa is for our race what the Far West is for America."[4]

The year 1909 had seen a change in the attitude of the Right, which until then had been in the habit of joining the extreme Left in criticism of a policy that tied down precious troops and resources away from the threatened eastern borders. The altered view of Africa was that its material and human resources would help to compensate France's weakness in Europe. In Africa, the Right now thought with Delcassé, a new world could be called into existence to redress the balance of the old.

It was the solution to the problem of France's feeble natality, the answer to her numerical inferiority before the philoprogenitive Germans. A speech of Delcassé pointed out that on this would depend France's continued existence as a great power.[5] The speech met with great success, and Jaurès was moved to ask his colleagues: "Why did you let him down, if you applaud him today?"[6] Perhaps, as the *Berliner Tageblatt* suggested, the applause was due in part to persistent resentment against the policy that had led to the sacrifice of Delcassé.[7] Nonetheless, a more forward-looking sentiment brought the Right to the side of the government in future debates.

Nor could France by this time have got out of Morocco easily. The privileges she had obtained entailed responsibilities, and large sums of money had been invested. With vested interests so great, there could be no serious talk of cutting losses and getting out.[8] The persistent nightmare of Morocco[9] had to be accepted and used to the best advantage. Thus, colored troops would be employed to compensate the "resources of national recruitment which have become insufficient." A trial project to that effect was introduced in the Chamber, where it excited heated debate.[10] Meanwhile, France was drifting ever deeper into the nightmare: Pichon explained a fresh armed intervention by the need to impose respect.[11] This need, and the security of French subjects, soon called for yet another intervention. In April, 1911, a French column had been ordered to march on Fez. There had been warnings by the press and by Parliament against doing this, and a growing awareness in certain circles of dangerous undertones in the German and Austrian press.[12] But the step had been decided. Morocco should be secured. As far as possible, Europe should be faced with an accomplished fact, as by Austria's annexation of Bosnia-Herzegovina.[13] Even if it meant war, the country should be ready for it. The country was, in fact, no more ready than it had been forty-one years before.[14] But the mood in Paris grew similar to that of 1870.

At an end-of-June demonstration by student organizations in the Latin Quarter, a public of more than three thousand drowned with their refrain *Vive l'Alsace! Vive la Lorraine! C'est l'Alsace qui nous faut!* the end of the speech of Professor Henry of the Ecole des Sciences Politiques: *Debout Gaulois! Debout Français! Face aux Barbares! Le Progrès de Lyon* was enchanted by the sight of this youthful gathering communing over their patriotic ideal.

The month of June had been troubled, and there had even been the beginning of an insurrection in the countryside, caused by legislation trying to limit the vine-growing area whose wines could be properly labeled Champagne. In the Aube, hard-hit by the new regulations, the red flag had been brought out, and even the German flag had flown outside a *mairie*. Angry peasants proclaimed that they would rather be subjects of the German emperor than of the oppressive Republic. Such disturbances and such childish expressions of ill-temper did not last long, but at the time they seemed grave enough.

Yet, unlike the *coup de Tanger*, the news of Agadir when it came did not create a panic, although the possibility of war, considering that tempers on both sides were high, was far greater and preparedness not more improved than in 1905. Auguste Gerard has called the summer of 1911 the first general mobilization of French patriotism. Paul Cambon who visited Paris that September drew in his letters quite a different picture from the one only six years before:

> Aujourd'hui de Selves m'a raconté qu'il avait vu Clemenceau, Pichon, etc. ... que tous y compris Ribot reprochaient amèrement au Cabinet d'avoir négocié, alors qu'avec l'appui de l'Angleterre et de la Russie on pouvait tout braver.

Politicians were not alone in their new intransigence. Reports from the countryside brought surprising accounts of a bellicose and determined mood among the peasants:

> ... Xavier [Charmes] que j'ai vu hier, arrivant d'Auvergne, m'a dit qu'il était stupéfait de l'état d'esprit du paysan dans ce pays, le plus pacifique du monde. Fleuriau arrivant de Saintonge dit la même chose. Berkheim te rapportera des impressions semblables, et il est non moins stupéfait que moi d'un emballement avec lequel on ne peut raisonner.

In town or country, no one would listen to reason, and normally prudent businessmen, even the ponderous members of the Board of the Orléans Railway, echoed the general mood.[15]

If looking for any one date from which to count the birth of nationalism as a widespread, chauvinistic feeling, I would pick the fourth of November, 1911, the date of the signing of the Franco-German agreement on

Morocco, Congo, and the Cameroon. By negotiating with the Germans, Caillaux had hoped to achieve a more lasting understanding. Morocco, as a bone of contention, would be eliminated, German ambitions in Africa to some extent assuaged, and relations between the two countries eased, or so the negotiators thought. As it turned out, the accord of November, 1911, rubbed existing rancor and distrust to the raw. Both in France and in Germany the press denounced what it took for a diplomatic defeat, the public protested at the humiliation of allowing concessions to the other party, and neither government could nor dared guide public opinion into calmer channels.

In fact, governments would soon be doing their best to excite it. Not that the national tempers needed much encouragement in this direction. Those witnesses who judged the French nation from Paris and by Paris, saw the rise of what Henri Bazire was to greet as the new nationalism. This would carry Poincaré to the Elysée, the necessary votes to the passing of the Three-Year Law, and the inevitable (it was not so then) into the pages of our history books.

On the day when von Schoen, the German ambassador in Paris, handed de Selves, the French foreign minister, the note announcing the German intervention at Agadir, Jules Cambon, French ambassador in Berlin, was in Paris. Six months later a letter from his brother Paul to a friend tells of his reaction: "Imagine," writes Paul Cambon, "that as soon as the news of the German demonstration was out, Jules hurried to Schoen, made a scene, and called the German action a *cochonnerie*." Schoen complained at the Quai d'Orsay of the rudeness of this language. De Selves merely replied: "He is displeased, but admit that he has good reason to be so."[16]

The general reaction of the Paris press was almost uniformly firm and calm.[17] *L'Humanité*, in which Jaurès had bitterly remarked, "Il n'y a plus une seule faute à commettre," gladly noted the general *sang-froid*.[18] The *Echo de Paris* registered "neither surprise nor alarm." *La Libre Parole* found "no reason for emotion." In the *Action française*, Maurras explained: "In fact, what we do or do not do, does not seem to matter. . . . Agadir is sufficient proof of that."[19]

In his excellent account of the facts of the Agadir crisis, E. Malcolm Carroll surmises that the real excitement and resentment of the affair only followed the publication on November 8, by *Le Matin*, of the secret terms of the Franco-Spanish entente of 1904, and the public realization that not all Morocco would be France's share of the Franco-German bargain. This does not seem to have been the case. Nor do I believe a practical disappointment to lie behind the new mood, but rather a new popular or, better still, a newly popular, awareness and resentment of Germany and the threat of war—feelings that all evidence shows to have grown up in the late summer and autumn of the year, before any news of a settlement, let alone of its drawbacks.

An interesting light is provided by the statement of Adolphe Messimy during the debate on the reintegration in the army reserve of Lieutenant Colonel du Paty de Clam, the prominent anti-*Dreyfusard* retired from the army in 1906.[20] Messimy, who had been minister of war in the Caillaux cabinet at the time of the Agadir crisis, explained that on July 20, 1911, du Paty made a demand for reinstatement in the reserve service, "based on the sharp state of tension in which we found ourselves at the time, following the *coup d'Agadir*." Du Paty's was one of hundreds of similar letters from officers no longer on the service lists.

Among these, Messimy particularly remembered a request of General Bazaine-Hayter asking for an active command, and a letter from General de Negrier, couched in these terms: "I am told I am too old for a command. I simply ask to be sent to the frontier as a cavalryman, to show the young soldiers of France an old division commander, *grand'-croix de la Legion d'Honneur*, knows how to die." In the period between July 20 and September 1, not one day passed without the ministry's receiving ten to twenty requests of the same kind.

All thought that war was for the morrow. Exasperation against German bullying was general. *La Libre Parole* was persuaded that a general awakening of the national spirit was taking place.[21] But the Right-Wing press had to acknowledge that the Left was now as jealously patriotic as the Right.[22] Germany was odious, the more so as the crisis had once again opened old wounds. At Nouvion-en-Thiérache, Lavisse declared that France could never give up Alsace; no true friendship was possible between Germany and France, he said. France could have accepted the accomplished fact, but she had refused.[23] And the *Dépêche* reminded its readers that, whatever the issue of the present incident, they had long endured the ill-humor, bad faith, and arrogance of Germany, by whom they were constantly threatened with war.[24] *La Libre Parole* also thought of war: "There are many who look up their Service Books. . . . If this is to go on, we might as well get it over at once."[25]

As to which side was the injured one, conviction was general. Brossé expressed the feeling in *L'Aurore:* "France does not want war, but she would not refuse it at the cost of her honor. Her mind is made up. If war were to break out, it would be because we are attacked by an unscrupulous enemy who still believes that his force is sufficient excuse for all his brutalities."[26] *Le Matin* noted the tacit political truce and the full awakening of the national spirit. France owed her fresh-found unity to Mr. Kiderlen-Wächter.[27] Paul Deschanel agreed: "The German fife," he said in a speech to his constituents, "has rallied France."[28] Delcassé at Port-Vendres, Mascuraud at Le Mans, expressed the same opinions;[29] while at Isoudun, Klotz, then minister of finance, spoke of the "grave and joyous confidence the nation in arms has in itself." Couyba, minister of commerce, declared the unity of all Frenchmen before the necessities of national defense.[30] Charles Maurras agreed: German provocations had tightened French unity.[31]

The new atmosphere struck an English visitor and friend of France, Mrs. Vernon Lee, who published in the *Nation* a letter describing the change in attitude of her former *Dreyfusard*, pacifist, antimilitarist, antinationalist friends in whom she now found the "willingness, the barely repressed longing, for war."[32] Paul Desjardins replied: "What lies between the Germans and ourselves is not Morocco; not even Alsace. . . . It is their outrageous fashion of weighing upon us and upon all by the right of their might."[33]

L'Aurore did not deny that a "breath of warlike ardor" had affected everyone.[34] The conclusion of the Franco-German accord had done anything but calm the passions aroused in the preceding months.[35] Could such conflicts as those which divided France and Germany ever be settled peacefully? *L'Eclair* warned its readers to be on their guard.[36]

The debates on the ratification of the convention of the fourth of November made it clear that, for once, all parties wished to dissociate internal from external politics.[37] Albert de Mun, who had hoped for so much from the first news of Agadir,[38] spoke to blame the government and the regime which had led France into such straits. He spoke at peril of his life for, suffering from heart trouble, he was forbidden public speaking; but it seemed to him that "at no moment during the last forty years has the state of Europe seemed more troubled and more threatening."

No one in the Chamber believed in the accord which they felt they must ratify. Pelletan asked in *Le Matin*: "Is there anyone sufficiently naïve to see in it the pledge of an enduring peace?"[39] *Le Progrès* echoed him: "The treaty of the fourth of November solves nothing. . . . France has never been more nervous, nor more fully resolved."[40] Ernest Judet considered the accord distressing to French patriotism, and injurious to national dignity.[41] Edouard Drumont thought a general war inevitable in a future that the agreement had done nothing to bring less implacably near.[42]

The French reaction had not gone unnoticed abroad. The French ambassador in Vienna wrote of the notice that had been taken in the

Austrian capital of the "admirable mobilization of French patriotism during the past months."[43] From Berlin, the military attaché warned his superiors of the growing chances of conflict. In a further, personal letter to Messimy, he wondered whether a renewed German attempt to change French policy by military pressure would not lead to war "considering the present state of French opinion."[44]

In military circles, a crisis was confidently expected in spring of 1912; preparations for the coming conflict went ahead.[45] The Austrian military attaché, who knew Paris well, commented to his German colleague: "Strange how excited people here still are. At my Club, at parties, in shops, even at my barber's [one would have thought it the obvious place] —everywhere I am asked, *Aurons-nous bientôt la guerre?*" Other military attachés, the Italian and the Russian, apparently shared this impression.[46] Major Winterfeldt, the German attaché, warned his superiors that the new chauvinism was not, in his opinion, a superficial, temporary phenomenon, but deep-rooted, growing, and flourishing at that very moment. He attributed it to general nervousness, positive hatred of Germany, and a very sensitive national pride.[47]

As the speaker who presented the November agreement for the ratification of the Senate said: "There is not one of us who does not feel deeply and painfully the sacrifice this treaty imposes."[48] It was as a defeat that the agreement was treated, not as a reasonable compromise. "We negotiated under the cannon of Agadir . . . and a French government accepted this, forty years after the Defeat. . . . It is the counterpart of Fashoda!"[49]

The lesson was clear: "There are times," said the dean of the Senate, "when the country must rely on its armed forces to maintain its economic policy abroad, and the prestige of its moral and intellectual expansion in the service of peace."[50] Antonin Dubost, taking his seat as president of the Senate, concurred: "The whole country expects us to put its military and diplomatic protection above everything else." Loud and general agreement ensued.[51]

Writing in *L'Echo de Paris* on January 12, 1912, Albert de Mun found that during the last six months the country had undergone a profound change—a change of which it was not unaware. If through lack of readiness the opportunity of war and of revenge had been missed when most favorable for France, preparations for the inevitable should henceforth be ceaseless and untiring.[52] The article sounded the first—perhaps as yet unconscious—notes of de Mun's campaign in favor of Poincaré, a campaign that the latter's premiership encouraged.

The fall of Caillaux and the new Poincaré cabinet found the press

sounding a new note, especially in Republican politics.[53] Internal affairs
gave way to foreign. Political promises and programs had come to
nothing so often that they met with increasing scepticism. Now it seemed
that internal affairs would look after themselves, if only the new ministry
could settle the imbroglio of foreign policy. The new interest in foreign
affairs permeated a political world heretofore preoccupied almost solely
by local and national questions. Judet noted: "There has never been so
much talk of foreign affairs."[54]

As ever in times of foreign danger, national union had been sought and
found round a moderate Republican. André Siegfried has pointed out
that the nationalist sentiment was essentially Republican: "Not reactionary, but tending to give precedence to the unity and indisputability
of the army, over the instability of political parties. Not anti-Republican,
but national-Republican."[55] This is a good description of the point of
view of Poincaré himself. A firm Republican and partisan of the religious
policy that had so deeply marked the character and physiognomy of the
regime, his first concern was unity at home, the better to face the foreign
menace of which he was deeply persuaded.[56]

"The unity of sentiment in France is a danger for Germany," had
written Barrès.[57] "It is also the negation of parliamentarianism." This
explains both the support and the opposition the new leader met. The
key words of his ministerial declaration were "force," "authority,"
"discipline."[58] The prime minister found his support in the center and
on the Right, but on the moderate, conservative Right: the *Action
française* of January 17, 1912, was not at all pleased with his admittedly
nationalist but Republican point of view. But the *Action française* was
still on the lunatic fringe of the Right. More authoritative voices spoke
in favor of the new man: Paul Beauregard expressed the Right's conviction that what the country needed was a ministry that would insure
France the prestige it now lacked. Louis Millevoye, a nationalist, believed the dominant question to be that of unity before the foreigner;[59]
and *Le Temps* made his implication explicit when it spoke of national
unanimity in support of Poincaré's policy of appeasement and discipline.[60]

Apart from the inevitable Dupuy, the men of the Alliance Démocratique were not much in evidence in his team. But Millerand and
Briand, both of whom had by now left their distressing past well behind,
served just as well. After an unfortunate lapse while Monis and Caillaux
governed, the forces of order reasserted their grip on the levers of
power—an evolution beginning with Rouvier in 1905 had at last brought
a member of the Alliance to the presidency of the Council pending his
further promotion.

The Italian war against Turkey in Tripolitania furnished the new ministry with their first opportunity to express the recently acquired national pride. The Italian navy had stopped French passenger steamers in order to seize Turkish passengers and suspected war supplies. French official protests merely reflected opinion at home. Poincaré's attitude was extremely firm; so was his language to Barrère, the ambassador in Rome, who appeared too readily inclined to accept the Italian point of view. Poincaré seems to have felt that his own attitude was a reflection of popular excitement. On January 27, 1912, he wrote to Barrère: "You do not seem to know the state of French opinion. If there are any more incidents of this kind, we cannot guarantee order either at Marseilles or in Tunis."[61] However, the firm tone of his statements in the Chamber satisfied Parliament.[62] Albert de Mun welcomed the "wind blowing from Lorraine, wholesome and invigorating, toward the Quai d'Orsay."[63]

Italy was the first to feel French intransigence, but the reasons for French behavior were still, and would remain, at least self-consciously defensive.[64] Millerand at the ministry of war was doing his best to raise the confidence of the people in its army, and of the army in itself.[65]

It is likely that Germany had perceived by then the growing Frankenstein monster of its own creation, and would have favored improved relations between the two countries.[66] But, as Poincaré wrote to Jules Cambon in Berlin, no understanding was possible between the two countries while the past lay unredeemed between them.[67] If this mood was shared by the Cabinet, a majority in Parliament, and a large section of the press, trends within the politically-conscious minority were not all in the same direction. The German chargé d'affaires in Paris wrote ominously of the growing chauvinism,[68] but he did not deem worthwhile to mention—unless it had escaped his attention—the attendance at the funeral of Aernoult. Aernoult was a soldier who had died in an African disciplinary company and whom *L'Humanité* had promoted to martyrdom. Attendance at his obsequies was said to exceed one hundred thousand. Yet at a time when nationalist movements quarreled over the exact number of participants in their demonstrations, which hardly exceeded two or three thousand, it would have been worthwhile for the Germans to note the number of sympathizers that Socialists and Syndicalists could turn out on a Sunday afternoon for a political demonstration of a pacifist and antimilitarist nature.

This is proof that if the nationalist revival was influential, its scope was very limited.[69] It is probable, on the other hand, that many of the men and women who followed Aernoult's bier, also followed the military bands, which, that same weekend, played through the streets the tattoo reintroduced by Millerand. The significance of this martial revival was not misread by contemporary observers who took it as designed to increase public pride in the armed forces and, through it, national self-confidence. *L'Echo de Paris* commented: "Do not think the restored tattoo is mere child's play; it is the sign of a revival."[70] Approval was general at first, but soon Maxime Vuillaume warned his friends on the Left against certain unexpected results that seemed less desirable from the Radical point of view:

> Everyone is glad to see what is generally called the patriotic revival. . . . The people cheer the tattoos, and this is excellent. Yet reservations are called for. A note of chauvinism has crept in. Demonstrations have taken place which recall the heyday of Boulangism. This is dangerous, and one may well think twice before reviving tattoos in other towns.[71]

Enthusiasm for the army reached a peak on the day of the spring review held at Vincennes on the tenth of March. The correspondent of *L'Eclair* could remember no popular enthusiasm like it since Longchamps in 1899.[72] *La Libre Parole* and *L'Echo de Paris* felt the wind filling their sails.[73] Even *Le Temps* allowed itself to move majestically with the others, and noted the new national sentiment and the fresh patriotism of French youth.[74]

> I have never seen in Paris such a remarkable manifestation of military patriotism as that of last Sunday. The change in the national temper of the French people since last summer is one of the most notable events of contemporary Europe.

wrote the *Daily Telegraph*'s correspondent in Paris.[75]

The prevailing mood expressed itself in other spheres. There was a renewed interest in religious drama.[76] A spate of patriotic plays appeared in the theaters. Literature bowed to the prevailing fashion. The *chansonniers* naturally took it up, and bookshops for their part saw the sales of books exalting bravery and action in general going up. All this engaged the attention of the press.[77]

In the political world, the election of Paul Deschanel to the presidency of the Chamber, left vacant by the death of Brisson, indicated the growing weakness of the Radical group,[78] and pointed to the trend that would carry Poincaré to the Elysée seven months later.[79]

The Socialists watched Radical disintegration without displeasure. Radical newspapers watched with anxiety.[80] The Republicans were gradually taking over nationalism and using it in their own interests. Etienne Rey, the fashionable playwright and author, saw the "best of nationalist doctrine now in the hands of the Republican party."[81] But this was the result of a steady rightward evolution on the part of the Republicans themselves.

Charles Maurras was justified in commenting that Republican policy was that of the Action française without the king.[82] Paul Deschanel's presidential address in the Chamber praised the lay schools that respected freedom of conscience (applause on the center and Left) and were fully aware of their duty to the fatherland (applause on center and Right).[83] In the same sitting, Poincaré announced that it was the intention of the government to institute a national holiday dedicated to Jeanne d'Arc—a patriotic holiday, as he took care to point out.

All this contributed to persuade the German public that the French desire for revenge was unappeased.[84] Certainly the government in France regarded it as such.[85] Both the popular press and the debates of the Chamber supported its policy and the determined effort it was making toward material and moral rearmament.[86] Such rearmament went unopposed by some influential pacifists, who argued that a strong defensive force made war less likely.[87]

Poincaré's visit to Russia in August, 1912, was generally taken to be a part of such concrete preparations,[88] and the courteous salute of the German fleet on meeting the presidential cruiser in the Baltic was interpreted also as a reminder of Germany's interest in, and position between, the two allies. Poincaré had declared at Nancy:

> Rien de solide et de durable ne s'édifie sur le mépris des traditions ... c'est folie que de vouloir rompre le charme entre le passé et l'avenir. ... La patrie, comme l'humanité, est faite plus de morts que de vivants.

A number of apparently unrelated measures confirmed this point of view. The reinstitution of the *Concours Général*, abolished some years before, gave satisfaction to conservatives for whom it carried both sentimental and cultural values. At Boulogne, the annual procession in honor of *Notre Dame, Reine de France* was revived after ten years' abandonment, under the presidency of Monsignor Lobedey, Bishop of Arras. Special trains brought in more than twenty thousand visitors for the occasion.

The revived interest in Russia, and the transfer of the third French Naval Squadron from Brest to Toulon, led to a great deal of comment in the press.[89] This naturally affected the newspaper-reading public. Hanotaux saw that, by press campaigns and other artificial means, the peoples of the world were precipitated toward events being rendered unavoidable. His warnings had no effect.[90] No more did those of the Socialists whose voice, loud and influential among industrial workers, was not allowed to affect national policy. An article in *L'Humanité* of September 9, 1912, noted that the chauvinistic tone, formerly a monopoly of the Right-Wing press, was now a characteristic of the great dailies. It concluded: "If there is so much effort to instill us with belligerency, it must be because the government envisages war."

The articles of Jaurès became increasingly pessimistic. Some French Socialists, affected by the growing helplessness of their foreign comrades, wondered, too, whether the contending international rivalries would not end in a violent clash.[91] Georges Sorel, who believed that peace was merely an interlude, and that only mediocrity or cowardice retarded general acceptance of this fact, watched Socialist struggles to avoid the unavoidable, and waited with spiteful curiosity to hear their eventual justification of the change in attitude which he knew this would entail.[92]

In September, a crowd in Nancy surrounded the car of Princess Colloredo-Mansfeld who was driving through the town, tore off the red, white, and black flag it was flying, and trampled it in the gutter. The protests of the German chargé d'affaires in Paris brought an embarrassed admission from his friend, Paléologue, that relations between the two nations were not all that one could wish for.[93]

The Belgians, anxiously watching developments that would so closely affect their own fate, did not consider the mass of the people to be in a warlike mood. The farmer, the bourgeois, the shopkeeper, the businessman, knew what a war would cost them. But the country had been rendered confident in its eventual success; and one had to reckon with turbulent youth, with the military, and with those who had nothing to lose.[94]

The government also had to be reckoned with, for it had to influence opinion to support its rearmament plans. To achieve these ends, the government called on the press.[95] We know now that the changed tone of the great dailies was due partly to the use of Russian funds that, disbursed by Klotz, the minister of finance, were used to encourage certain organs to adopt an attitude friendly to the policy of Poincaré. It should be remembered, however, that money alone seldom served actually to change a newspaper's policy: it encouraged friendly papers, it paid off attempts at blackmail, it persuaded the hesitant to take sides. But it is reasonable to suppose that, had no money been used, the over-all attitude of the press would have been much the same. This is a mere supposition and, as evidence is lacking for a thorough discussion of the matter, no opinion can be more than that.[96]

The Russians were worried about the use of their money for ends only indirectly concerned with their own, and showed concern about the new mood prevailing in government circles.[97] It seems certain that Poincaré wanted to act in a way that would prevent the possibility of Russian doubts and recriminations, such as had followed the Bosnian crisis of 1908.[98] But the outbreak of the Balkan war led, in any case, to an increase in anti-German demonstrations and in patriotic fervor. The victories of French-trained Greek troops over the German-trained Turks appeared as French victories over the Germans.[99] Jules Isaac recounts the general impression that the risk of war had become much greater, but that the balance of power had been inclined to French advantage. "From there to accepting the risk of war was only a step—too easy to take."

Sommes-nous prêts? Haut les coeurs, patriotes français! The tattoos degenerated into demonstrations, accompanied by loud shouts of *A bas l'Allemagne!* There were so many rumors that the Germans, alarmed, made inquiries. Their findings were crowned by a report of the chief of staff, General von Moltke, to the effect that actual preparations for war had not been found in France.[100]

Already toward the end of summer, Alfred Capus had spoken of 1912 as leaving the memory of a reactionary year in the social and the moral field.[101] This vague term "reactionary" is widely used to express a mood nearly as vague—a reaction against the politically forward movement in which the Left had, however halfheartedly, tried to lead the nation; against change; against (though this was as yet an implication realized by very few) the ideals of 1789 and 1898; and certainly against the men who had ridden to power on their strength. As André Siegfried pointed out in the book he was then writing, the reactionary spirit of the time when taken in its most general sense had made great strides, chiefly among the middle class, which had long ago lost all traces of a revolutionary spirit and was only concerned with retaining what it had gained.[102]

Jacques Bainville also characterized 1912 as the reactionary year. He too found the middle class profoundly penetrated by the reactionary spirit. Far from being a passing or a superficial one, the movement had grown in strength and speed.[103] The movement, it should be added, was not new. What was new was the awareness of it, only now apparent on every side. Once it had become self-conscious, it would forge ahead even faster than before.

Such is the view of the France of 1912: reactionary, militaristic,[104] convinced that war was inevitable, a war against Germany;[105] all this accompanied by the new nationalism that Henri Bazire explained and announced in the pages of the *Libre Parole.*

Chapter X

OF HEROES AND HERO-WORSHIP: 1912–1913

> The triumphs of extreme nationalism and racialism in our time,
> furthermore, were facilitated by the attitude of many statesmen
> and politicians who were not in sympathy with their aims, but
> either believed that it was too dangerous for their own position
> and that of their partners to take energetic measures against them
> or even considered them as necessary evils. (Friedrich Hertz,
> *Nationalism in History and Politics.*)

By a simple but penetrating self-appraisal, the new nationalism saw itself to be an entity, admittedly sharing a name with another movement, but peculiarly different in kind and probably in aim. It did not repudiate the name—indeed it accepted and used it as the most apt and convenient—but it broadened its application, rendered it less specific and denied restrictive implications that would make it exclusive. Exclusive it certainly was not, and might well have proclaimed that "Tout qui est Français est notre," for its self-confessed origin was an awakening of patriotism, and its self-conscious nature was vague—a mood, an atmosphere, an *ambiance* rather than a doctrine.

This is the essence of the nationalist revival, and the stumbling-block to those for whom the term carries echoes of *fin-de siècle* nationalism, echoes that (as is their nature) must mislead. Appropriately enough, the best description of the vague phenomenon was provided by a moderate Catholic in the pages of a new *Libre Parole* whose own nationalism had changed even as the character of the new nationalism had changed.

Writing at the end of 1911, Henri Bazire pointed to the birth of a "new nationalism."[1] He attributed it to external causes and, in particular, to the general impression that Germany would never allow the country to live in peace:

Facing the revelation of the foreign danger, *a new nationalism is born.* . . . It does not stem from transports of enthusiasm, nor from a political movement, but essentially from an awakening of patriotism, and of reasonable patriotism. . . .

Nationalism and patriotism were used as equivalent terms,[2] for that was how they appeared to him:

On nous dira, votre nouveau nationalisme se confond tellement avec le patriotisme qu'il se dilue en lui, c'est une moyenne de l'esprit public qui pénétrera plus ou moins les partis, mais d'où ne sort ni un programme positif, ni une méthode d'action suffisamment précise. ... Vous allez encore nous parler d'ambiance.—Pourquoi pas?

His article was the first analysis of the new atmosphere. It called forth confirmation and warm agreement from readers and friends.[3] The spate of investigations that flowered the following spring led him to reiterate his opinion: the new nationalism was different from the old one; it overflowed the limits of the old parties; and it looked beyond the anxieties of internal politics.[4]

Of the investigations that had confirmed Bazire in his opinion, there are a great number from which to choose. They all concluded that outlook had changed and was changing, that action was popular, national consciousness widespread, and doubt, reflection, indecision, and weakness were abhorred.[5] Sports played an important part, both as a cause and a reflection of the general attitude. A contemporary article, "Sport et Patriotisme," pointed out the close connection between one and the other, insisted on the importance of the widespread "air fever," but added that other athletic pursuits also were, physically and morally, "games for the fatherland."[6] It quoted the words of a boxing critic: "Tomorrow the great Club will be France itself, and I am certain that whatever the game there is no better side to help win."

The influence of sporting principles went hand in hand with a warlike and activist political allegiance. Young people regarded war as a game to be played as well as possible, after methodical training. A young playwright, J. Raymond Guasco, author of a French namesake of Shaw's *John Bull's Other Island*, explained to Agathon: "War is not cruel, stupid, hateful. It is merely sport *pour de vrai*."

National sentiment had become lively, almost irritable. The words "Alsace-Lorraine" would be greeted with cheers in the schools, and lecturers now hardly dared to mention German methods or ideas for fear of the murmurs and catcalls. A master in a Paris Lycée reported that in his class of forty pupils, twelve or fifteen were or wanted to be *camelots du Roi*, five or six were *Sillonistes*. The rest were "Republican," *le Marais*. All these young people admired glory, adventure, and martial things.[7] This may not seem particularly surprising, but to men who themselves at a like age had read the Barrès of *Un Homme Libre* or *Le Jardin de Bérénice*, the contrast seemed striking.

The same admiration for glory and martial adventure was evident in the fascination that France's Moroccan enterprises held for young people. To Alfred de Tarde, colonial enterprise was a derivative for France's traditional imperialism, an upsurge of the stifled energies of the race. His explanation is, above all, psychologically interesting as a document, because it shows what Frenchmen thought of themselves. It is certainly true that, as he said, thousands of young men who had never left France had been thrilled and excited by the reading of what were revealingly called "colonial epics."[8] "Ils avaient reconquis le sens de l'héroïsme à la pensée de ces terres où coulait le sang français."

Lyautey was one of their heroes. Cheered by the students of the Ecole des Sciences Politiques, he exclaimed: "What I like about the youth of today is that it does not fear war—neither the word nor the fact."[9] Such an attitude was thought highly desirable by those who saw in the youth of the day the soldiers of the morrow. The warlike spirit burning bright was what they wanted, and general appreciation of the grandeur and the glory of war. "In the present state of the world," said M. de Lamarzelle in the Senate to the loud approval of the Right, "the horrors of war must be veiled by its grandeurs, by its sacrifices, by its glories."[10] At the beginning of 1911, all this was still relatively new. Agathon had not yet examined contemporary opinion in schools and universities to find no student who might still profess antipatriotism.[11] *L'Eclair* greeted the movement toward a cult of vigorous action and noble sacrifice, and declared with satisfaction that "heroes are once more in the fashion."[12]

An instance of this was exemplified in the all too brief glory of Ernest Psichari, son of Renan's daughter and of a well-known philologist. Leaving his home and studies in 1903, he joined the 51st Regiment of Colonial Infantry as a private. He reënlisted in the regular army the following year, became a sergeant but, being impatient for action, obtained a transfer to the Colonial Artillery as a simple gunner. Soon promoted to sergeant-major in his new unit, he was included in an exploratory mission to the French Congo from which he returned in 1908 with a brilliant record and the Military Medal. After a stage in the Artillery School at Versailles, he was commissioned a Second Lieutenant. Immediately, he left for Mauretania once more.

He had already published a book on his Congo journey. A second book, *L'Appel des Armes*, appeared in 1913. At this time it was already outdated by its author's conversion to Catholicism, which had occurred in the meantime, but it expressed extremely well the sentiments described above. Very honest, seeking ever to justify his existence and to serve his country, Psichari with his youth and unusual experience was a symbol and an admired example to the young men of his acquaintance, a promise to the older.[13]

In an article entitled "Réveil de l'Heroisme," Henri Massis quoted Psichari at length. The spirit this latter incarnated had stirred, Massis said, in many young men since the tense days of the past summer. Young men no longer thought so highly of intellectual things, no longer believed in the primacy of thought over action. That sort of nicety did not make sense to this generation. "We think . . . that we must love our country with real love, and seek heroic actions. . . . Tempers have changed these last ten years. . . . Resentment has grown in our hearts with a force our elders never knew."[14]

A new cult of Napoleon, not unknown in the days of Boulangism, a certain revival of Bonapartism in student circles, and a recrudescence of its political activity, were aspects of such inclinations.[15]

The Rousseau Bicentenary celebration on June 31, 1912, furnished the young adventurers an occasion to manifest their opinions, and provided the Action française with yet one more opportunity to prove that in the Latin Quarter it was mistress of the streets.[16] Barrès had opposed the vote of credits necessary for the celebration. Rousseau's was an anarchic system of thought, the mainspring behind all anarchies since its conception. This was not a man to glorify or an idea to celebrate at a time when the tide against anarchy was at its flood. "I can see nothing in your project suitable for the France of 1912," Barrès had told the Chamber. And perhaps he had been right.[17]

But, if students and young writers were nationalists, older or more mature men did not necessarily share their enthusiasms or their interests. The subjects of the numerous *enquêtes* were themselves selections of a minority of a minority. Agathon, the most influential of these investigators, told his readers that there was mention in his pages "only of educated youth, of such young men as we were in a position to know the real thoughts, and such confidences as we could obtain. To be honest, they are picked men. We did not intend to trace the portrait of the average young man of 1912."[18]

Restricted as its object was, the influence of Agathon's work was vast, for, as the author explains: "It may be believed that the influence of such an inquiry matters as much as its exactitude. It is itself an act."[19] Regarded as a means of propaganda, of pressure on public opinion, the *enquête* and its fellows were surprisingly effective in the restricted circles at which they aimed.[20]

In a later work, Henri Massis explained the motivating conception of Agathon's *enquête*: "A myth, but an effective myth capable of exerting an influence, of directing minds, of revealing them to themselves, of increasing their energy and their faith."[21] We have firmer evidence than that of Romains' *Men of Good Will* to show that Agathon's inquiry achieved its end. The book brought echoes, not only from the Right but from all sides, and deeply influenced by its apparent proof of the popularity and importance of patriotic ideas certain politicians who later remembered its conclusions in Parliament. Albert de Mun, Edouard

Herriot, the young senator from Lyon, and Paul-Boncour wrote to the authors to express the impressions Agathon's findings had made on them.[22] Romain Rolland, whose opinion had not been asked, volunteered his sympathy for it and for the ideas it represented.[23] André François-Poncet wanted Agathon to know that, having shared their experiences, he shared their feelings too.[24] Even Ernest Psichari wrote from the Adrar: "All your strokes must lead us one day to the glory of war and, to be frank, to a revenge from which we must never turn our eyes."[25]

The revenge Psichari called for was to take on human form in the person of Raymond Poincaré. By his Lorrainer origins, the firmness of his personality, the notoriety of his patriotism and integrity, he would become the symbol of the new nationalism, of the patriotic revival.[26] Whatever his symbolic character, his most solid asset was the military policy of his minister of war, Alexandre Millerand, immensely popular, and the discreet rumors of the latter's intention to strengthen the army by lengthening the period of service under the colors.[27]

The two-year period of military service had been one of the most generally popular measures introduced by the Radical and Radical-Socialist majority of 1905. In fact, though the measure had been initiated by Radicals, there were few who, looking toward their seats as Combes advised them to do, had not been prompted by electoral wisdom to cast their votes for it. Although General Billot called the law a national peril and asserted that it weakened the army, the Senate had voted 232 to 37 in its favor.[28] In the Chamber, only the extreme Right and the Bonapartists had voted against it, and the law passed by 504 to 34 with 27 abstentions.[29] Since then, there had been no complaints concerning its effects. Successive judgments showed general satisfaction, shared by official circles and the general public.[30] The year 1911 brought the first suggestions that a longer period of service would increase the country's threatened security.[31] In *L'Eclair* Judet attacked the two-year service, "with which we shall never be ready," and called for a reform.[32]

The new aggressive spirit of the army, the theories of its leaders stressing the importance of the first clashes, of the offensive of the active army ready for battle as against the slow-moving reserves, all, no doubt, contributed to the growth of the reform demand.[33]

The *Action française* was one of the first papers to welcome the as-yet-discreet campaign for a revision of the Two-Year Law. Inspired by an article of General Maitrôt in *Le Correspondant*, it published two long articles in May of 1912 in which a return to three-year service was suggested.[34] The Right-Wing press was naturally favorable to the idea, so much so that *L'Aurore*, through the pen of its editor, Brossé, found it necessary to warn its readers against the new *affolement nationaliste*, and to answer those critics and polemists who completely discounted the military value of reserves.[35]

The Reichstag, which in 1911 had voted to increase the effectives of the German army by thirteen thousand men, voted a new law in June, 1912, which increased by one-tenth the military forces of the Reich. From a chronological view of events, it seems clear that the three-year offensive in the Chamber, beginning June 18, 1912, was not unrelated to the Reichstag vote of June 14. Fear of growing German power, of Germany's warlike preparations, and the uneasiness aroused by the menacing words of German military experts, were its seeds—not nationalist agitation that, on the contrary, fed on the same sources. Nor did the nationalists in the Chamber seem to think at the time that a proposal for prolonging the duration of military service had a great chance of success.[36] Those who tried to obtain such a prolongation merely for the cavalry arm six months later[37] stressed the restricted scope of their proposal. Their reception was uncertain, although Millerand's apparent sympathy worried the Radicals.[38]

The time was one of stress. The coming presidential election monopolized increasingly all interests and political activity: budget, laws under consideration, everything, passed into the background. Politicians were busier outside the Chamber than in. From mid-November onward the presidential election was the subject of every conversation in that little world.[39] The Right, persuaded by Albert de Mun of Poincaré's essential moderation and believing that he would introduce three-year service, decided to vote for him.[40] The nationalists also supported him, although contrary to some suggestions, there was never any open alliance or understanding between them and their hero.

Maurras has written in a recent book that there was never an alliance, that there were never even talks between him and Poincaré at this time. There was what Maurras calls "reciprocal circumspection based on the national interest." Anti-Republican as it was, even the Action française "could not treat a government that rearmed like governments that had disarmed."[41] It does seem however that Poincaré's regard for Maurras and the Action française went beyond mere circumspection, and there is some reason to believe that Poincaré might have liked a closer understanding with the Action française as early as 1911, an understanding perhaps based on his consideration for the thought and person of Maurras.[42] Certainly during the war of 1914 he saw Maurras and showed great consideration for him. But conditions had changed much in the intervening years.

The election of Raymond Poincaré to the presidency of the Republic was interpreted in all quarters as a victory of the Right over the Left.[43] In voting for him, many had voted for the continuation of a policy of national union, increasing armed strength, and defiance toward Germany.[44] To them, as to their opponents, the election seemed a nationalist victory. *Le Progrès* saw in it the first great maneuver of the nationalist party.[45] Joseph Denais in the *Libre Parole* saw in it the defeat of the bloc and all that it had stood for.[46] To Caillaux it meant war after the general elections. If we are to believe him, Fallières shared this impression. To Briand, apparently, the departing president admitted: "Je crains bien que la guerre n'entre derrière moi à l'Elysée."[47]

These words need not be taken to refer to the personality of the president-elect so much as to the uneasy international situation. In Paris early indifference to the Balkan conflict had, by the autumn of 1912, changed to sympathy for the Balkan allies in newspaper-reading as in newspaper-writing circles right of the Radical-Socialists. Allied victories began to persuade people that French interests might be involved in the fortunes of Balkan armies. The tone of the press was not unconnected with the changed tone of the Quai d'Orsay and the new feelings of the moderate group eager to spare the old alliance and interested in new possibilities.[48] Yet in the rest of the country, interest was slight, the warlike spirit nonexistent. In the Gironde, Trarieux found only "quiet fatalism . . . passive resignation," and no thought of war. "It is only a question for them of distant barbarians who are settling obscure quarrels." The correspondent of the *Berliner Tageblatt* and the German ambassador also noticed the peacefulness of public opinion, though not of the Paris press.[49]

Yet Poincaré seems to have shared Fallière's forebodings. To Russian Ambassador Izvolsky he expressed the opinion that it was of the greatest importance that French opinion should be prepared for the war that might at any moment break out of the Balkan hostilities.[50] We know that at the time he spoke, at the end of January, 1913, well-informed circles in France showed a lively anxiety about Germany's military preparations.[51] These were almost the direct result of the victories of the French-trained Balkan armies over their German-trained Turkish enemy, which constituted indirectly a German defeat. To make up for this defeat, Germany increased her armed forces. To make up for the increase in Germany's armed forces, France too would have to follow suit. The vicious spiral continued.

The nationalist revival was the activator of this vicious spiral in French affairs, and Poincaré was almost its creature, certainly its accredited standard-bearer in the eyes of the general public.[52] The publication of Gaston Riou's *Aux Ecoutes de la France qui Vient*, coming as it did from a young Protestant leader,[53] persuaded men like Herriot and Lucien Maury that courage and action had come to be regarded by the younger generation as ends rather than means.[54] *Le Temps* concurred: its correspondent connected the mood examined and expressed by Riou with the presidential election of January, and concluded that the spirit of a *risorgimento* burned in the younger generation.[55]

Another pointer to this fact was the widespread enthusiasm for the then-beginning conquest of the air. Individual exploits appealed to the public mind, they were exciting, they could be quoted as examples of superior national worth. The men who flew the new machines were not just adventurers. To nationalists they served a higher purpose as symbols of the glorious nature and destiny of the French nation. "They further patriotic sentiment," wrote Agathon. "The airplane is, above all, in the eyes of the crowd a war engine."[56]

A teacher in the Lycée of Versailles also found that his pupils' "idealism and love of courage" now took the form of flying-madness.[57] So popular were flyers that a by-election of 1912 had seen the candidature of one, Vedrines, in the constituency of Limoux. Defeated by his Radical-Socialist opponent, he had yet managed to secure seven thousand of the twenty thousand votes cast.[58]

The import of the new arm was recognized at once by enthusiasts; Gabriel Bonvalot commented at length on the usefulness of airplanes as the "fourth arm" and praised the patriotic motives of those who encouraged the development of the air arm and the growth of France's offensive power.[59] One of the Michelin brothers gave one hundred and fifty thoussand francs to the *Aéro-Club de France* for four air-target prizes; "the aim of this being to draw the attention of the public to the undisputable interest of the airplane as a weapon of war." The dean of the Senate paid homage to the flyers whose example stimulated the happy emulation of French youth.[60]

As early as 1909, Paul Doumer had foreseen the importance of aviation in the general scheme of national preparedness, and *Le Progrès* had noted the political import of the new developments. The very nature and possibilities of these developments brought them to the notice of nationalists, eager in every field to assert the supremacy of France over other countries. The implication of force and war did not escape them. Already in September, 1908, a Ligue Nationale Aérienne had been founded by René Quinton.[61] And the respective states of French and German aviation were constantly compared.[62]

The Germans were not slow to notice the chauvinistic possibilities of the subject, and the use to which it was put by nationalists in France. In an interview to *Le Matin* of April 6, 1911, the Reichstag deputy Liebermann von Sonnenburg, one of the leading figures of the Pangerman party, had said: "Talking of airplanes, it seems to us that they have recently led to the growth of a vigorous chauvinistic movement in France." It was merely one aspect of a greater trend.

This trend was evident to all observers.[63] The publication of Agathon's *Enquête* in February, 1913, intensified it. The theatrical critic of *Le Temps* noted the growing taste for martial shows:

> Le peuple reprend goût aux spectacles guerriers ... cet amour de l'héroisme ... détermine un courant dont le théatre subit la répercussion. Partout où sonne le clairon, où retentissent les cris de révanche et de victoire, à l'Ambigu, chez Réjane, chez Guitry, la foule accourt. ... Ainsi tout recommence.[64]

L'Echo de Paris had also noted the trend in an article by Léon Cury, who had been similarly struck by the new taste in paintings: "Once more we meet the cavalrymen rising in their stirrups, mouths open wide in a war cry, steeds dashing forward in a wild charge."[65] A Belgian report from Paris on May 5, 1913, confirms the impression:

> Des théatres nombreux donnent des pièces de nature à surexciter les esprits, et à aggraver une situation déja trop accentuée. Il n'est pas une revue, ou une représentation de café-concert qui ne se distingue pas dans ce sens, et les tirades les plus chauvines soulèvent des applaudissements frénétiques.[66]

Allies also noted the changed atmosphere with mixed feelings. A British dispatch of the same year reported exactly the same things: the general emphasis on *revanchard* subjects, their commercialization, the success of ultrapatriotic and anti-German shows. To this somewhat disquieting report, two illuminating minutes are appended:

(1) The jingo spirit to which Sir F. Bertie refers is a distinct danger to the peace of Europe. G. H. Villiers.

(2) Perhaps, but Ministers must foster and take advantage of this spirit, to pass the burdensome measures which will ensure some equality of fighting efficiency between France and Germany. George Clerk, Eyre Crowe, Arthur Nicolson, Edward Grey.[67]

For his part, General Sir Henry Wilson, returning from a visit to General Foch, told Sir Arthur Nicolson that his French interlocutors hoped that war would not be too long postponed.[68] And the Russian ambassador in

London, Count Benkendorff, wrote to Sazonov: "Of all the Powers, France is the only one which, not to say it wishes for war, would see it without regret."[69]

The presidential message that Briand, as prime minister, read to the Chamber on February 20, 1913, said: "No people can be really pacific unless it is always ready for war. We must turn toward our army and navy, and spare no effort or sacrifice to consolidate and strengthen them." *Le Temps* echoed: "The reëstablishment of three-year service for all arms seems the only possible solution to counterbalance Germany's military efforts." This brought a resounding answer from Jaurès, in which he railed the "puppets of reviving nationalism and the patriots of the blustering press, who think the Three-Year Law the only way of underpinning French security."[70]

It would be too repetitious to quote all the press comment, argument, and mud-slinging that introduced and surrounded the campaign. With the exception of the extreme Left, the press was almost solidly in favor of the proposed measure. Progressive Radical newspapers like the *Dépêche de Toulouse* came out early in favor of a measure that would counter the "German danger."[71] Warm support also came from the Republic's representatives abroad, and particularly from Berlin where Jules Cambon wrote to put the question in a negative but effective light.

The issue had attracted so much notice abroad, he wrote, the question had now been put in such a way that, if the duration of service was not seriously increased by the debate, the German press would take it as a proof of French weakness. Assuming that a strong France would be a deterrent to war, it followed that to avoid giving an impression of weakness was in the interest of peace. Strengthen France, prepare for war, and give no ground to enemy anticipation of easy pickings. That, according to Cambon, was the best hope of peace. But fail to increase the duration of military service, show yourself yielding and weak, and peace will be in danger. This seems to have been Cambon's thesis when he wrote:

> The question of three-year service has been put in such a manner that, unless we seriously augment the duration of service, the German press will see it as a default on our part. It is most important in the interest of peace, that the German people should not be given this impression.

From Vienna, Dumaine wrote in the same vein; from Bruxelles, Klobukowski; while from Cairo, Defrance reported hopeful encouragement from the Sirdar, Lord Kitchener.[72]

The Germans, it is true, followed the fortunes of the measure with understandable interest. Their ambassador, writing from Paris at the beginning of March, thought that the law would go through, but that it was causing a real upheaval in the political world and in public opinion.[73] This upheaval was reflected in the dispatch of the Belgian minister in Paris, Baron Guillaume:

> One meets only people who are certain that an early war with Germany is fatal. They regret it, but they are resolved to it. They demand the immediate and undisputed vote of any measure likely to increase the defensive power of France. The most reasonable argue that they have to arm to the teeth in order to scare their opponents, and prevent war. . . . Last night I met M. Pichon, who said that there must be ever more armament, to prevent war.[74]

The Paris correspondent of the *Times* (London) described this atmosphere in an article, "The National Revival in France," which evoked further comment in the leading article of that issue.[75] The leader viewed the *revanchard* trend with misgiving and warned against chauvinistic excesses:

> Well-informed men have seen the growth of the new spirit for a considerable time. . . . We rejoice at the self-reliant spirit of the "New France". . . . But it is with regret that we see [these] tokens of true patriotism accompanied by provocative speaking and writing, and by plays of the character our correspondent describes.

Two days later, on the fifth of March, an official note in the morning papers announced the government's decision to introduce the Three-Year Service Bill. It was tabled the very next day by the minister of war, Etienne, in the face of violent and prolonged opposition. The debate on that occasion is well worth reading for the violence and the bitterness of the exchanges.[76]

Ernest Judet was right to think that the revival of nationalist spirit and of military pride were changing the face of France, or at any rate of Paris.[77] The students of Parisian Lycées produced a petition for the passing of the Three-Year Bill; indeed, as *L'Humanité* commented: "Les lycéens de Paris sont les enfants de choeur du nationalisme ressuscité."[78] Perhaps they believed, as Sydney Smith had written of another controversial measure, "that Gerunds and Supines will be abolished, and that Currant Tarts must ultimately come down in price. . . ." Their elders in the municipal council, under a similar misapprehension, followed suit and voted thirty-six to twenty-nine a motion expressing the hope that Parliament would pass the new bill as soon as possible. Academic circles proved more resistant to the enthusiasm, possibly not so much because of a more reasonable frame of mind as because of a contrary enthusiasm. They sinned by excess in a different direction, and Paul Passy was suspended from his chair at the Ecole des Hautes Etudes for an inflammatory article in the April issue of *Espoir du Monde*. But the pacifist activities and petitions of the teachers excited less interest than those of their pupils.[79]

The readers of Agathon's *La Jeunesse d'Aujourh'hui* were told: "On ne trouve plus ... dans les grandes écoles d'élèves qui professent l'antipatriotisme. ... A la Faculté de Droit, à l'Ecole des Sciences Politiques, le sentiment national est extremement vif, presque irritable." Roger Martin du Gard, whose novel *Jean Barois* appeared in the same year as Agathon's study, makes one of his hero's young nationalist interlocutors a *normalien*. This would have been unheard of ten or fifteen years before or, at any rate, most untypical. Now, under the direction of the loudly patriotic Lavisse, the Normale seems to have been about evenly split while, as Agathon relates, other great schools, particularly traditional citadels of privilege like the Ecole des Sciences Politiques, leaned heavily to the new enthusiasm.[80]

In the lycées, too, as mentioned earlier, the new spirit had been gaining ground. To a certain extent this was due to the generation of teachers brought up in the patriotic traditions of Bert and Ferry. Men like Malet or Canat at Louis-le-Grand could not fail to communicate some of their patriotic enthusiasm. But in general the student's enthusiasm was more ardent than the teacher's—Condorcet, where Baudrillart made the prizegiving speech in 1912, Janson de Sailly which had listened to Faguet, were among the first to produce petitions in favor of the Three-Year Law and, at the request of his son Philippe, Barrès himself had drawn up that of the Catholic lycée.

At a different social level, the new enthusiasm is less apparent than the reaction against it. The *instituteurs* were not as a group sympathetic to nationalism. Their interests leaned rather toward the social demands of a working class from which many of them stemmed, with which they had economic interests in common, and toward the pacifist, internationalist, and antimilitarist ideas they had carried out of the Dreyfus Affair and out of their own experience of military service. Their unions had long caused concern and indignation in conservative circles, and in the summer of 1912 things had come to a head when at its congress of Chambéry (August 16–18) the Fédération des Instituteurs Syndicalistes pronounced in favor of open antimilitarist propaganda. Reactions came promptly and from all quarters.[81] But while individuals were proceeded against, nothing had been done to tackle the fundamental cause of the trouble, the official teaching programs, until Barthou used the parliamentary recession of 1913 to send out a circular on textbooks which tried to bring the books into line with the government.

Meanwhile, and particularly in Paris, the excitement continued to grow. The dispatches of the German ambassador teem with references to the growing nationalist fever. Jonnart, Pichon, and Barthou, with whom he discussed this, were forced to admit its reality, but asked that it should not be taken as an indication of belligerence. This did not allay the fears of von Schoen.[82]

It was not the idealist nationalists who could affect public opinion in this manner. Their newspapers had no great circulation nor great influence in the political world.[83] From this point of view, the Socialists had by far more popular support. The Socialist-Syndicalist demonstration on the Pré Saint-Gervais gathered some 150,000 supporters, come to protest against the extension of military service and the idea of a Three-Year Law. Even allowing for a proportion of picnickers, the public that the opposition to the bill commanded was so great that some Syndicalist revues proposed that the momentary success might well be used for the dissemination of other, less popular items of the party program.[84]

The Socialist Congress of 1913 was held at Brest. The congress unanimously adopted a resolution denying all interest in revenge and calling for most vigorous action in the country and in Parliament against the Three-Year Bill, for Franco-German understanding, for a national militia, and for international arbitration treaties. Some thoughtful people, while they sympathized with the Socialist aims, found them impracticable. Gustave Lanson thought that they took no account of the public temper:

The Socialists pretend that Germany and its Emperor want peace. The majority of this country thinks that the guarantee of peace lies solely in our military force. . . . The German peace, the peace that the German people and the Kaiser sincerely desire, is a peace where no resistance will be opposed to German economic ambitions; where the permanent show of her force, dispensing her from its use, would insure it without danger of universal domination.[85]

The Socialists, aware as it were of a conspiracy to smother their voices and, when that was impossible, to ignore them, became increasingly violent. Some of their leaders called for sabotage and mass desertions.[86] In all the services antimilitaristic propaganda redoubled its activity, feeding now on the growing resentment of men due for release, who were being told that they would have to serve another year.[87] The government reacted with vigor: May Day demonstrations were forbidden. One of the official telegrams to this effect explained: "The government does not want that, by popular demonstrations, any pressure should be exercised on members of Parliament concerning matters awaiting discussion."[88]

The annual Socialist rally at the Père Lachaise cemetery having been forbidden for this reason, Vaillant and Willm interpellated the government on behalf of their party: "We consider the Three-Year Law, the maintenance of the Class under the colors, and other kin actions on the part of the government and the nationalists, to be a real beginning of civil war waged against the working class." And Vaillant compared the Boulangist, the Dreyfusist, and the present periods, all "times of nationalist and militarist reaction."[89]

Instead of Père Lachaise, the Socialists gathered once more on the Pré Saint-Gervais where, if crowds were no less numerous, the speakers were even more heated than they had been the previous time.[90]

Chapter XI

THE DEBATE: 1913

Il n'y a de certitude que dans l'état de passion. (Charles Ferdinand Ramuz, *Journal, 1909–1914.*)

ALL THIS TIME opinion throughout the country was uncertain, troubled,
fearing the threat of war, disliking the sacrifice and waste of a third year
of military service. Whom was one to believe? The detractors of two-year
service, Generals Cherfils and Maîtrot,[1] or those who praised its results,
General Bonnal, General Niox, and even General Zurlinden?[2] Millerand,
who warmly supported three-year service in 1913, had declared in 1912
that the reserve were troops of wonderful solidity.[3] It was around the un-
reliability of the reserve that much of the debate turned. Colonel Rousset
had glowingly described the maneuvers of 1912 as the triumphant bloom
of an army full of health and vigor; nine months later he was expressing
his profound conviction that the effects of the law of 1905 were frightening.[4]

Insinuations of obscure and sinister interests involved in the fortunes
of the bill did not meet with much notice from a public for which nothing
was more natural than the advancement of private interest from a position of public trust. Poincaré had been the counsel of Saint Gobain,
Millerand of Le Creusot. This latter had in 1910 presided over the annual
banquet of the Comité des Forges, and made a strong appeal in favor of
rearmament and preparedness, which had been very naturally appreciated by the assembled company. Etienne, the minister of war who
guided the bill through the Chamber, was president of the great enterprise, les Tréfileries du Havre. Paul Doumer, who had reported on the
proposal in the Senate, was an administrator of the Comité des Forges
and of the Chambre Syndicale des Constructeurs de Matériel de Guerre.[5]

All this seems to have struck later historians much more forcibly than
it did contemporaries, some of whom were not unaware of the fact or of
the power of occult interests.[6] They probably knew that there was little
to be done about factors that would always exist.

During another period of crisis, M. Bergeret had explained to the Abbé
Lantaigne that, if the Republic was easily militaristic, it was yet not
warlike. This applied equally well to the supporters of the Republic.
"When considering the chances of a war," Bergeret had said, "other
governments need only fear defeat. Ours fears equally, and with good
reason, both victory and defeat. This salutary fear insures our peace."[7]
Bergeret had overstated his case, but his description of Republican

psychology may help to explain the quandary in which too many honest Republicans found themselves.

An inquiry organized by *Le Temps* in April of 1913 produced varied results. After publishing comments that were favorable to the Three-Year Law from such Right-Wing strongholds as Epernay or Calvados, the correspondent of *Le Temps* met with more doubt about the proposed measure in the Nivernais. The strongest opposition came from working-class quarters. It was not based on antimilitarism (which, the reporter noted, was practically extinct), but on practical objections to its need and utility.

In the countryside, where people were much friendlier and their patriotism was unquestioned,[8] there was lively suspicion of possible nationalist intrigue, of a nationalist nigger in the patriotic woodpile. "What does most harm to the project," one of its ardent supporters declared, "is that in many places it has been presented as a nationalist scheme." Great efforts were made to make it appear to the peasants as an anti-Republican and reactionary measure. This impression, its supporters feared, would not pass unless the law were voted by a majority that was clearly Republican.[9]

But politics were made in Paris, like the election of M. de Gromance, and vocal public opinion was heavily concentrated there. Maurice Reclus has left useful indications on the ideas of a section of the Paris "world" that did not belong to either extreme, but which, in the good old Republican tradition, insisted on being both Republican and patriotic.[10] Himself of this world by right of birth, Reclus was in a good position to know its crosscurrents and its reactions, to understand the social and cultural links which brought Barrès and Déroulède together with Deschanel and Clemenceau in the *salon* of Mme de Loynes, Jules Renard together with Léon Daudet over the dinners of the Goncourt Academy, linked the Republican with the legitimist aristocracies through such families as the Blanc or the Casimir-Périer.

From that broad yet narrow world that lay between Casimir-Périer's son and the son of Mme Péguy, the chair-mender of Orléans, solid support could be expected, thought Reclus. Such people, like Péguy himself, "were successively for Clemenceau against Jaurès and the Combistes; for Millerand when he reëstablished the military tattoos that had in the author of *Notre Patrie* a resolute and enthusiastic partisan; for Barthou, in spite of the fact that [they] did not care for him at all—because Barthou championed the Three-Year Law; for Poincaré against those who still upheld the bloc."

Thus, Péguy, who had broken with Millerand during the Dreyfus

Affair, was reconciled with him during the struggle for the Three-Year Law.[11] This period of struggle also saw the publication of *L'Argent* (*suite*), last in the great line of Péguy's polemics directed to waking up his country to the danger he had first felt in 1905 (*Notre Patrie, Louis de Gonzague*), a danger that he felt threatening from Germans abroad and from Germanophiles and weaklings at home. To Péguy patriotism was simplicity itself. The reality of glory would be to enter Weimar at the head of a platoon of infantry.[12]

Geneviève Favre tells in her *Souvenirs* of a walk he had taken with her, Maurice Reclus, and Ernest Psichari, who was then home on leave, to the Invalides on Ascension Thursday, 1909: "In the Great Court, then in the Chapel, they evoked the glories of the past, they predicted that war was near, and the certain triumph of France over Germany."[13]

Péguy's convictions and his insistent purity led him ever further away from his friends and associates of the Affair. He was himself not an easy man with whom to get on. However, when faced with the choice between his Left-Wing *Dreyfusard* past and those Catholic influences of the Right, which had been heartened by the publication of his *Jeanne d'Arc* in 1909 and were pulling toward nationalism, Péguy chose the former. This choice, and the fact that there had to be a choice, appears in *Notre Jeunesse* and probably in his break with Georges Sorel.[14]

His relations with the nationalists remained good.[15] He had to be allowed to go his own way, but his greatness could not be gainsaid. Then, his good friend, Joseph Lotte, editor of the *Bulletin des Professeurs Catholiques de l'Université*, was a great sympathizer of the Action française. Péguy himself had thrown the Action française a bouquet at the end of *Notre Jeunesse* which Maurras did not fail to appreciate. But relations between the two men never developed beyond mutual respect and admiration. Henri Massis tells that, beginning in 1911, Péguy had a special copy of all his books bound for Maurras, "*homage à peu près unique.*" This did not leave the recipient unmoved. Maurras sent back, among other books, his *Une Campagne Royaliste*, with this dedication: "A M. Charles Péguy, que je ne puis confondre avec qui que ce soit."[16]

In *L'Argent* (*suite*) Péguy was chiefly concerned with the home front. "It cannot be denied," he wrote, "that we have before us a violent and profound renascence. . . ."[17] Who was to lead this necessary national "reintegration"? He himself was doing a great deal to guide and inspire it.

Ruder inspiration came from a series of incidents that poured oil on the fire. On April 3, 1913, the Zepplin L-Z-16, having left Friedrichshafen on a trial flight with three army observers on board, crossed into French territory near Belfort, passed over Xertigny, Passavant, Epinal,

Baccarat, and Manenviller, flying at different heights and turning oddly over a part of France full of military installations. After some six hours of this, it landed at Lunéville, where it spent the night under military guard and whence, refuelled at once from Germany by permission of the French government, it left the following morning. Crowds had gathered when it landed, crying *A mort!* and throwing stones. Even after the landing area had been cordoned off, the booing continued and more stones were thrown. None of this is very clear as efforts were made to hush up the incident, but it seems that if the stones found any victims, it was among the French soldiers guarding the Zeppelin.[18]

The next incident occurred at Nancy, on Sunday, April 13. Two parties of German tourists from Metz were insulted and molested, without the police bothering to intervene or the local authorities to notify headquarters in Paris. After a great outcry in Germany had followed the return of the indignant travelers, measures were taken from Paris to punish the police and the prefect of Nancy.

The Sunday following this, German officers who were leading a troop of boy scouts, marched them, band, flag, and all, into French territory. It was a childish affair, but it troubled inflamed tempers where in normal times it would have received scant notice. Two days later, on April 22, a German army biplane from Darmstadt landed at Arracourt, pleading that it had got lost in the fog. The likely explanation was accepted, and and the plane allowed to proceed to Metz. But, once again, the commonplace was treated as significant, *mise en épingle* for all to see.

These incidents, indicative of the mood of the eastern provinces, happened very apropos. For the daily press, for the apostles of the Three-Year Law, they were exactly what Klotz had ordered. Nor is it unlikely that they contributed to the zeal and promptness which Joffre noted with satisfaction in the fulfilling of military requirements. "La crainte est le commencement de la sagesse," the chief of the French general staff commented.[19]

Joffre himself thought there was good reason for fear. He personally had long expected war, long prepared for it. In February, 1912, he had told the Russian military attaché that he was getting ready "in case war breaks out in spring. All the arrangements for the English landing are made down to the smallest detail, so that the English army can take part in the first big battle."[20] Now many politicians, affected by the prevailing atmosphere or by private information, were coming round to his way of thinking.[21] There were many factors in such resolutions. Certainly, the dispatches of Jules Cambon had greatly influenced the cabinet's resolution to propose the Three-Year Law. The dispatches were to stiffen politicians in support of it and to furnish some of the official arguments.[22] A large number of books also brought their polemical contribution to the arguments already in circulation.[23]

The bill was becoming a symbol. The dogma of three-year service was becoming an article of faith. Driant shouted at Jaurès: "You have heard General Pau say No. If he says No, all your reasoning is worthless." Whoever refused to accept the dogma was expelled from the community of patriots. Aulard complained in *La Dépêche* that one could not discuss it rationally without being attacked as a traitor, a *sans-patrie*. "Everything is a matter of faith," he wrote. "One has to believe and not to reason, to avoid being branded an heretic."[24]

Some patriots were peculiarly exalted: General de Castelman proclaimed: "Give me seven hundred thousand trained men, and I will conquer Europe." General Pau said to d'Estournelles de Constant: "Try to understand me, Sir: I do not want to wage war with married men."[25] But excessive as such statements and attitudes may appear, bear in mind the basic cause of the excitement. On May 29, the question of the credit that would permit the retention under the colors of the Class due for release, came before the Senate. To pay the troops, the government asked for extra credits. To the criticisms this demand aroused, these were the first replies: M. Jenouvrier—"It costs less than a defeat!"; a senator from the center—"It costs less than an invasion!"[26]

But, as Clemenceau was to point out, the law of 1905 had been a social reform as much as a military one.[27] The fight against its revision had a social significance as great as its pacifist or moral meaning. Socialists and Left-Wing Radicals opposed the law for its political, not for its military, implications. On this ground, first the disintegration, then the reintegration, of the Radical party took place and, if the Radical leaders tended to side with the moderate wing, their troops moved in large numbers nearer to the Socialist position.

Franklin-Bouillon spoke for many of his Radical colleagues when he said: "We are already, and cannot be anything but the opposition."[28] Some interpreted this merely as a struggle for the spoils and perquisites of power, with those on the outside seeking to displace the men or the parties in power. No doubt personal interest was involved: it always is. But as a rule the debate was kept on the plane of principle and of the pressing danger.[29] Besides, many of the deputies plainly represented the feelings of their constituencies.

Franklin-Bouillon, from the comparative security of Seine-et-Oise, could afford to take a stand that a Chaulin-Servinière in the west could not, though he would later subscribe to the "unified" program of Pau.

The representatives of the eastern provinces were solidly in favor of the measure, and an almost equal solidity appeared in the west (though not in Brittany, where social claims were making headway and the Catholics split by internal dissensions). Eventually these deputies would vote for the bill, the unanimity of the five eastern departments marred by only one vote, that of the ten western departments only by four.[30] The southwest also came out heavily in favor of the measure.

Briand fell on March 18, voted down in the Senate after a debate on proportional representation. But it is worth noting that a Radical organ had commented only two days before that electoral reform was no longer the sole object of the political struggle. It had suggested, *en connaissance de cause*, that the eventual vote of the Senate would be influenced by considerations other than proportional representation, for instance, the Three-Year Bill.[31] The vote following Briand's declaration in the Chamber on January 25 had given him a majority of 324. But the make-up of the majority had shown the dependence of the cabinet on a coalition of the center and Right.[32] This goes a long way to explain its fall in a Senate still dominated by old-fashioned Radicals and Radical-Socialists. It was clear to all that Briand had left power after a vote showing that his policy did not have the confidence of the Republican majority.[33]

His successor, Louis Barthou, appeared as a confirmation of the dread nationalist reaction.[34] The Left maneuvered to cut the government off from its Right-Wing allies by introducing a number of motions on education. Lay education was a touchstone that no Republican government could oppose without exposing its reactionary character, nor support, they thought, without forfeiting the alliance of the Catholic Right. But the Right put the passing of the Three-Year Bill above any other consideration.[35] The government replied to the tactical motions of the Left by accepting them and by echoing the Left-Wing speakers in convinced tones, while the Right coöperated by abstaining in relative silence.

Apart from pretexts for delay or maneuver, the Three-Year Law had banished all other preoccupations. Pelletan noted that there was hardly any more talk of proportional representation. There was, however, a good deal of discussion over the Three-Year Bill in the Chamber, where the opponents of the measure tried to delay the defeat they could not prevent.[36] Convinced that the law would only bring war nearer, they introduced numerous amendments and argued at length over every article.[37]

Certainly there were in both Germany and France nationalist groups that fanned popular passions, but the opponents of the bill knew, or thought they knew, that their opposition represented the majority feeling in the country, and that this feeling would grow.[38] The country was interested in the type of law which would permit the fishing season to begin a day sooner and thus allow fishermen to get an extra Sunday's fishing.[39] The service bill may have been necessary: the general public saw it as a nuisance.

The class of 1910 had reacted to the prospect of another year's service with rebellious talk, and mutinies had actually broken out at Toul and at Rodez. This brought anxious pressure from deputies affected by opinion in their constituencies. As soon as he could, Barthou decided to release the Class of 1910, but any good will won on the swings was lost on the roundabouts: to release the third-year men, the age of call-up had to be shifted from twenty-one to twenty, which brought some talk of cradle-snatching.[40]

Aulard wrote in the *Dépêche*: "The Three-Year Law will be passed against the great majority of the Republican party." And Maurras himself felt certain that the strong pacifist minority in the Chamber represented a majority in the country. Candidates supporting the Three-Year Bill obtained a minority of votes at by-elections. A Socialist petition against a Three-Year Law gathered .730,000 signatures and was submitted to the Chamber.[41] Neither this nor the crowds that turned out for Socialist protest meetings could move the Right-center coalition determined to pass the bill for the good, if against the will, of the country.

Article 18, containing the principle of three-year service, passed on July 7, 1913, by 337 votes to 223. On July 19 the law itself was voted by 358 votes to 204. It provided for three years' active service, followed by eleven years in the active reserve; then for seven years in the territorial army followed by seven years in the territorial reserve. It affected alll Frenchmen between twenty and forty-eight years of age, and was to last until 1923.

The press, Socialist and Radical-Socialist newspapers apart, was well pleased. The measure was far from ideal. Even so, it appeared as an improvement on the past and, perhaps, a promise for the future.[42] Thomson, in *L'Homme Libre*, voiced the sentiment of its Republican supporters: "C'est pour ne pas revoir les Prussiens aux portes de Paris, que nous avons voté le service de trois ans." But, to do this they had accepted the nationalist lead or, at least, nationalist doctrines.

Barrès, at a banquet in honor of Henri Galli of the *Patrie française*, expressed the pleasure of the nationalists:

It is certain that first Boulangism, then nationalism, have failed, but it is equally certain that all their content and goodness have survived them. Our terminology can be rejected, our doctrines are being realized. We find them in the work of Millerand, in the speeches of Poincaré, in the noble transports of those very men who, only yesterday, opposed us and who today work to realize what we wanted. What does it matter to us that the nationalist party fades away if, at the same time, we see the opposing parties being nationalized![43]

The progressive "nationalisation" of the Republic and its doctrines, was also predicted by Edmond Barthélémy in his review of Jacques Bainville's latest book, *Le Coup d'Agadir et la Guerre d'Orient*. The royalism of the Action française could not be taken seriously, but the men and the methods of the Action française could. And the critic saw that organization furnishing France's most eminent statesmen before ten years had passed:[44] he was reasonable but mistaken in thinking of it as a nursery for future *hommes de gouvernement* on the lines of the Socialist party.

The national-republicans, afraid of the explosiveness of nationalism, would have liked to repress or disavow it, but feared to hand their opponents the sole use of this magnificent political weapon.[45] If Caillaux justified his opposition to the government by the assertion that this latter was merely carrying out the will of the reactionary parties, Thomson, a more moderate man, was himself looking anxiously at the government's supporters, discerning behind their nationalism, *ce patriotisme de café-concert*, the shadow of the general on a black horse who had elicited the same support.[46]

Clemenceau accused Barthou of being a nationalist in disguise: "M. Barthou declares he is no nationalist, knowing well what his fate would have been had he said the contrary. At once the nationalist opposition, represented by one of its leaders, M. Barrès, hurries to calm his fears and to assure him that this will not be held against him." And *L'Homme Libre* published a large cartoon, entitled "Neo-Nationalism," which showed Barrès talking before a bust of Barthou to a great concourse of priests, bishops, and choirboys assembled under the banners of the Sacré Coeur and the Ligue des Patriotes: "Qu'importe le nom, si nous avons la chose!"[47] *L'Eclair* of July 24 commented on these campaigns: "The extreme Left tried to stifle the majority between its patriotic action and its electoral fears."

Such articles as that published by *La France Militaire* under the heading "Gesta Dei per Francos" were helping the arguments of the extreme Left. While *La France Militaire* wrote:

It will be a beautiful war which will deliver all the captives of Germanism: Danes and Poles, Alsatians and Lorrainers, Czechs and Tyroleans, Dalmatians, Croatians, Serbs, and Bosnians . . . ! And for this fine war, France will once more be in the van, as of yore . . .

the vice-president of the army commission defended the project before the Senate, arguing that without the German military projects of February, the Three-Year Law would never have seen the light of day.[48] Defensive patriotism and offensive nationalism had become difficult to distinguish.

Edouard Herriot resented the atmosphere in which these last debates took place. Parliament he said, had become a sort of military academy. People met each other with the question: "Have you read Bernhardi, or von der Goltz?" A few speeches had sufficed to render warlike the most pacific of assemblies.[49] The result of it all was a favorable vote on August 7, 1913, by which the bill became law.[50] The comment of Maurras was melancholy: the vote had been against the Senate's inclination, it showed no enthusiasm, implied no unanimity, or even quasi unanimity. Had the Senate returned the bill to the Chamber, that might have well been the end of it.[51]

CHAPTER XII

THE DECISION: 1913–1914

Et la revanche doit venir, lente peut-être,
Mais en tout cas fatale, et terrible à coup sûr;
La haine est déja née, et la force va naître:
C'est au faucheur à voir si le champ n'est pas mûr.
(Paul Déroulède, "Vive la France.")

THE VOTE OF THE THREE-YEAR LAW was not the end of the agitation its discussion had aroused. The Left, defeated by a hostile coalition, promised to win the second inning after the elections. Upon these ramifications, political life would be focused from now on. The months between August, 1913, and May, 1914, were one long electoral campaign. *L'Echo de Paris* told its readers:

It is unbelievable to what extent the towns and the countryside are concerned with the new military law. It is the only general subject of discussion. I have heard a hundred conversations about the Three Years, the twenty-year call-up, family allowances, and the bonuses for reënlistment.[1]

The nationalists felt certain that, with Poincaré in the Elysée, all was set fair for their continued success. A new word had been coined, *Poincarisme*, to define the national revival, the new pride in the army and the fatherland. It was criticized or approved, but on the whole the nationalists appreciated the help it had brought to their cause.[2] Among others, Maurice Pujo, leader of the *camelots du Roi*, rejoiced to see that the "state of mind that has been called *Poincarisme* has benefited the fatherland, but not the Republic. . . . The best proof of this is the considerable increase in the number of our supporters, the genuine bound upwards of our organization during this period."[3]

The attitude of Poincaré was appreciated by many who saw in him the pledge and warrant of his country's strength and safety. Gabriel Hanotaux wrote: "Peace must reign over the world; it cannot reign except by the will of the strong; therefore let us be strong. . . . Pacifism is not an idle fancy, but neither is nationalism a regression."[4] Barrès wrote to Poincaré to express his gratitude for the way in which the president had revived the country's dignity and pride.[5] Meanwhile, men of a different mind like Paul-Hyacinthe Loyson saw a greater danger for the Republic in the actual nationalist crisis than in the crises of the days of Boulanger or Dreyfus.[6]

On September 9, 1913, Combes wrote to Caillaux asking him to take over the presidency of the Radical and Radical-Socialist party. The election of Caillaux to this post at the party congress held at Pau, and the resolutions voted there, were declarations of war against the new law.[7] Pelletan had proposed an electoral alliance to this purpose with the S.F.I.O. On the Socialist side, Albert Thomas published *La Politique Socialiste* in which he advocated the revival of the old bloc and Socialist participation in a bourgeois ministry. While such ideas on both sides came to nothing, the "unification" of the Radical-Socialist party, marked by the expulsion from the party of all Radical members of the Barthou cabinet of November 30, introduced a policy of increasing (though still mostly tacit) coöperation between the two "unified" parties.[8]

The struggle in Parliament had now shifted to those financial measures necessary to implement the new law. Unwilling to introduce new taxes, unwilling most particularly to introduce anything resembling an income tax, the majority proposed a loan. The principle of this was finally accepted on the first of December, but only by 291 votes to 270. The next day the government was defeated because Barthou insisted that the bonds of the new loan should receive perpetual exemption from any tax, including an eventual income tax.[9]

The Radicals had stated before the discussion began that they would vote for a limited issue of 900 million francs for extraordinary armament expenses, but that they would vote against any formula, printed on the bonds, committing Parliament to future action. Their attitude was motivated by the pending issue of an effective income tax. The Barthou government had insisted on a total sum of 1,300 million francs to cover not only the extraordinary armament expenses but also expenses incurred in Morocco, with a promise printed on the new bonds freeing them from all future taxes.

Poincaré himself, as well as Cochéry, the president of the budget commission, were against this latter idea; and both men advised the government not to go against the current opinion. Any intransigence would only involve them too deeply in an issue already rejected once before—on March 25, 1908, because it affected the *principle* of a general income tax. When Barthou fell, Poincaré murmured while shaking his hand: *C'est un suicide.*[10] Jaurès was not unduly elated:

> The Left offered a curious sight yesterday; an odd mixture of passion and timidity. Against Barthou it had been challenging, it had stood up to him, proclaimed its will to cast him down and, at times, one could have thought oneself back in the great days of Republican inspiration. Then, when Vaillant greeted the cabinet's fall with the cry "Down with the Three-Year Law" it felt uneasy, constrained, as if wondering what to do with its victory.[11]

Barthou had maneuvered badly: he had forced his own unnecessary defeat by facing many of his "republican" supporters with the logic of their own actions. Ready to support him in fact, they refused to support him in principle. Principles, after all, made up a large part of their electoral stock-in-trade, and they could not allow the prime minister's foolish intransigence to spoil the *appearance* of their record. They voted against him, but when they realized the implications of their action, many of them felt lost.

La Dépêche commented: "M. Barthou, qui avait pu vivre d'une série d'habiletés, est mort d'une serie de maladresses."[12] *Le Progrès* attributed his fall to a Republican reaction against the continuation of a reactionary policy which furnished one more pledge of his loyalty to the Right.[13] Aulard, in *La Dépêche*, assured his readers that, as with Briand, the actual occasion of Barthou's fall was not the real cause but merely the orange peel on which he had slipped.[14] Certainly the scene following the announcement of the government's defeat justified this point of view: the cries of *A bas les trois ans!* and *Vive la République!* indicated the significance that the vote held for many.[15]

The moderate reaction that, with a brief interruption in 1911, comprised the dominant trend of French politics since 1905, coming to a head in the Briand and Barthou cabinets of 1913, had been broken. The Three-Year Law would be cast down, the faithful reinstated in the tabernacle of patronage: good Republicans could breathe freely once more. The new prime minister was Gaston Doumergue.[16] *L'Aurore* forecast his policy:

One question dominates all others in the loud concert for the new government's opponents: the Three-Year Law. Well, the Three-Year Law is above all The Law. The government is there to apply The Law. The congress of Pau has said that the [Three-Year] Law must be altered as soon as circumstances permitted. It has not said that it should be broken, nor would any sensible person follow such advice.[17]

The question of revision, like that of proportional representation, would be left to the new Chamber of 1914. *Le Progrès* would have preferred a firmer stand against the law, a proposal to turn gradually back to two-year service. It agreed, however, that opposition to the law would have been impossible.[18] Doumergue realized this. He stressed the Republican character of his administration and implied its caretaker nature.[19] As for the Three-Year Law, the debate would remain closed. In fact, far from doing anything against it, new measures were envisaged "to carry the defensive force of the nation to its highest point."[20]

Yet some people felt the atmosphere in governmental circles to have changed: many doubted the sincerity of Doumergue's adhesion to the law. In the Senate, such opponents of the three-years' service as Gouzy and Pic-Paris supported him.[21] Violette, though no longer a party member, spoke for many Socialists when he stressed that the new cabinet had in their eyes one essential merit—that of interrupting the succession of ministries of the Left governing with a majority of the Right. His words met with loud approval on the left of the Chamber.[22] *L'Humanité* itself, harder to deceive, was far from satisfied:

> We should have known! The ministers' words have nothing in common with their language when they were still in opposition under Barthou. They have not even the strength of character to impose on themselves the course of action which they wanted a week ago to impose on others.[23]

In fact, power had operated a real change in the attitude of the new ministers. This could have been due in part to the confidential information to which their new position in office gave access. Dispatches from abroad had been growing steadily more pessimistic as the year progressed. Already in September, Klobukowski had written from his listening post in Bruxelles that the news of a conflict would surprise no one.[24] November had been a critical month: at Saverne, a small town in German-occupied Alsace, the clash between officers of the German garrison and the local population had grown into an issue of international notoriety. German brutality, Alsatian resentment, had once more excited opinion in France and Germany.

During the same month, Jules Cambon had had an extremely serious conversation with his Belgian colleague in Berlin, Baron Beyens, which he reported in a dispatch of November 22, 1913. In this he informed Foreign Minister Pichon that the Kaiser, who in spite of his mercurial temper had been considered a moderating influence on German policy, had come to think war inevitable and necessary.[25] Poincaré relates that Cambon's dispatch was kept only for himself, the prime minister, and the foreign minister. However, certain words spoken between Pichon and Izvolsky indicate that before long the news became more widely known—within a restricted circle.[26]

In any case, the Kaiser's new attitude appears to have been an extremely public secret. Poincaré recounts in his memoirs that, when dining one evening with Eugène Lamy, perpetual secretary of the Académie française, and a few other fellow-immortals, Ernest Lavisse said to him: "My German friends warn me that the Emperor is sinking more and more deeply in the toils of the military party. We must be careful."[27]

Hora novissima, tempora pessima sunt, Vigilemus. It was a time to be on guard: but the guardians were preoccupied. Elections were approaching and the battle promised to be desperate. Meanwhile, though its sponsors were out of power, the new Three-Year Law benefited from an unexpected respite. Robert de Jouvenel could well think that the parliamentary struggle was largely put on for a show. After speaking their brave words, the erstwhile opponents seemed to have settled down side by side. The Republicans, reassured by Doumergue, content with a larger share of the spoils, were grooming the new law as if they had always wanted it and had no intention of doing without it. January 3, 1914, found Maxime Vuillaume writing in *L'Aurore*:

The law is the law. Besides, the congress of Pau never demanded an immediate return to the Two-Year Law. It asked for a return in stages, when circumstances should permit. It asked that the reserves should be organized. It never meant to rise against a law that had been voted by Parliament.[28]

But surely, that had been exactly what the resolutions of Pau had meant! After all, they had been framed and carried after the law had been voted by Parliament, and no one then had spoken of it as inviolable.

But such tergiversations did not calm the fears of those supporters of the law who thought their work threatened by the new Republican power. Where were the good old days of national and patriotic exaltation, so well reflected in the election of Poincaré, and of which the Three-Year Law was the concrete manifestation? Alas, what was now left of past hopes, asked Albert de Mun in a despondent mood.[29] But a Socialist surveying the scene found no more reason for hope than Albert de Mun. To the threatened peace he saw only one alternative: the end of the Republic and the reëstablishment of the monarchy by those strong nationalist-royalist forces of which the *Action française* was the thrusting point. Marcel Sembat wrote *Faites un Roi, Sinon Faites la Paix* to persuade his readers of the necessity of a Franco-German understanding. Many were more impressed by the fanfare of the title than by the argument of the book.[30]

But the offensive against the Three-Year Law was being organized in Socialist ranks. Other claims were being left in the background: henceforth the password would be *A bas les trois ans!* The Socialist Federations of the Seine and of the Rhône submitted to the Socialist National Congress motions aiming at the reconstitution of the bloc for the *anti-troisanniste* campaign. The congress unanimously adopted a resolution on electoral tactics, making it clear that the campaign was directed mainly against nationalism and the Three-Year Law, and calling for coöperation against them with all republican forces.[31]

When *L'Echo de Paris* asked, "We should still like to know whether the government is for or against the Three-Year Law," *L'Aurore* replied happily and vaguely:

The Three-Year Law is not a dogma; it is not intangible. But, at the present moment, our general staff, having seen its ideas accepted by Parliament, has naturally organized everything in such a way that it would be impossible to return *de plano* to the law of 1905. Whether we want it or not, this is so. . . . To return to the Two-Year Law, the whole job must be started right from the beginning. To expect that this could be realized by a tap from a magic wand would be playing politics at the expense of national security—a thing which my friends and I would never do.[32]

These were political bedside manners at their best. Of course, far from refusing to play politics, these gentlemen were in politics up to their eyes. There is no doubt that the issue of the Three-Year Law was a burning poker, so hot that many did not know by which end to pick it up. Apart from those few who had taken a clear stand, apart from those few whom the particular characteristics of their constituency helped or forced to make a choice, many candidates could not choose their phrases carefully enough. Jacques Piou writes of those days:

There were no elections like those of 1914. . . . Except in regions where the memory of invasion had survived, and in those where pacifism was the rule, the most profound divergencies faded into discreet shadows. Some did not want to hurt family senti- ment; others were circumspect about national sentiment; all knew that Europe was all ears.[33]

Le Temps's correspondent in Berlin wrote that the government's inten- tions regarding the Three-Year Law preoccupied German opinion. The Berlin newspapers published long reports from their Paris correspon- dents. The French press, too, realized quite clearly that of all electoral issues "La plus grave, la plus angoissante, est sans contredit la question des réformes militares."[34]

The election campaign was temporarily diverted into other than mili- tary channels when Mme Caillaux shot and killed Calmette, editor of *Le Figaro*, on the seventeenth of March. Calmette had published private letters from Caillaux to his wife, showing the writer's political integrity in a very bad light. He threatened to publish further incriminating documents that Caillaux thought would be disastrous for his reputation, coming when they did. Calmette dead, Caillaux resigned immediately from the office he held as minister of finance in the Doumergue cabinet.

The debate following the murder brought out the dregs of Republican politics. Barthou read a letter (which should not have been in his pos- session in the first place) showing that, when minister of finance under Monis, Caillaux had used his influence in favor of the fraudulent finan- cier, Rochette. A friend of Caillaux, the deputy Ceccaldi, countered with a story of how Barthou had helped to shield a deserter belonging to his family.[35] No one seemed much surprised at the revelations of the debate, though some may have been pleased at the quantities of platform ammu- nition they supplied.

Caillaux had been attacked to prevent his introducing the income tax dreaded by his enemies. The campaign of *Le Figaro* had been one of blackmail, probably supplied with material by Barthou, perhaps by others also. So much was perfectly clear. Clemenceau, who was no friend of Caillaux, wrote:

> He had become, more by the work of circumstances than by his deliberate will, the best qualified representative of the most radical solution to the income tax problem. It was as such that he was ferociously attacked by a great number of people who, while knowing a great deal about the stories they have now told, would never have thought to say a word had he chosen to take his stand in the opposing camp.

Le Progrès told its readers:

> Rest well assured that it is not concern for the public good which inspired the righteous. They simply wanted to trouble the end of this Parliament, and to slow down the vote of the projects of financial and fiscal reform. They have, as a matter of fact, been successful.[36]

The threat of an income tax had alerted all sides. Among those who disliked it were many Radicals who had accepted it as part of the party program while there had been no likelihood of its realization, but who, when faced with the possibility of its introduction, did not care for the idea at all.[37] However, the danger had been effectively averted for the moment. In its last sitting before the general elections, the Chamber carried off with a righteous swing the conclusions of the commission of inquiry appointed to look into the dirty linen aired on and since the seventeenth of March. It then adjourned, rolled up its sleeves, and got down to real work.

Internal affairs entirely dominated the national debate, but they were obviously affairs and issues which had been shaped by external events and external pressures. Only Jacques Bainville at the time thought to remark: "Perhaps one day history will find reason to wonder that the election of 1914 held no account of the brewing storm—no more than the yokel of Daumier had done when he voted Yes in the plebiscite of 1870."[38] Another observer of the foreign scene also had his gaze, for once, turned toward events at home. Gabriel Hanotaux expressed the feelings of a replete minority, but still an influential one, when he saw

> ... the uncertainties of the present hour appear so much more cruel, as they have succeeded with startling speed to the hopes conceived only a year before. The rise of a national party, the election of M. Poincaré, the vote of a law of abnegation and patriotism, all led one to anticipate a revival. It was an hour of hope and confidence such as few we have known; and a few months have sufficed to spoil everything....[39]

The last act staged by Parliament before getting on with the elections had little effect on public opinion. Radicals assured themselves with some optimism:

Paris, Boulangist and Nationalist, no longer governs France, and the influence of the great Paris press which commercial interests have turned Nationalist does not carry beyond the department of the Seine. The calumny campain that we have undergone has produced in the provinces an effect contrary to that which had been hoped for, and the elections will only strengthen the positions of the Left-Wing parties.[40]

This may seem to be traditional preëlection optimism, but it did not in the circumstances appear unjustified, nor the optimism too bold.

The Fédération des Gauches, founded in December, 1913, to associate such "national republicans" as Briand, Pichon, Etienne, Chéron, Joseph Reinach, and others under the paternal wing of Jean Dupuy, the owner of *Le Petit Parisien*, began to melt away. Between April 11 and May 10, the name of Maujan had disappeared from the list of its vice-presidents where it had figured with those of Barthou, Millerand, Klotz, Poirrier, and Lourties. The stars could afford to stand by themselves. Lesser lights found the over-patriotic associations of the new federation compromising in the eyes of their republican electors.[41]

An article in the *Dépêche* of April 21 throws a light on opinion in the Fourteenth Arrondissement of Paris, whence Steeg had just been returned to the Senate. The Fourteenth lies roughly between the Latin Quarter to the north, and the Ceinture to the south, where the road begins through the Porte d'Orléans toward Sceaux and Robinson. It had seen much hard fighting in the days of the Commune, chiefly around Denfert-Rochereau, and it was very close to the center of the new nationalist agitation in the Latin Quarter. In this mixed population of workers and middle class, nationalist sentiment was strong and susceptible, memories of Agadir still fresh, desire for national readiness general. This was also true for the Socialists, most of whom had forgotten antipatriotism and discarded the slogans calling for "insurrection rather than war." The issue was no longer regarded as one of ends, but of means. The extreme Left was for the *Nation Armée*, but everybody agreed that the Three-Year Law should not be touched until something had been made ready to take its place. The task of the next Parliament would be to perfect the Three-Year Law, while building up alongside it a structure that would permit its revision. Such was the impression of the *Dépêche*.

On the occasion of the visit of King George V and Queen Mary to Paris in April of 1914, just before the elections, the crowds in the streets were heard to cry *Vive l'Armée* as much as *Vive le Roi*.[42]

Gustave Téry who, with Jean Piot, had opposed Caillaux at Mamers in the Sarthe and had seen him win by 12,297 votes to the nationalist's 295, commented bitterly:

Give and take. Not a word about questions on the agenda, not a word about the country's interests—of the interests of this country called France, not Mamers or

La Ferté. Who will represent the constituency? The most worthy? No—rather the best able to do his electors a good turn, to render personal services. . . . No program. A deal. No phrases. Just a calculation: total 107,170 francs and a few cents [which Caillaux had obtained for the locality]. There is no answer to it.[43]

Incapable of discerning the most worthy, even if there should have been a choice, the French elector with his usual logic chose the most useful. In this connection, *L'Echo* quoted the words of an inhabitant of a small town in the south who had helped elect what *L'Echo* called a "Socialist of the worst kind." "Oui, monsieur. Nous sommes très dévots ici. Mais les élections c'est de la politique."[44]

The second ballot would decide the make-up of the new Chamber. Socialists and Radicals were determined to reforge the old unity of the bloc. Gustave Hervé, in an interview, outlined this aim:

We want three things: the return to two-year service, income tax with a controlled declaration, the rout of the clericals. On these issues Radical and Socialist programs are the same. Hence, the need for the bloc. We must work together at the second ballot, with no care for our personal interests.[45]

And the deputy of the Jura, Ponsot, lumping all the Right under a common label, resumed the content of the struggle: "For the Republic, against the nationalists."[46] For their part, the nationalists appealed to the electorate to vote for France and safeguard it against the unholy alliance of the Left. Fortune, credit, national honor, prestige, army, existence itself, all depended, it seemed, on the Three-Year Law.[47]

The results after the second ballot appeared to be a great success for the reconstituted bloc, and particularly for the S.F.I.O., which had gained 34 seats and now numbered 101 deputies. The Radicals and Radical-Socialists returned 228 strong, having gained 11 seats. Of these 228, only 172 belonged to the "unified" party and were officially pledged to the program of Pau. But in the first flush of victory, such distinctions went unnoticed. In a Chamber that numbered 602 deputies, it seemed that, if they would, Socialists, Radical-Socialists, and Radicals could have a steady majority for whatever measures they envisaged. And, fortunate coincidence, their programs were almost identical.[48]

The Socialist victory had been striking. *L'Echo* commented ruefully: "There is a considerable and worrying phenomenon—the progress of revolutionary Socialism among the rural population. In certain regions the peasant has become revolutionary, and votes for the S.F.I.O."[49] And General Percin, the Radical candidate at Neuilly-Boulogne, standing down in favor of the Socialist Morizot, explained: "Two thousand electors refused me their votes because I stood as a Radical, and they have enough of Radicals. These two thousand electors have become Socialists because the Socialist party has a program, and the Radical party has none."[50]

Commenting on the results, Bainville wrote in the *Action française*: "In Paris pure republicanism is already almost entirely eliminated, and the fight is circumscribed between the nationalist idea and the collectivist idea."[51] There were no doubts of what had been at stake. Joseph Reinach in an interview on his own defeat at the polls said: "The electoral fight turned on the Three-Year Law." And *L'Aurore* affirmed: "The military law remains the pivot of all possible combinations."[52] Obviously, the chief issue of the new nationalism remained the chief issue of the political situation. Nor can we understand its full significance apart from the background of action and reaction, fear and resentment, against which the great debate had been and still was carried on. For those who carried the law, it was unthinkable that it might be lost now in face of the continuing German threat. Albert de Mun tried to discern the intentions of Jaurès: "What will Jaurès do? He tells us every morning, and at least thanks to his frankness positions are clear. The great objective is the Three-Year Law. . . . Thus the law is at the present moment the criterion of all politics. Its fall would be the victory of Jaurès with all his program of internal and external disorganization."[53]

Jaurès himself made his proposals plain: the Doumergue ministry was to carry on backed by the two great parties of the Left. Based on the manifest will of the country, it could present to the Chamber a clear, vigorous program that Left-Wing Radicals and Socialists would be able to support and carry through. As for the program, the Socialists only asked that it should conform to the Radical resolutions of Pau.[54] But this was too much to expect of a profoundly-disunited group of "unified" Radicals. Writing on May 31, on the eve of Parliament's opening, the *Dépêche* found that "although the elections have been very clear, the deputies on the Left seem to find it difficult to decide what stand they will take." In fact, the Radical head office had never been as firm on the Pau program or on party discipline as the congress had intended it to be. It had sown dragon's teeth of indecision with results now beginning to appear only too clearly.

Candidates had been accorded the party's benediction without any requirement that they should first accept the program of Pau. Many had voted for the Three-Year Law. Some supported it still.

In the east, the only "unified" Radical to demand even a gradual return to two-year service, heavily qualified by proposals for preparatory measures like premilitary training, was Schmidt in the Vosges. Nearby, in Saône-et-Loire, Henri Poncet had declared "je voterai la réduction de

la durée du service militaire dès que les difficultés extérieures auront
disparu," thus adjourning the operation indefinitely. Across the country
in Finistère, where two Le Bails, father and son, represented the family
borough of Quimper, there had been uneasy reconciliation of the program of Pau *pour le principe,* and of the Three-Year Law "tempered by
long periods of leave." But the Finistère, which had long drifted toward
the Left, was not as solid as the department of Mayenne, where another
supporter of the program of Pau, Chaulin-Servinière, found it wiser to
say nothing at all about its revisionist implications.

Other *unifiés* opposed, when they did not ignore, other parts of the
official party platform.[55] The experience of unification had been a failure.
The party's membership still contained those moderate elements that
had prevented any coherent action before the elections.[56] Political homo-
geneity was hard to achieve with men like a Fould, who stood for the
party in Hautes-Pyrénées, or a Louis Dreyfus, the friend and electoral
neighbor of Jacques Piou in the Lozère. *La Lanterne* had rightly commented: "The party is bicephalous. One head is Radical, another
Radical-Socialist. . . . Thus, in fact, there are Radical-Socialists and
Radical anti-Socialists."[57]

To impress the latter, nothing was too good. Poincaré himself, speaking at Rennes on June 1, descended into the political arena with a plea
for the integrity of the law. In order to defend her independence, her
rights, and her honor, France "needs an army composed of ample effectives capable of rapid mobilization; she needs also troops with adequate
instruction, drilling, and field training." This was a departure from the
presidential tradition of political neutrality, and on June 3 Jaurès called
the speech unconstitutional and exceeding the presidential functions. In
the words of Georges Michon, "c'était déclarer, en face d'une Chambre
nouvellement élue que, même contre la volonté du pays, il ne laisserait
pas toucher à la loi de trois ans." Michon, no friend of Poincaré, may be
making too much of his words, but the action of the President was
certainly more than openly partisan. However, at a time when even the
stolid Joffre could threaten resignation *si la loi de trois est remise en
question,* such niceties counted for little.[58]

On June 2, Doumergue resigned. He had held the fort, kept it clean,
and now the election truce was coming to an end. Of the problems facing
his successor and the new Chamber, the most pressing was still that of
the Three-Year Law. It reared its ugly head before Deschanel's presidential allocution had ended. His speech was followed by an exchange of
A bas les trois ans from the Left and *Vive les trois ans* from the Right.
Jaurès commented: "Until this law of national division is settled . . . all

responsible government will be impossible." *Le Progrès* thought the same: "The situation is dominated by the military question, which has acquired exceptional importance. One must be for or against the three years, for or against immediate measures to reduce the duration of service."[59]

On resigning, Doumergue had advised Poincaré that Viviani might make a good successor. He had not voted for the Three-Year Law, but he was no less determined to maintain it than Doumergue himself.[60] Viviani himself acknowledges that the outgoing premier was right in his judgment: "I undertook the formation of the ministry, with the purpose of leaving the recently voted law intact."[61] But this was not generally realized.

Viviani tried to form a cabinet, but failed to obtain the collaboration of Bourgeois at the ministry of foreign affairs,[62] and also that of Lebrun and Peytral, because he refused to declare the law to be intangible. Having at last assembled a cabinet which included J. Dupuy, Thomson, Malvy, Messimy, and René Renoult, he met with refusal on the part of two Radicals (Justin Godard and Ponsot) to accept his attitude on the same question. Their objection was his weakness in accepting the law at all. The attempt had to be given up.[63]

Viviani's failure was a relief to the supporters of the law, ignorant of his private inclinations. The Ribot cabinet that succeeded it was greeted by them as a victory. De Mun exclaimed: "The Three-Year Law is safe!"[64] Overlooking the scene, the *Times* of June 10 decided that the "real issue in the Chamber—for or against the present army law—has been fairly joined," and went on to predict a solid majority in favor of the law.

The new ministry exemplified a moderate attempt to combine respectable Republicans of the lay-school variety, with the Delcassé-Peytral faction that insisted on the inviolability of the Three-Year Law. Formed on June 9, it was beaten three days later on its first appearance before the Chamber. The debate was long, violent, and fruitless. Beaten by 306 votes to 262, and again by 395 to 145, Ribot retired.

> *Admiral Bienaimé: C'est la ruine de la France!*
> *(à gauche et extrème gauche:) Vive la République!*[65]

To the *Times* of the thirteenth of June, repenting perhaps its earlier optimism, the "event [was] of great gravity and may have very serious results both for France and for Europe."

The situation was indeed serious. The atmosphere of the president's approaching visit to Russia would be spoiled by prolonging the crisis, or by an immediate revision of the Three-Year Law.[66] In any case, the general feeling seemed to call for a breathing space, a break to recover

from the exertions of the recent elections.[67] Viviani was persuaded to try
again. He agreed to try on the same basis as that on which he had failed
ten days earlier. On June 14, *L'Echo* published an interview with Viviani,
and with his finance minister designate, Noulens:

Viviani: We are resolved to apply the military law as it is.
Noulens: No one has any intention of going back on it. There is no danger to be
feared. . . . You can have full confidence in Messimy [the future Minister
of War]. . . .
Question: It seems that the formula of your ministry is not the same as that of your
first combination?
Viviani: I do not remember the exact terms, but it is roughly the same; formulas,
after all, mean little. Everything depends on the way one applies them:
you can have complete confidence on this subject.

The Radicals, scared by the Ribot episode, tired of shuffling, accepted
Viviani. *La Lanterne* became less intransigent: "Perhaps it is all a question of words," it wrote. Then it went on to suggest a possible compromise
by which the Right would keep the Three-Year Law in exchange for
allowing the introduction of an income tax.[68]

Viviani's new position displeased the Socialists, but brought him cheers
from the center and the Right.[66] In *L'Eclair* of June 17, Ernest Judet had
already pointed out that the formula that made Radicals accept the
second Viviani cabinet was not notably different from the formula that
had caused the failure of the first. In the *Libre Parole*, Bazire was relieved: "The essential is that the Three-Year Law is safe." *L'Echo de
Paris* was also thankful for the respite, while *L'Aurore* hemmed and
hawed:

The immediate return to two years cannot find a majority at the present hour.
There is a majority for all measures likely to prepare this revision, but most of those
who sincerely want a lightening of the military burden are afraid of themselves.[70]

Jaurès saw Viviani as relying on a resigned majority, afraid to reject yet
another government.[71] *Le Progrès* considered with assumed curiosity this
majority that had been refused to Ribot for his program, and granted to
Viviani for his almost identical one. The failure of Ribot, it commented,
had been a triumph for the bloc. The success of Viviani dislocated it on
the morrow of victory.[72]

But the composition of Viviani's cabinet troubled the Right. There
were too many ministers who had opposed the law or who, like Messimy,
had had counterprojects of their own. The appointment of General
Pedoya, an old opponent of the law, to head the army commission,
seemed an ominous indication that the reduction of the period of military
service was not far from the government's mind. Augagneur had until
recently been the law's determined opponent.[73] His newspaper, *Le Lyon*

Républicain, had not changed its tone. The opposition felt it had reason
to be uneasy. Ernest Judet found his fears confirmed by an article in the
Lyon Républicain suggesting that the government intended to revise the
military law as soon as the Parliamentary recess was over.[74]

Clemenceau also commented on the article and, after having marked
the cleavage in Radical ranks over this issue, indicated his opinion that
the ministry would move toward a revision directly upon the opening of
the autumn session.[75] Poincaré himself must have had his doubts: before
he left France in July he had called the minister of war, Messimy, to the
Elysée and warned him that a conflict was imminent. Above all, he had
insisted, the Three-Year Law must not be touched.[76] How much of this
was argument, one wonders, and how much forethought?

Recess had come with the vote of credits for Poincaré's Russian trip.
The Socialists refused to vote these, in order to show their distrust for
the personal contact and secret treaties which involved France in affairs
far beyond her knowledge and will.[77] But, as Maxime Vuillaume remarked a little later, "Socialist resolutions need frighten no one. They
are . . . purely formal."[78] Jaurès had said as much several years before:
"The workers' movement has become parliamentary—so parliamentary
that one cannot seek in its motions the real expression of its thought."[79]

Most Socialists now agreed with Varenne, who wrote in *Le Journal:*
"If war threatens, we shall do the impossible to prevent it. If it breaks
out in spite of us, we must only think to save our country."[80] This was a
different language from that of 1905, or even of 1910. War hovered over
Europe, the military problem remained in the foreground of parliamentary preoccupations, but the country was getting used to the mass of
dark clouds in the east.[81]

Expected for so long, war came unexpectedly, the clatter of its approach drowned in the clanging concert that had lasted for so long. On
Sunday, July 22, Daniel Halévy was visiting a village in the Cévennes:
he heard the local deputy make a speech at a local banquet without
saying a word about the Austrian ultimatum to Serbia, and without his
audience expecting it. The following Sunday, July 29, a young student
could still write to his friend:

> Je suis tout surpris encore de t'avoir entendu dire que tu croyais à la guerre; mon
> Dieu, tu as mieux lu que moi les journaux et tu es moins sujet aux illusions. Serait-ce
> que je m'abuse, je ne crois pas la guerre possible.[82]

The polemic on the Three-Year Law continued. On the eve of war,
L'Echo of July 31 published an article by General Maitrôt: "Le Retour
au Service de Deux Ans—Imbécilité ou Trahison?" while *L'Aurore* still

featured a series of articles by General Percin, demanding the instant revision of the Three-Year Law.

To the newspaper-reading public, the first glimpse of the crisis came when a week of full-page accounts of the trial of Mme Caillaux gave way to dark headlines. "Never has the international situation been so serious," they were suddenly told.[83] Faced with the possibility of war, with a decision outside their control, their first reaction was of the "it cannot happen to me" variety.[84]

Jaurès, incurable optimist, refused to believe that war was possible, let alone probable. Before leaving Vandervelde after the Extraordinary Meeting of the Socialist Bureau in Brussels on July 30, he told the Belgian Socialist: "It will be like Agadir: there will be ups and downs, but things cannot not be settled." Then he went to spend an hour with the Flemish Primitives in the Museum, before catching his train back to Paris.[85] On the same day Poincaré, who had canceled the second part of his Baltic cruise, returned to Paris, to be greeted by relieved and tumultuous crowds, by anxious and harassed caretaker ministers.

Public temper hovered between the anxious and the excited. Colonel House visiting Paris a month earlier had found French statesmen pacific, the French people less so.[86] An attitude had been built up, increasingly exasperated by constant and repeated threats, increasingly matter-of-fact about the possibility of war. One thing led to another, and the atmosphere now imposed its own conditions. Merrheim, who led the C.G.T. minority during the 1914–1918 war, said that the working class itself was now nationalistic. It was, in his words, "soulevée par une formidable crise de nationalisme."[87]

In what was to be his last editorial, Jaurès warned his readers against themselves and against their brethren:

> The greatest danger at the present hour lies not in the events themselves. It is not even in the real inclinations of the chancelleries nor in the real will of the peoples; it is in the growing nervousness, in the growing fears, in those sudden impulses born of fear, of acute uncertainty, of prolonged anxiety. Crowds can yield to [such] a crazy panic, and it is not certain that governments are not yielding too.[88]

And it does indeed seem as if men did not go to or cheer the war for the sake of Alsace-Lorraine or for the sake of Serbia: they went to war to clear the air. Because they had lived with the menace for so long, they were glad to see it face to face, tackle it, and get it over (as they thought) once and for all. The pacifists and the Socialists saw their troops run away from them to follow the drums and the flags. Jaurès himself was shot by a madman and, while his dead body lay on a marble-topped table in the Café du Croissant, the men who had once cheered themselves hoarse at his words now cheered all that he had tried to avoid. Across the Rhine, his erstwhile Socialist comrades also cheered the patriotic speeches of their country's leaders.

The nationalists now lived their hour of triumph. They too were surprised, but the outbreak of war was the justification of all their campaigns, their efforts, and their hopes.[89] Barrès was jubilant: "Il éclate enfin, le jour espéré pendant quarante quatre années!"[90] A great prelate echoed his words, or at least his mood: "I think these events very fortunate," wrote Monsignor Baudrillart in *Le Petit Parisien* of August 16, when war had already been raging for two weeks. "I have awaited them for forty years. France is remaking herself and, in my opinion, this could not be achieved without the purifying war."

The Socialists finally looked over and beyond their lost leader. Aggression had cleared away their last remaining doubts.[91] Jules Guesde and Marcel Sembat entered the "national" government to collaborate with former antagonists like Briand, Millerand, and Delcassé in the struggle for the life of France.

With the war, a chapter closed, but a glorious period began for the nationalist forces. The war justified their patriotic foresight. During the dangerous years war brought, their attitude called for everybody's respect. Men as far apart as Poincaré and André Gide came to regard them as the stoutest defenders of the nation. Then the outbreak of the Russian Revolution stressed their importance as guardians of the established order.[92]

The sky-blue election of 1919 was deeply penetrated by the doctrines that nationalists, and in particular the Action française, had preached for nigh on twenty-one years. But beyond 1914, their story is outside the scope of this study. Its aim is to show, on the one hand, the revival of nationalism and the nationalist movement, on the other the atmosphere that aroused them, and that they in turn created.

CONCLUSION

Herbert Hoover relates how in 1931 Filipino politicians came to Washington to carry on a noisy, emotional propaganda in favor of a bill granting full independence to the Philippines. But then they came to see him, asking him to veto the bill, explaining that the islands were not yet economically ready for independence, and that if they stood alone they would be in danger from either Japan or China.

"I was utterly astonished, and said so. I asked why they were lobbying with Congress to pass the Bill and carrying on propaganda to that end. . . . They replied that independence was their political issue in the Philippines, and that unless they promoted it their leadership would be lost to more dangerous elements. I was disgusted, and said I would call in the entire Press at once and repeat their statements. To which they replied blandly that they would say I had entirely misunderstood their remarks. I told them I hoped they would never come into the White House again." (Herbert Hoover, *Memoirs*, II.)

THE STORY THAT HAS BEEN UNFOLDED is that of nine years seen from one particular point of view. For this purpose I have, as it were, isolated the particular circumstances that interested me and followed them and all events relating to them through the years. The historian who does this must in some sort wear blinkers. He must eliminate irrelevant material; he must select from a great deal of relevant material that which most clearly shows the development of his subject.

Some readers may feel that this particular study of a national phenomenon centers unduly on the capital of the nation and ignores other politically significant areas. In this instance, however, the reasons for focusing a study of French politics on Paris are particularly strong: whatever its very real connections with other regions, the nationalism of 1905–1914 was a product of Paris. It never went much beyond, and, even in Paris, it remained a minority movement, trying tò compensate in violence and vociferation for the paucity of its numbers. This metropolitan and minoritarian character allowed it to strike up alliances, largely tacit, here and there, but it could never aspire to electoral success based on the great mass of lands and small towns wholly enfeuded to the Radicals or to other political groups. But through Paris life, thought, and society, it dominated and influenced the representatives of the provinces that by itself it could not impress.

If the new nationalism of the prewar years was largely the return to political favor of a patriotic platform and patriotic vocabulary, then those regions whose patriotism had not wavered in the interval are less significant than those that experienced a change. Where national pride, respect for the army and other established institutions, and awareness of foreign danger, have all remained constant, little sign of development or revival could show.

Such regions are, generally speaking, the departments west of a line from the Seine Inférieure in the north to the Vendée in the south; the eastern departments of the Meuse, Meurthe-et-Moselle, Haute-Marne, Vosges, and Haute-Saône; and certain departments south of the Massif Central of which the most steadfast is the Lozère, usually together with the Ardèche and the Aveyron. A more hesitant southwestern group (south of Vienne, west of Garonne and Tarn) of which the firmest are the Basses-Pyrénées and which follow the pace of the Poincarist revival until after the elections of 1914, might be added.

Going back as far as 1898, the Republicans of these areas (with occasional defections in the southwest) were standing firmly against the anticlerical, antimilitaristic policy of the Republican victors of the Dreyfus Affair, voting against the anticlerical measures of Waldeck-Rousseau and Combes, in favor of the Three-Year Law in 1913 and in favor of its Ribot defenders in 1914.

In this connection, significantly, of those "unified" Radicals and Radical-Socialists who did *not* attack the Three-Year Law in their election addresses, the overwhelming majority hailed from those regions or from nearby. These men knew perfectly well that a firm stand against the Law would endanger their election. They might deplore the temporary necessity of the measure, as Messimy did in the Ain, Péchadre in the Marne, Paul Laffont in the Ariège, Noulens in the Gers; or, like Abel Lefèvre in the Eure accept it only with strong reservations; or again keep mum, as did Chaulin-Servinière (Mayenne), Garat (Basses-Pyrénées), Magniaudé (Aisne), Puech (Seine), and Jovelet (Somme), whose policy is clear. It becomes even clearer when it is remembered that the motion that defeated Ribot on June 12, 1914, stood in the names of the discreet Puech and of Dalimier, who, in Seine-et-Oise, had also temporized on the subject of the Three-Year Law. They could be brave once the elections were over, and discretion has ever been the better part of valor.

The east, most affected by the loss of Alsace-Lorraine, remained the region where the thought of revenge was in least danger of fading. When there were signs of a German peril, it was the east, most immediately threatened, most aware of the threat, that gave the strongest support to the demand for increased preparedness. As François Goguel has pointed out, the east, republican but not radical during the first twenty-five years of the Republic, moved toward the Right in reaction to the Dreyfusist spirit dominant at the turn of the century. The extremes of Dreyfusism shocked the moderates there, its antipatriotic overtones went against their deepest convictions, its antimilitarism could not be understood by men who lived in the shadow of the German army.

A map will show the reality of this shadow over the eastern departments and its apparently distinct influence. Their proximity to the German border made them support Rouvier in 1887 against a warmongering Boulangism that filled them with unease, but the same proximity made them favor a *Poincarisme* of preparedness and national pride. That this awareness became less acute west of Meurthe-et-Moselle, where not Germany but Belgium lay across the border, can be inferred from the different electoral language and orientation in the Ardennes and Nord.

The north was torn in the years before 1914 by the travail of new problems fighting old forces, religious and social realities being faced by a new industrial revolution. Parties of the center, if not of the Right, had always been reasonably strong in the north, and normally the Republicans of northern departments fell in the ranks of the Poincarist coalition. But the issues of 1914 meant electoral defeat for supporters of the Three-Year Law and success for its opponents in all departments except the Pas-de-Calais and the Marne, which is not really in the north.

Other changes in the electoral map were due largely to fortuitous causes. Thus in the Sarthe, which Caillaux by personal influence had swung against nationalist causes, the election of 1914 showed a revival of the Right. But this was because of the special effort made by Caillaux's enemies to defeat him in his electoral fief. In this they failed, and in the circumstances his survival might well be reckoned as a nationalist defeat. Another instance of personal influence exerted in a different direction is that of the Independent Socialist André Lefèvre who swung the Bouches-du-Rhône behind the Three-Year Law—though he was not strong enough to keep them there too obviously after the 1914 elections.

However, the real novelty in the electoral geography of this time was the vote of a majority of Parisian deputies for the Three-Year Law that the Left and extreme Left opposed with all their might. And this swing toward the Right on a military issue was confirmed in 1914 when Parisian nationalism, surrounded by a belt of largely hostile suburbs, yet projected its influence toward south and east, into Seine-et-Oise, Loir-et-Cher, Yonne, and even into the Sarthe. This is why it seemed that in terms of political orientation the most significant change occurred in Paris and the Paris basin (an area where Paris newspapers, orators, and echoes could most easily reach), and this is where the workings of the "nationalist revival" might be most profitably examined.

A survey of the different forces affecting political orientation cannot ignore the social factor and the various attitudes and sympathies of different social classes insofar as these can be apprehended. To begin with, acquaintance with the life and literature of the time portrays the reality of a class division and class-consciousness sometimes of a very meticulous kind. The main divisions here will have to be classic almost to roughness: the aristocracy, the middle classes, and the rest.

During the years covered by this study, the aristocracy had not lost all political, and still retained a great deal of social, influence, particularly in the countryside. Purged of its eighteenth-century scepticism, the nobility had moved through royalism to Catholicism, the defense of the Church having proved a better proposition than the restoration of monarchy. The great bastion of their power lay in the west, especially in Anjou, Maine, and Vendée, where they still made elections in the twentieth century much as the Earl of Brentford made them for Phineas Finn at Loughton in the nineteenth.

This aristocracy, whether legitimist or *rallié*, was fundamentally anti-republican, patriotic by tradition, and not at all "nationalist" in a party sense. The constructive part of the nationalist platform they had always advocated as a matter of course, unless they had taken it for granted to the extent of not thinking it worth the mention. The rest was probably a matter of indifference to them. They naturally showed some interest in the integral nationalism of the Action française, but where their power was absolute, as it was in the west, they had no need of it and could afford to ignore it in political practice. It was in the southwest where their influence was thin that such men as Lur-Saluces and Cabrières saw in the Action française a useful channel for their policies. In western towns where the Action française did wield some influence, there was not alliance but competition and struggle, in which the Right divided and in which the erstwhile weaker party, the Catholic middle class, defeated the stronger aristocratic faction by securing the support of the new nationalists.

This serves as a useful reminder of the influence of the Church. This influence had been exerted on behalf of the Republic to bring about, however halfheartedly, the *ralliement* by which an important section of the Catholic Right left the royalist camp and accepted the established order. But the institutional traditions and the class connections of the leaders of the Church made it and them lean heavily toward the Right even before pacifist Radicals had provoked their enmity by anticlericalism. Throughout the life of the Third Republic, ecclesiastical influence appears openly, though not officially, on the side of nationalism.

It was the Catholic alliance in the more specifically Catholic parts of the country (Normandy, Brittany, Basque country, Catholic cantons of the Cévennes and Vosges) which gave the nationalists heart. But, once again, Catholicism was the local reality, nationalism simply its occasional political expression and not the only one. We can find the Catholics putting up a "free-thinking Republican," as they did at Rennes in 1914, to secure the defeat of the distrusted Catholic, Louis Deschamps, or indulging in internecine struggles like the fight preceding the election of Paul Simon at Brest in 1913 against another Catholic.

But whatever forms Church policy and power might take, however ferocious the family quarrels in which it might indulge, it remained Catholic, and nationalist if at all *because* it was Catholic.

Altogether, this official Right of aristocracy and Church hardly alters its orientation in terms of political attitudes and language during the twenty-five or thirty years before 1914. The twentieth century finds it maintaining much the same positions as it held a decade before and would hold more than a decade later. There is little or no question of change about it: it could at most await the swing of the pendulum which eventually restores its ideas to the favor of political fashion.

The second of the social order, the middle classes, tremendously diversified, melting into their rivals at both ends, provided most of the personnel of the political, academic, and administrative worlds, and hence most of the material for a study of contemporary politics and political opinions. Some of them need not be considered—*grands bourgeois* like Casimir-Périer or Pouyier-Quartier whom only the nobility knew not to be of their own. Below them, *haute* and *moyenne bourgeoisie* had in common a snobbery that made the sanction and frequentation of the aristocratic world one of their dearest aspirations. Vulgar academicians, ignorant of social niceties, may have considered the salon of Mme Verdurin to be the height of fashion, but Mme Verdurin herself knew better, and did her best to shed her awkward Dreyfusist connections.

It was, however, less the social aspirations of the *bourgeoisie* than a new community of interest which made it move toward positions held by the aristocracy for forty years: 1848 had done much to shake the Voltairianism of the *bourgeoisie*, and 1871 had confirmed this movement. At first religion had been good for the people, then it had provided for the children's education, at last it had appeared as the essential element of a moral and social discipline which seemed so signally lacking in modern democracy.

It was also worth considering that, by going to Church and to Church functions, one could meet the local *châtelain* and even perhaps penetrate into the little world of the nobility. Nobility and *bourgeoisie* met in defense of the Church, as some of them had met in defense of the general staff, and common political interests sometimes opened doors that neither material nor cultural interests had prevailed upon before.

But beyond the political, material concerns also drove the *bourgeoisie* from the ranks of the party of movement into the lines of conservative defense. In the years after 1871, layer after layer of the middle class came to the conclusion that enough had been done to alter the face of France and that further change should be opposed. The "old bourgeois aristocracy" of the country towns had its day with Thiers and MacMahon, disapproved of Ferry's anticlericalism, and went into opposition with Jules Simon in the 'eighties. Their fellows of the industrial and commercial world—Thomson and Etienne were survivors of this *Gambettisme d'affaires*—did not follow them until the defeat of the moderate Méline and the critical years of the Dreyfus Affair persuaded them of the primary importance of social defense with all its implications.

The lower sections of the middle class, the real Third Estate, took longer to come round. It harbored few of the social ambitions of the upper layers and was easily persuaded into a "radical" policy as long as this radicalism stuck safely to democracy and anticlericalism. The appearance of working-class demands was enough to frighten them away, not from radicalism that was by then no more than a harmless label, but from further reform. This class was not only antisocialistic but antistate, and one of the reasons for such an attitude is expressed in Pauline Bergeret's words to her father: "L'Etat, mon père, c'est un monsieur piteux et malgracieux assis derrière un guichet. Tu comprends qu'on n'a pas envie de se dépouiller pour lui." Thus, though by 1905 it was the radicalism of this class which dominated government and Parliament, its mistrust of the state power toned down its programs of social reform and turned it insensibly into a conservative force.

In its lower reaches, this layer merged with the working class, and this lower-middle class of small shopkeepers, shop assistants, and office workers, afraid of oppression from above and of losing their identity in the proletariat below, without exactly abandoning the hope of forward movement, offered by its vulnerable and incoherent nature just those opportunities, just that temper of mind, on which all the Boulangisms and all the demagogues could try their hand. A program such as carried the nationalist Lacrisse to victory in the ward of the Grandes-Ecuries could appeal to all these groups:

Défendre l'armée nationale contre une bande de forcenés. Combattre le cosmopolitisme. Soutenir les droits des pères de famille violés par le projet du gouvernement sur le stage universitaire. Conjurer le péril collectiviste. Relier par un tramway le quartier des Grandes-Ecuries à l'Exposition. Porter haut le drapeau de la France. Améliorer le service des eaux.

It seems fairly clear that, by the early years of our century, the middle class, whether notables like the Siegfrieds of Le Havre or on the confines of the working class like the market gardeners of Bobigny on the outskirts of Paris, had left the reformist Republican camp, had left the "party of movement." They were either concerned to obstruct changes they feared would endanger the established order, or prepared to attack the established order to bring about vague but violent changes. The paradoxical result was that both these tendencies brought grist to the nationalist mill: the conservative because it found in nationalist energy a not unattractive reassurance, the cataclysmic because it was tempted by their equivocal programs and by the passion of their demagogy.

One section of the middle class cannot well be included under any of these categories. That is the great and growing body of state employees who were beginning to develop not only a strong feeling of common interest but also a concrete syndical structure—in the civil service, the teaching profession, and so forth. Although as a class their traditions were strictly bourgeois, perhaps owing to the centralization of their services, the low level of pay, the size of the organizations of which they were a part, the analogy of their working conditions to those in great industrial enterprises, their sympathies went to the parties of movement and social reform, sometimes indeed of violent reform.

When speaking of the "rest," one nods in passing to a great indifferent mass of town- and especially country-dwellers, whose parsimony as a rule outweighed patriotism and social spirit, and who swayed with the wind of the active minority and of local tradition. However, the influence of the increasingly organized workers' parties, largely united by the S.F.I.O. in the political field, became more effective, and the Independent Socialists (more independent, most of them, than Socialist) were also important. Though any Syndicalist would claim that Parliamentary Socialists did not represent the working class, they interested the working class enough to secure ever greater electoral support and to frighten all the defenders of property and of the established order with the prospect of an impending Ragnarok.

Different as these varied groups and interests were, they had one thing in common: a basic or growing distrust for the system of government, condemned by some for being too harsh and by others for being too weak; condemned by Royalists and Socialists on principle and by others because it seemed unable to secure for them whatever they desired.

Men who were in temporary possession of the levers of power may have believed that the system could work well enough; and there were those, like Barrès and Jaurès, who thought that any radical change would probably be for the worse. Understandably, the need for national unity had been felt increasingly. Faced by a foreign threat, spurred also by the threat or the promise of internal change, a growing section of the politically significant minority could agree on slogans that, even when called Poincarist, were in effect nationalist. This is the essence of the development, but obviously, in its analysis, the *how* has been considered more often than *why*. Perhaps *why* is not a question that historians care to ask: they have good reason to know its pitfalls. One approach, however, I should like to call the *how-why* approach, because it goes beyond a mere account without aiming at—or believing in—an ultimate explanation. This much every reader is entitled to expect, this much every student is expected to offer.

Certain obvious drawbacks were inherent in the nature of the subject: the initial difficulty of defining and following what is essentially an atmospheric condition; the relative value of evidence provided by press and Parliament; the limited amount of information available concerning personal and local opinion and its changes; the necessity of describing a pattern of fluctuating opinion based on such limited evidence and therefore of attributing to a few sources an importance greater perhaps than they deserve.

I have not drawn any definite conclusion on the relationship between public opinion and public policy, but I have tried to show how much one affects the other, how opinion created for policy's sake may eventually influence policy that in turn will influence opinion. Much more clearly, it can be seen how little most issues of foreign policy affect and are affected by the opinion of the general public. Where foreign affairs are concerned, the great majority of the public were ignorant, indifferent, or both. It took hard work to create a stir even in limited circles; to create a lasting mood or opinion took longer, generally speaking, than the nine years here examined. It was only after the foreign issue had been transformed into an internal one that its burdens and decisions confronted the French as a whole. Even then, they needed more time to come to terms with the issues than they actually had.

On the other hand, the circumstances forcing me to follow the manifestations of nationalism chiefly in the pages of the press and in reports of parliamentary debates had certain advantages. There could be no better way to depict the interaction of the various issues, events, or circumstances and the narrowness of the circle in which these matters were debated.

It is possible to see the effects of this nationalism in the political world; to discern its growing influence in literary and academic circles, hand in hand and often confused with the antiscientistic reaction typified by Bergsonism, that intellectual Boulangism as Benda called it; to follow

the politics of the diplomatic corps and of a Quai d'Orsay deeply influenced by Delcassé, disappointed by the settlement of 1911, eagerly
supporting the new Poincarism of 1912 and offering their anxious aid to
the Three-Year Law. The new atmosphere is also reflected in the military
policy of the "Young Turks" and of Colonel de Grandmaison, who
preached attack as the best method of defense and the one best suited to
the impetuous national spirit. It was the job of the soldiers to prepare
for war; they cannot be accused of warmongering when they were
merely doing their job. But the spirit in which this was done mirrored the
confident chauvinism of the time, exalted the patriotic virtues, and
attacked men—even General Michel—suspected of not being whole-
heartedly sympathetic.[1] That Michel was attacked for being too far
Left, too close to Jaurès,[2] shows the quick recovery Right-Wing sentiment made in the army after General André's removal. But, whatever
their political opinions, it is fair to speak of the officer corps as a whole,
if only by an understandable *déformation professionelle*, as sympathetic
to the new nationalist spirit.

More significant in this connection was the assurance of Alexandre
Millerand that the "army is France."[3] The army seemed to endorse a
temper that Millerand's great patron, Waldeck-Rousseau, had reproved
within memorable time. Once again many officers, like Lieutenant Psichari, greeted recruits with a broad hint that attendance at Mass every
morning was expected. Once again, a General Bonnal could say in public,
addressing the fifth congress of the Action française on November 29,
1912, that war would be a good thing as it would deliver Alsace-Lorraine
from the Germans and France from the parliamentary yoke, and find a
ready echo in the military press.[4] This may not be what Millerand had in
mind, but it could have been.

For different reasons antiparliamentarism was not absent from the
political feelings of the aristocracy and the upper *bourgeoisie* that furnished the officer and diplomatic corps with most of their personnel, in
addition to staffing ministerial cabinets, the higher grades of the civil
service, the editorial boards of the great periodicals, and the boards of
the great companies. Influential in and influenced by a society with
strong national and religious sympathies, Protestant as well as Catholic,
these men often combined several such occupations with a political
career. Thus Xavier Charmes, a high civil servant, and Paul Cambon, a
diplomat, sat on the boards of great companies; E. M. de Vogüé and
Francis Charmes not only edited great conservative reviews but carried
their views into parliament; great bankers and industrialists like Guil-
lain, Schneider, Doumer, Etienne, Aynard, Jonnart, Pierre Baudin, were

active as ministers, *rapporteurs*, or presidents of parliamentary commissions; platoons of highly placed soldiers and officials resigned to enter politics, like Caillaux and Messimy, or to enter the service of great banking and industrial establishments. All this is perfectly natural, indeed commonplace, yet we cannot overestimate the importance of this great network of personal relations and influences working in a narrow world that Péguy once estimated at eight or nine hundred people, although it may be stretched to several thousand.

To certain sections of this world, nationalism proved useful either as camouflage or as a ticket of admittance to democratic politics. Royalism and even Catholicism, electorally worthless, heeded the counsel of Henri Léon:

> Notre force est dans notre principe. ... Un monarchiste ne peut pas se dire républicain, même pendant l'Exposition. Mais on ne vous demande pas de vous déclarer républicain progressiste ou républicain libéral, ce qui est tout autre chose que républicain. On vous demande de vous proclamer nationaliste. Vous pouvez le faire la tête haute, puisque vous êtes nationaliste.

The argument was good and, of course, Lacrisse "céda par patriotisme."[5] Paul Doumer, *rapporteur* of the Three-Year Bill in the Senate, also used it to refresh his respectability after opposition to Brisson and Fallières had somewhat blotted his political copybook. Whatever suspicions good Republicans still entertained of him in spite of his position on the Comité des Forges gave way to his quotations from Victor Hugo:

> ... Je ne veux plus rien voir
> Que la grande patrie et le grand devoir.

On the other hand, to the lovers of social order, frightened by the prospect of violent change, nationalism seemed to campaign in favor of just those forces of order, authority, discipline, and tradition in which they saw the best hope for themselves and for their country.

The incidental growth of lawlessness, itself attributable to economic causes, permitted gangsters, *apaches*, to be equated with anarchists, then with Socialists, and Socialists to be discredited by continual reference to their *apache* "supporters." As a matter of fact, the lawlessness so alarming to the public was only an expression of a greater lawlessness, a general slackening of morals and of principle at this time, as apparent in the politics of the Republic as it was in its streets.

Cause and effect constantly reversed roles, both producing new effects and influencing the original cause. Thus, foreign danger affected the country and the government. Vocal sections of public opinion, aware of foreign danger, began to change the attitude of the government. Increased awareness of danger in official circles led to official encouragement of propaganda to increase the public awareness, so as to permit the necessary preparations. Public and government reacted to each other's pressure as they had begun by reacting to outside factors, i.e., to the impression of insecurity given by German armaments and foreign policy.

But German armaments themselves were due, at least professedly, to Germany's own fear of aggression. Having seen their defensive reaction bring an increase in French armaments, the Germans answered by a further increase in theirs, which brought the obvious French reply. In armaments and mounting tension the game continued.

But countering and overbidding could not go on forever. With everyone preparing war to insure peace, the means inevitably became the end, even for those to whom the end had been more than a word.

The development that I have surveyed is at least twofold. Nationalism, a spirit or doctrine rather than a party, after brief periods of success at the time of Boulangism and of the Dreyfus Affair, had become unpopular and lost most of its influence by the beginning of the century. The party of that name, beaten in 1902, massacred in 1906, had ceased to count for anything. Then, a double threat caused a reaction in its favor, or at least in favor of the ideas for which it stood.

On the one hand, the Tangier crisis led to a new awareness of the German danger, increased insistence on armament and national security, and the waking of memories about the two lost provinces, never forgotten, but allowed to fade a little during the years. On the other hand, the unification of the Socialist party caused the dissolution of the bloc. The Socialist party moved ever further left, in order to keep up with its followers and with the more extreme and popular leaders. The Radicals, in whose ranks the moderate faction would soon feel free to coöperate increasingly with moderates further right, drifted to the center. The separation of Church and state, having left them without aim or battle cry, also freed the way for union with the Right, over the corpse of the accomplished fact.

Whether this could eventually have produced a coherent Conservative party cannot be ascertained. I have no way of knowing with certainty how far the last prewar cabinet, that of Viviani, had been influenced by the prevailing atmosphere. It does seem, however, judging by French parliamentary mores, that what had been done could only with difficulty have been undone, and that all politicians of any experience knew as much at the time.[6]

One thing is certain: had the revision been attempted before the outbreak of war, it would have had to be well-protected by vigorous patriotic assertions and aimed at perfecting the application of the law, not at restricting it.

At the same time the growing importance of social problems, of economic problems, of workers' claims, scared the by-now-deeply-conservative middle class into looking round for champions who could defend the established order. It did find "strong men" to hold the helm, men who became ever stronger. In addition it found the nationalists, doughty defenders of this order and enemies of their enemies; and nationalist doctrine—the only effective lever, in circles or circumstances where doctrine mattered, against the Marxists.

Thus, this was a nationalist revival encouraged by the Right, by the greater part of the press, by Catholic opinion, and benevolently watched by the property-owning middle class. It benefited when it came from a revulsion in certain circles against antimilitaristic and antipatriotic excesses, which could be as obnoxious as the excesses to which the nationalists themselves were prone. Patriotism, justified by this reaction and by the foreign threat, became fashionable once more and success brought more success.

But nationalism, whether movement or atmosphere, remained strictly limited, chiefly to the neighborhood of Paris, until the crisis of Agadir served to spread the spirit throughout the country. This is where the distinction between the traditional nationalism of Barrès and Maurras, and the new nationalism of Bazire, Millerand, or Poincaré is a useful one. The latter nationalism really affected politics and politicians, though it was not expressed in election results. Not firm, not concrete, it influenced, suggested, insinuated; it seldom expressed itself directly through the machinery of democratic government. This is an intriguing aspect of the phenomenon—one which deserves greater attention than I have been able to give it—because it is connected with the fundamental problem of political power and control in a democratic system of government.

The new nationalism need not have been an undemocratic phenomenon. Given time and opportunity, the defensive patriot will become almost identical to the offensive nationalist, especially when emotionally prepared for the change by a certain traditional or historical background. It is difficult to say how much time such a change would need—a hundred years' war perhaps, at any rate a period sufficient to stamp upon a national community "not merely a consciousness of distinctiveness and individuality but also such a feeling of hostility to the out-group, to the alien, to the rival national community across the border, that common ground between the two is difficult to find and mutual understanding difficult to achieve."[7] A short but grave period of crisis might also suffice, although unless it is repeated it will soon be forgotten.

This is well illustrated by French popular opinion at the beginning of the twentieth century: the French had forgotten their antagonism to Germany, which was as yet too fresh for tradition and supported only by infrequent crises. Active popular antagonism was turned against England, the secular enemy who had recently inflicted a bitter humiliation at Fachoda and whose colonial activities kept Anglo-French rivalry before the public eye.

Because Fachoda had shown that France could not afford two enemies, a powerful group of men planned and brought about the Entente Cordiale, which, as it turned out, involved a reaffirmation of the German danger. But awareness of this danger did not penetrate deep or fast enough from the viewpoint of the politicians who had to work within the democratic system.[8] The politician had to exert on the public a pressure almost identical to the pressure put on him by his awareness of necessary measures and policies. He had to communicate an apprehension, a feeling, a set of conclusions, a simplified version of his policies, and compress them into an atmosphere propitious to his purpose. One of his tools was the propaganda of those doctrinaire nationalists who had survived into the new, changing situation. By the end of 1911 such activities had become fused in what is called the nationalist movement.

The nationalistic movement was not sustained by propaganda alone. It was carried forward by events from which the propagandists manufactured their stock in trade. From the beginning time and tide favored the nationalists; again and again their cause was buoyed up by some fortuitous event when it seemed about to sink beneath the weight of public indifference. Certainly Tangier, Casablanca, Bosnia, Agadir, and the Balkan Wars all strengthened the hand of the nationalists. Because they were quick to extract the utmost advantage from them, these events became important milestones in the road that led the French to war.

Not that the leaders of the new nationalism, most of whom were politicians, not demagogues, wanted to drive the country into war: they wanted the country to prepare for war, which is a different thing. Getting ready was a dull and expensive business, and one not designed to excite public enthusiasm, the more so since the same political circles that preached preparedness opposed any rational measure to pay for it as an attack on their economic interests.

Besides, time was short in which to persuade a people, even with a profusion of crises, and it was thought to be even shorter. Only a relatively small change was brought about in the electoral orientation of most regions by the sometimes frenzied nationalist activities. And so, while democratic enough by nature and potentially so in fact, the new nationalism remained a minority movement and its votaries a minority group who claimed to express a General Will that did not know itself, and to impose it on society, which, if it accepted their enthusiasms, was refractory to their implications.

The delimitation of the phenomenon to the neighborhood of Paris may account for its intensity. Working within the democratic system of government which obtained in France, a few people had to put out a far greater effort to gain their end, to convince their public, to achieve a certain social and national preparedness, than they would have had to do under conditions that did not contest their oligarchic powers. Seen from this point of view, their problems have a much wider significance, and their struggle becomes a part of an almost universal endeavor to reconcile political realities with democratic myths and aspirations.

That the limits of nationalism were narrow and its influence slight outside the Paris basin does not diminish its importance or alter the reality of its influence. Public opinion is not the sum or the common denominator of individual opinions. It is seen to be, if examined carefully, a number of individual opinions forceful enough to make themselves heard. But public opinion can be influenced by the persuasiveness of such private opinions and, these, if they are sufficiently forceful or perseverant, may be so effective as to make themselves become really representative.

The struggle for power, even in a democratic society, is restricted to a comparatively narrow area: it is a struggle between a few men or tendencies for the possession of a power to be exercised over the many who will have relatively little to say.[9] What they do say, when they march up every four or five years to perform the mysteries of the democratic myth, is limited by the moment and affected more than they imagine by the action of the power that they pretend to control.

The press, if it is useful as a mirror of the times—sometimes I am moved to think, a distorting mirror—is itself used to shape the scene it pretends to reflect. The *Times* thought that it was "impossible to judge French opinion solely by the attitude of the Paris press. Newspapers appeal to the public opinion much more than they interpret it; they try to create it rather than express it."[10] And yet it may be worth remembering the opinion expressed by Lord Dufferin on this subject just twenty years before:

It is said indeed that too much importance should not be given to the utterances of the Paris Press, and that its teachings do not permeate beyond Paris. In the first place, this is not true. . . . But in any event, the Paris Press acts very powerfully not only upon the members of both the Chambers but also upon the public opinion of the Capital; and experience has over and over again exemplified the disproportionate ascendancy exercised by Paris over the rest of France.[11]

In any case, from the historian's point of view even tendentious writing is a useful indication—provided it can be recognized for what it is. The indicative value of the slant of a piece of news is often as great as the value of the news itself. Sometimes greater. Robert de Jouvenel has written: "The press makes public opinion as great dressmakers make fashion; inspired by the tendencies and the taste of the day." The prejudices of press and politicians reveal the dominant tendencies of their day.

By this criterion, the importance of the nationalist trend during this period was considerable. It impressed all who observed the political scene, excited them, thrilled or worried them, according to their aims or character.

In February, 1914, Jules Cambon told his colleague, the Belgian minister in Berlin:

Since the Dreyfus Affair, we have in France a militarist and nationalist party, which will not brook a *rapprochement* with Germany at any price, and which excites the aggressive tone of a great number of newspapers. The government will have to take them into account, and also the party they represent, should another incident break out between the two nations. The majority of Germans and Frenchmen want to live in peace, that cannot be denied. But a powerful minority in both countries dreams only battles, conquests, or revenge. That is the danger beside which we must live, as if next to a powder-barrel which the slightest imprudence might blow up.[12]

Cambon slurred over the situation, perhaps because he did not identify Poincarism with the old-fashioned "militarist and nationalist party," perhaps simply because he thought his version more diplomatic or potentially useful in future negotiations. I doubt whether the minority in France which dreamt "only battles, conquests, or revenge" was as powerful as it was noisy. There seems to be no way of assessing the real extent of the influence of doctrinal nationalists, but it would seem to have been slight. None of them held office or had a say in policy-making, and these seem reasonable criteria. The leading figures of the new nationalism might be called the authoritarian conservatives like Poincaré, Barthou, and Millerand, and it was they who apparently exerted a real influence over Parliament and the Paris press. It was therefore their attitude that mattered, and this was mentioned in a dispatch of the Belgian minister from Paris in May, 1914:

There is no doubt that these last few months the French nation has become more chauvinistic and more self-confident. The same men, authorized, competent, who two years ago showed lively fear at the very mention of a Franco-German conflict, have changed their language. They declare themselves sure to win.

It was the "authorized, competent" men who counted, whose change of attitude decreed, if it did not reflect, a change in national attitude or, at least, in national policy because they were in a position to act on their views. The dispatch closed by calling the reintroduction of three-year service "one of the most dangerous elements of the present situation. It has been lightly imposed by the military party, and the country cannot bear it. Before two years are up, they will have to give it up or go to war."[13]

They went to war, impatient to get it over, and eager for it as the first condition of peace.[14] France had certainly not sought war. Its government very probably did not want it. But it had helped to sow the whirlwind that Europe was to reap during the next five years.

Were the nationalists and those who supported them more than merely obeying a vaster sequence of causality? Was the nationalist atmosphere of prewar years not itself a whiff of a greater cloud? To this there is no answer, either in this conclusion or yet in the vaster story of which this is but a paragraph.

There is left only a choice of epitaphs—not for a sentiment, which lives on, but for the men, who after all are still the chief protagonists of history. Were they, as Marcel Sembat called them, "a lot of would-be saviors, who did not hesitate to sow alarming rumors and spread alarm, only to scare themselves before the abyss of their own creation"?[15] Or were they something greater, if only as the living proof of Bergson's words:

"I am inclined to believe that the role of fate has been exaggerated. Not enough attention has been paid to the very great importance of small, very small, accidental circumstances. It follows from this that men of action can greatly affect events and that the evolution of mankind is certainly influenced by the reconciliation of tenacious wills."[16]

NOTES

ABBREVIATIONS OF WORKS FREQUENTLY QUOTED

A.A. *Amtliche Aktenstücke zur Geschichte der Europäischen Politik, 1885–1914* (Belgische Weltkriege). Berlin: 1925. 9 vols.

Abominable Vénalité *L'Abominable Vénalité de la Presse, d'après les documents des archives russes, 1897–1917.* Edited by Arthur Raffalovitch. Paris: 1931.

Aussenpolitik *Oesterreich-Ungarns Aussenpolitik von der Bosnischen Krise 1908 bis zum Kriegsausbruch 1914.* Vienna: 1930. 9 vols.

B.D. *British Documents on the Origin of the 1914 War, 1898–1914.* Edited by Gooch and Temperley. London: 1926–1938.

D.D.F. *Documents diplomatiques français*, 1871–1914. 1ᵉ série, 1871–1900; 2ᵉ série, 1901–1911; 3ᵉ série, 1911–1914. Paris: 1929–1940.

G.P. *Die Grosse Politik der Europäischen Kabinette, 1871–1914.* Berlin: 1922–1927. 39 vols.

J.O.C. *Journal Officiel de la République française*, Débats, Chambre. Paris: 1900—.

J.O.S. *Journal Officiel de la République française.* Débats, Senat. Paris: 1900—.

L.N. *Un Livre Noir:* Diplomatie d'avant-guerre d'après les documents des archives russes, 1910–1917. Paris: 1922–1934. 3 vols.

Tableau Politique André Siegfried. *Tableau politique de la France de l'Ouest sous la 3ᵉ République.* Paris: 1913.

NOTES TO INTRODUCTION
(Pages 1–16)

1 Thus Georges Bernanos, *Scandale de la Verité* (Paris: 1939), p. 18, could write: "J'espère, je crois, que la France est le royaume d'élection du Christ. Je l'espérais, je le croyais, bien avant d'avoir lu une seule ligne de M. Maurras. Je ne force personne à partager cet espoir et cette croyance."

2 George William Sharp, *The French Civil Service* (New York: 1931), p. 112.

3 Walter Lippmann, *The Phantom Republic* (New York: 1925), p. 47.

4 *Action française*, Oct. 6, 1910: "Nous avons cessé d'être un 'parti' subsistant de ses forces anciennes et ralliant des cadres un fois comptés: nous sommes devenus une idée conquérante." Romain Rolland, *Péguy* (Paris: 1944), I, 246: "Mais n'allez donc plus nous conter maintenant que la guerre de 1914 nous a été imposée contre notre volonté. Soyez francs! Sachez et osez avouer ... que toute une jeune génération française marchait au devant, joyeusement. ..."

5 André Siegfried, *Tableau Politique*, points out that nationalism never got far in traditionally Catholic and monarchist regions. Cf. p. 495: "Depuis la Révolution en effet, le tempérament bonapartiste, boulangiste, nationaliste ... (quelque nom qu'on lui donne) est resté profondément injecté dans les veines du peuple français. Nous n'avons pu l'étudier malheureusement avec suffisamment d'ampleur en l'observant simplement dans l'Ouest, parce qu'il y manque de base: la Droite pure y est trop puissante, et les provinces du royalisme et du cléricalisme sont justement celles où il se développe le moins. ..."

6 This might be qualified with a query as to how *revanchard* the population of the eastern provinces really was. It must not be forgotten that in 1887, after the crisis following the German abduction of Schnaebele, the republicans in the east supported the cabinet that Rouvier set up almost solely to get rid of Boulanger, who was considered to be a threat to peace. Lorraine returned several Boulangists and nationalists to the Chamber; Barrès in 1889, Driant and François de Ludres later. In spite of this, the political temper of Lorraine does not seem *revanchard* in the sense of seeking a war of revenge, or wanting to take the initiative, although the idea of war might be more readily accepted there than in provinces farther from the frontier and the German peril. The east was certainly militaristic; it was certainly patriotic. But was it actively *revanchard?* A fuller answer to this question might be furnished by the publication of M. A. Railliet's work, "Géographie de la France Politique du Nord-Est."

7 An instance of this is the pressure exerted by colonial interests, led by Etienne, both within Parliament and upon the policy of the moderate republicans.

8 Cf. Charles Maurras, *Pour Un Jeune Français* (Paris: 1949), p. 130: "Entre Poincaré et nous il n'y eut jamais d'alliance ou de tractation, mais des ménagements réciproques sur le plan des intérêts nationaux. Nous ne pouvions traiter un governement qui réarmait comme les gouvernements qui avaient désarmé."

9 The influence of the Comte de Lur-Saluces, of Mgr. de Cabrières, or for that matter of Lucien Millevoye or Jacques Piou, receives little notice in the course of this study: such influence raises no new problems.

10 Georges Dupeux and Alain Bomier-Landowski, *Etudes de Chronologie Parlementaire* (Paris: 1951), pp. 78–81.

11 "The Influence of Domestic Politics on Foreign Affairs in France, 1898–1905," *Journal of Modern History* (Dec., 1942), pp. 449–479.

12 *A.A.*, V, 229, Paris, Jan. 16, 1914, and Brussels, Jan. 23, 1914: Maurice Barrès, *Cahiers* (Paris: 1929), VIII, 66.

13 That old Boulangist Paul Adam wrote in his preface to Francis Laur's *L'Epoque Boulangiste* which appeared in 1914: "Le présent donne raison à notre passé." It was natural enough.

[14] Barrès, *Cahiers*, VII, 75, and VIII, 81; Marc Sangnier, *L'Armée et la République* (Paris: 1912); Halévy, "Franco-German Relations since 1870," *History* (April, 1924), p. 28.

[15] Cf. the definition of Maurras in his article "Nationalisme Intégral," as it appeared in the twelfth fascicule of his *Dictionnaire* (Paris: 1932), p. 169. See also Henri Massis, *Maurras et Notre Temps*, I (Paris: 1951), 121. whence it would appear that Renan in his early enthusiasm for Fichte and Hegel in 1848 had been the first to translate the word into French.

[16] "Ce que M. Barrès a entendu par l'amélioration sociale, c'est en général la protection des intérêts de la petite bourgeoisie." Albert Thibaudet, *Barrès* (Paris: 1939), p. 275.

[17] Jacques Bainville, *Histoire de Trois Générations* (Paris: 1934), pp. 232–235: "Si jamais consultation populaire signifia une volonté de paix et de désarmement, ce fut celle-là. Le service de trois ans ... sortait condamné du scrutin."

[18] A similar explanation, with the Communists now taking place of the antirepublican Right, will go a long way to explain the similar difficulties of the Fourth Republic.

[19] *L'Echo de Paris*, Oct. 1, 1913.

[20] Cf. François Goguel, *Géographie des Elections françaises* (Paris: 1951), who makes the same suggestion.

NOTES TO CHAPTER I

MISE EN SCÈNE

(Pages 19–24)

[1] The extreme Left could never be extreme, for fear of opening the way to an extreme Right that would sweep away the system that was the reason of its being. A similar situation obtained after 1919, but it was the faction of the extreme Left which hobbled the normal working of the regime.

[2] *J.O.C.*, Nov. 6, 1886.

[3] *J.O.C.*, July 12, 1887, Clemenceau: "La presse allemande a systématiquement attaqué le ministre de la Guerre, de sorte que les esprits superficiels ont pu voir en lui l'incarnation de la patrie."

[4] *Tableau politique*, p. 487.

[5] John Harold Clapham, *Economic Development of France and Germany* (Cambridge: 1948), p. 240, gives figures of the steam power used in industry, including the generation of electricity, but excluding locomotives, trams, and marine engines: 1870, 336,000 h.p.; 1880, 544,000 h.p.; 1890, 863,000 h.p.; 1900, 1,791,000 h.p.; 1910, 2,913,000 h.p.; 1913, 3,539,000 h.p. "When to the latter figures are added the 750,000 h.p. generated by hydroelectric installations, nearly if not quite all created since 1900, it might easily be argued that an industrial revolution began in France somewhere about the year 1895." See also J. Weiller, *La Chronologie Economique de la Troisième République* (Paris: n.d.), and David Thomson, *Democracy in France* (London: 1953), p. 67.

[6] Cf. Pierre George, and others, *Etudes sur la Banlieue de Paris* (Paris: 1950).

[7] Charles Seignobos, *L'Evolution de la 3ᵉ République* (Paris: 1921), p. 197; Daniel Halévy, *Décadence de la Liberté* (Paris: 1931), p. 58; also Roger Thabault, *Mon Village* (Paris: 1944) (a study of the village Mazières-en-Gatine on the confines of western France), who confirms this view, p. 182: "L'Affaire Dreyfus qui souleva tant de passions en France fut pratiquement ignorée à Mazières. Elle était trop complexe et confuse, elle mettait en jeu trop de choses ignorées dans ce coin de campagne pour passionner les hommes du pays les plus attirés par les idées. Et ceux qui s'y intéressaient étaient trop peu nombreux pour pouvoir s'exciter mutuellement par leurs

approbations et leurs oppositions." On the Affair in general and its perplexing unimportance to so many at the time, see E. W. Fox, in Edward Meade Earle, *Modern France* (Princeton: 1951), p. 131 ff.

[8] Sorel's comment was: "Si Rochefort, esprit foncièrement vulgaire, s'est jeté dans les bras du nationalisme, c'était peut-être par esprit commercial. La grande majorité des français de 1898 et 1899 a été nationaliste. Rochefort a pensé à la vente de son canard. C'était un marchand de papier." Jean Variot, *Propos de Georges Sorel* (Paris: 1935), pp. 130–131.

[9] Nov. 27, 1893, "Principes Socialistes—Socialisme, Révolution, Internationalisme," conférence à Paris au groupe d'étudiants socialistes.

[10] Alexandre Zévaès, *Le Parti Socialiste de 1904 à 1923* (Paris: n.d.), p. 50.

[11] *J.O.C.*, April 8, 1895: "Ne croyez pas, lorsque nous affirmons ici notre haine de la guerre, que nous soyons résignés pour notre pays à la brutalité des faits accomplis. Nous n'oublions pas, nous ne pouvons pas oublier. Je ne sais si quelqu'un oublie, mais ce n'est pas nous! Nous sommes dans la necessité douloureuse de dire: la nation française est mutilée. Nous n'oublions pas la blessure profonde reçue par la patrie."

[12] Marcel Sembat, *Faites un Roi, Sinon Faites la Paix* (Paris: 1913), pp. 151–152.

[13] Already in 1890 the Boulangists who assert that they belong to the extreme Left, as did Barrès at Nancy, Turigny in the Nièvre, Castelin in the Aisne, vote with the monarchist and Catholic conservatives on such monarchist issues as the proposal to repeal the law that had sent the princes into exile; *J.O.C.*, Feb. 10, 1890.

[14] On Oct. 8, 1905, the *Revue de l'Enseignement Primaire* demanded "qu'on proscrive de l'école cette religion de la patrie." To understand the significance of this it is necessary to know that six years before the *Revue* had celebrated "la flamme sacrée qui brûle d'une égale ardeur dans ces deux sanctuaires de l'honneur national, l'École et l'Armée," and insisted on the "union fraternelle qui doit exister entre l'Armée et l'École, ces deux incarnations de la Patrie." (Sept. 10, 1899.) By Sept. 30, 1904, at its congress held in Amiens, the Ligue de l'Enseignement Primaire had passed to other leadership and other sentiments. Its motto, "Pour la Patrie, par le Livre, par l'Epée," was significantly discarded. Cf. also *ibid.*, July 2, 1905, and Clemenceau in *L'Aurore*, Sept. 14, 1905.

But René Goblet in the preface he wrote shortly before his death for Bocquillon's *Crise du Patriotisme à l'Ecole* (Paris: 1905), p. viii, said: "Qui aurait pu penser qu'après trente ans de république nous assisterions à une crise de patriotisme à l'école, c'est à dire, qu'il deviendrait nécessaire de défendre l'école contre l'accusation d'enseigner le patriotisme!" This leads to the supposition that there was no lack of patriotic teaching in schools, but merely certain campaigns against overdoing it, which in turn bred their own reaction.

[15] Eugène Tavernier, *Cinquante Ans de Politique* (Paris: 1925), p. 316; Emile Bocquillon, *La crise du patriotisme à l'école* (Paris: 1905).

[16] Maurice Paléologue, *Un Grand Tournant* (Paris: 1934), p. 33.

[17] Joseph Caillaux, *Mémoires* (Paris: 1942), I, 144, n. 1.

NOTES TO CHAPTER II

The Reminder: 1904–1905

(Pages 25–34)

[1] *L'Européen*, April 26, 1902.

[2] March 19, 1914.

[3] Louis Dimier, *Vingt Ans d'Action française* (Paris: 1926), pp. 264–265, tells of trying to reorganize the league. Plateau, one of the leaders of the *camelots du Roi*, advised him: "Il m'avertit de m'attendre à du désappointement, tout cela n'existant

que sur le papier. C'était trop dire. Je dus constater pourtant que pas un quart des membres inscrits sur nos contrôles n'avait signé l'engagement à la monarchie, ni depuis bien longtemps payé de cotisation. C'étaient les deux conditions de la Ligue. En Provence, des sections allaient par trois cents membres, dans lesquelles venant au fait on n'en trouvait pas dix."

⁴ Charles Seignobos, *Etudes de Politique et Histoire* (Paris: 1934), p. 365.

⁵ A moderate republican, Alfred Mézières, senator of Meurthe-et-Moselle, referred to it some years later as "une crise infiniment pénible pour l'amour-propre national. Beaucoup de Français en gardent encore un souvenir amer, celui d'une humiliation infligée à leur pays."

⁶ Maurice Paléologue, *Un Grand Tournant* (Paris: 1934), p. 196. See also on p. 13 his note dated Dec. 29, 1898.

⁷ Preface to Emile Bocquillon, *Crise* (Paris: 1905), xiii ff.

⁸ Paul Bourgeois, deputy of the Vendée, Doyen d'Age, in the session's opening address, *J.O.C.*, Jan. 10, 1905.

⁹ Jan. 11, 1905.

¹⁰ Paul Deschanel, *J.O.C.*, Jan. 13, 1905: "Le président du conseil n'a qu'à montrer la droite et les nationalistes, et ce geste ... suffit pour qu'aussitôt les urnes se remplissent, comme par enchantement, de bulletins agréables au gouvernement."

¹¹ The "Affaire des fiches" is well covered in Mollin's book, *La Vérité sur l'Affaire des Fiches* (Paris: n.d.); there is also a brief, clear account in Jean Galtier-Boissière, *Histoire de la 3ᵉ République* (Paris: 1935), pp. 172–175.

¹² Dimier, *Vingt ans d'Action française*, pp. 145–154.

¹³ *La Revue*, Jan. 15, 1905, pp. 151–174.

¹⁴ March 12, 1905.

¹⁵ *L'Aurore*, March 23 and 25, 1905.

¹⁶ *Le Petit Parisien*, March 24, 1905; *J.O.S.*, March 31, 1905; *La Dépêche*, March 27, 1905.

¹⁷ C. Laurent commented cheerfully in *Le Matin*, April 2, 1905: "Il ne sortira rien de grave, on peut le croire, de cet incident qui n'aura été, après tout, qu'une tempête autour d'un paquebot."

¹⁸ *Ibid.*, June 6, 1905.

¹⁹ Cf. Jaurès, *J.O.C.*, April 6, 1905, and Guyot de Villeneuve, *J.O.C.* April 7, 1905.

²⁰ *J O.C.*, April 18, 1905.

²¹ *J.O.C.*, April 19, 1905, J. Delafosse: "Voilà la vraie cause ... Le Maroc, c'est le prétexte, c'est l'occasion. ..." In fact, the closeness with which German action over Morocco followed the Russian defeat at Mukden appears to have been coincidental. This view is taken by George Peabody Gooch, *Franco-German Relations, 1871–1914* (London: 1923), p. 43; Goldsworthy Lowes-Dickinson, *The International Anarchy, 1904–1914* (London: 1920), p. 125; see especially Raymond J. Sontag, *American Historical Review* (Jan., 1928), pp. 278–301, for reasons of German delay in taking action before March, 1905. However, the favorable possibilities of the situation were not ignored by the German General Staff. Cf. *G.P.*, XIX, 1, 175; W. Kloster, *Der deutsche Generalstab und der Präventivkriegsgedanke*, pp. 40–42, quoted in Ernest Llewellyn Woodward, *Great Britain and the German Navy* (London, 1935), pp. 82–83.

²² *J.O.C.*, May 16, 1905, Charles Benoist: "Tout le travail parlementaire se trouve suspendu. On dirait vraiment qu'il n'y a plus dans ce pays qu'une seule question digne d'être étudiée, celle de la séparation des Eglises et de l'Etat!" Simyan: "Oui! tant qu'elle ne sera pas reglée, cette question devra absorber tout notre temps."

²³ *L'Echo*, June 13, 1905: "Un vent d'alarme a passé sur nous tous. La leçon a été brutale." *Le Matin*, June 19, 1905: "On se remet à parler de guerre, ce qui n'était pas arrivé depuis longtemps."

²⁴ "Louis de Gonzague," *Cahiers*, Jan., 1906: "It does not depend on us . . . it is out of our hands . . . we can only go on doing what we were and are doing . . . and be prepared." See also Jules Isaac, *Problème des Origines de la Guerre* (Paris: 1933),

p. 22 ff.: "Pour qui a vécu ces événements (en France) et interroge ses souvenirs, historien faisant appel à son propre témoignage, il n'y a pas de doute: l'année 1905 marque un changement du destin; l'acheminement à la guerre part de là."

[25] Henri Massis, *Evocations, Souvenirs* (Paris: 1931), p. 274. Massis, later to become the most faithful disciple of Maurras, moved even as a young student in the very different circles of both Barrès and Péguy.

[26] *D.D.F.* 2e série, IX, part I, 34; *G.P.* XX, 429; *Kreuzzeitung*, June 7, 14, 21, 28, 1905; *Le Figaro* and *L'Eclair*, June 15, 1905; *L'Echo*, June 9, 21, 23, 1905.

[27] Cf. Lt. Col. Rousset, *Le Gaulois*, Dec. 11, 1906, writing on "l'Alerte de 1906:" "Ce péril subit suscita un émoi dont seuls ont pu mesurer la violence ceux qui, à cette époque, fréquentaient les avenues du pouvoir. Dans les couloirs de la Chambre, silencieux et mornes, errait une foule inquiète, qui se ruait aux nouvelles, collant sur les cadres où d'heure en heure s'étalaient les télégrammes des figures ravagées par la peur." This should no doubt be taken with a pinch of salt; but the gist of it remains.

[28] Paléologue, *Un Grand Tournant*, pp. 368 and 373.

[29] *Le Matin*, Oct. 7, 1905, published what purported to be the inside story of the negotiations. This account presented the fall of Delcassé as a surrender to German pressure and helped to create the impression of national humiliation, which was to be variously accepted or assailed thereafter. Cf. Oron James Hale, *Germany and the Diplomatic Revolution* (Philadelphia: 1931), p. 132.

[30] Paléologue, *Un Grand Tournant*, pp. 386-387. Paul Revoil, the French representative at Algéçiras, minister at Tangier and governor-general of Algeria, would soon be appointed ambassador, first in Berne, then in Madrid.

[31] The amnesty was a broad one, and it would be incorrect to represent it merely as an act of defiance. It was, however, at least partly occasioned by the crisis, and its emotions were invoked in the cause of national unity. Cf. the words with which the garde des sceaux, Chaumié, defended the project before the Senate, *J.O.S.*, July 11, 1905: "Songeons, Messieurs, au retour qui s'accomplit dans nos âmes lorsque, à un moment donné, une émotion patriotique gagnant tout d'un coup le pays, on songe au patrimoine commun que tous seraient demain prêts à défendre. ... C'est pourquoi le gouvernement vous convie à le suivre dans l'oeuvre d'apaisement et de réconciliation nationale à laquelle il a à coeur de travailler." The Senate voted for the project 243 to 14, and the Chamber was kept from following suit only by the offensive speech of a nationalist deputy who broke the temporary party truce.

[32] *A.A.*, VI (Erster Ergänzungsband), 31.

[33] J. L. de Lanessan, *Histoire de l'Entente Cordiale* (Paris: 1916), pp. 209-240; Thomas Barclay, *Thirty Years* (London: 1914), *passim*.

[34] *Westminster Gazette*, June 22, 1905; *Patrie*, June 27, 1905; Hale, *Germany and the Diplomatic Revolution*, p. 77 n.

[35] *L'Echo*, June 23, July 11, Oct. 6, 1905; *Le Temps*, July 10, Oct. 9, 1905; *Le Gaulois*, Oct. 5, 1905.

[36] Cf. *La Patrie*, Oct. 14, 1905.

[37] George P. Gooch, *Recent Revelations of European Diplomacy* (London: 1940), p. 294; *Paul Cambon par Un Diplomate* (Paris: 1937), p. 229. See also Metternich's letter to Bülow, *G.P.* XX, 2, 676, dated London, Nov. 2, 1905: "Die Franzosen als Nation haben unser Entgegenkommen zurückgewiesen. Es hat ihnen im Gegenteil Mut gemacht uns zu widerstehen, und sie glauben mehr als bisher an den Nutzen der Englischen Hülfe."

NOTES TO CHAPTER III

ALGEÇIRAS AND AFTER: 1905–1906

(Pages 35–43)

[1] George P. Gooch and A. W. Ward, *History of British Foreign Policy*, p. 456.

[2] *Studies in French History*, ed. Alfred Coville and Harold Temperley, 165–166.

[3] Gooch and Ward, *op. cit.*, p. 467; cf. also James E. Tyler, *The British Army and the Continent, 1904–1914* (London: 1938), *passim*.

[4] *G.P.* XXI, part 2, 543 ff.; Paul Cambon, *Correspondance*, II, 228.

[5] E. Lautier, "Les Mensonges de Guillaume II et M. Delcassé," *L'Homme Libre*, Oct. 9, 1922: "La cause de la guerre de 1914, c'est la chute de Delcassé en 1905. C'est rigoureusement la vérité que proclamera l'histoire." This is quoted with approval by E. Florent-Matter, *Les Vrais Criminels* (Paris: 1926), p. 167.

[6] July 31, 1905.

[7] *Le Temps*, Aug. 16 and 19, 1905; *L'Eclair*, Aug. 9, 1905; *L'Echo de Paris*, Aug. 17, 1905; *La Dépêche*, Nov. 5, 1905.

[8] Jan. 7, 1906.

[9] *Le Temps*, Jan. 19, 1906.

[10] Henri Massis, *Evocations* (Paris: 1931), pp. 186–187.

[11] David Thomson, *Democracy in France* (London: 1953), p. 73.

[12] March 28, 1905.

[13] *La Dépêche*, Feb. 10, 1906.

[14] Pelletan, *Dépêche*, March 16, 1909: "Ce que je reproche au comité éxécutif c'est de prendre des nationalistes ou des membres du grand parti Ribot, de les baptiser radical-socialistes, et de les faire élire par la vertu d'une étiquette qui est un mensonge."

[15] Daniel Halévy, *Décadence de la Liberté* (Paris: 1931), p. 70.

[16] *J.O.C.*, Jan. 13, 1905.

[17] *Le Matin*, Jan. 19, 1906.

[18] *Le Gaulois*, April 11, 19, 1906.

[19] *L'Eclair*, April 19, 24, 1906.

[20] April 19, 21, 25, 1906.

[21] Hardouin, *Le Matin*, April 24, 1906.

[22] May 7, 1906.

[23] May 4, 1906.

[24] In the *Libre Parole*, Dec. 9, 1909, Drumont recounted a visit to Lavisse in the days when Drumont was a candidate for election to the Académie française: "Je l'ai rappelé déja, mes visites coincidèrent avec le grand mouvement syndicaliste. J'eus l'occasion de constater ainsi combien la révolution sociale serait faite facilement. Tout le monde s'y attend. J'ai pris contact avec quelques hommes d'une incontestable valeur avec lesquels j'ai eu des conversations qui n'avaient rien de confidentiel, mais qui étaient généralement au dessus des banalités mondaines. Aucun de ces hommes ne manifestait cet effroi, cette terreur bourgeoise, qui jeta les conservateurs de 48 dans les bras de César Lavisse n'avait rien du conservateur bêlant. 'Il y a vingt ans que je l'attends,' disait-il, 'cette révolution syndicaliste.' Le mouvement lui apparaissait comme un développement logique de la longue évolution française."

[25] *J.O.C.*, June 18, 1909; echoes of the same feeling can be found in the *Letters of Princess Radziwill* (Bologna: 1934), vol. IV, pp. 94, 122, *passim*.

[26] *J.O.C.*, Jan. 14, 1905.

[27] *D.D.F.*, 2ᵉ série, IX, part I, 34.

[28] Anatole France, *Vers les Temps Meilleurs* (Paris: n.d.), III, 17; Georges Michon, *The Franco-Russian Alliance* (London: 1929), 326 n. 1.

[29] *G.P.*, XXI, part 2, 563; The American ambassador in Paris gives another aspect

of this point of view in a dispatch of Dec. 12, 1906 (Dept. of State, Numer. file 4, 40/30–31): "Thoughtful Frenchmen are beginning to ask themselves what practical good is to come from taking the side of England as against Germany between which two powers commercial rivalry may lead to a war of which France may have to bear the brunt when the time comes. The practical interests of France and Germany in the future clash nowhere, whereas the practical material interests of Germany and England clash in every part of the globe. Why should France place herself between the upper and nether grindstone in this inevitable conflict?" But this was the language of "reason," not of "la terre et les morts."

[30] *Le Temps*, May 8, 1906; A. Meyer in *Le Gaulois*, May 21, 1906; Driant in *L'Eclair*, May 21 and 22, 1906; *Le Progrès*, May 23, 1906.

[31] *Libre Parole*, May 22, 1906.

[32] *Dépêche*, May 10, 1906; for earlier governmental antipatriotism, see the discussion between Tournade and Berteaux, *J.O.C.*, March 16, 1905.

[33] Bouglé, on June 22, 1906; it should be said that the Socialist attitude conformed with that of the social class from which they drew their greatest support, just as the Radical policy coincided as a rule with the attitude of the middle class. To comment upon the implications of this would be to enter a field separate from the present study. A brilliant analysis of the reciprocal influence between a political party and its electorate may be found in Maurice Duverger, *Les Partis Politiques* (Paris: 1951).

[34] *Progrès de Lyon*, May 23, 24, 1906; *Dépêche*, June 22, 1906.

[35] *Progrès*, Sept. 29, 1905.

NOTES TO CHAPTER IV

THE INTERVAL

(Pages 44–51)

[1] Cf. J. Delafosse, *Le Gaulois*, March 15, 1907.

[2] March 29, 1907.

[3] April 4, 1907.

[4] *J.O.C.*, May 11, 1907: "Il n'y a à la surface du mouvement ouvrier que quelque formules d'outrance et de paradoxe, qui procèdent non pas de la condamnation de la patrie, mais de la condamnation de l'abus qui a été fait si souvent de l'idée et du mot. ... Les déclamations contre la patrie ne sont pas un péril pour la patrie; elles ne sont un péril que pour le prolétariat lui même."

[5] *L'Humanité*, July 1, 1907.

[6] Cf. Aulard, *Dépêche*, Aug. 8, 1907: "Les républicains sages n'osent plus se dire antimilitaristes, c'est à dire adversaires de la prétention des chefs de l'armée à régenter la cité, parce que l'usage s'est introduit, et jusque dans le langage officiel, de traiter d'antimilitaristes ceux-là, et ceux-là seuls, qui veulent déconsidérer, affaiblir, détruire l'armée. Il n'y a plus de mot courant, populaire, pour exprimer le sentiment si juste, si républicain, si français qui était exprimé par le mot antimilitariste."

[7] Cf. *L'Humanité*, Aug. 12, 1907.

[8] *L'Echo*, Sept. 25, 1908.

[9] *Le Matin*, Aug. 17, 1907: "C'est surtout comme étant antisocialiste que nous combattons l'antipatriotisme dont Hervé a doublé son antimilitarisme."

[10] Aulard, *Dépêche*, Sept. 5, 1907.

[11] *L'Echo*, Sept. 20, 1907: "Le parti républicain me paraît dès maintenant assez fort pour se passer d'auxiliaires plutôt compromettants," wrote Delpech. Dated Sept. 11, this letter suggests that there might well have been no campaign without it. *L'Echo* had scouted out the ground with an article on Sept. 3; the next articles of the series came on Sept. 13, 15, and 20. Had not Delpech's letter been in their hands "pour la bonne bouche," would *L'Echo* have published its articles of the 13th and 15th?

[12] Cf. *L'Humanité*, Oct. 12, 1907: "Ce que nous avons voulu, c'est tout en nous dégageant formellement de l'hervéisme, ne pas nous séparer du parti socialiste." (Steeg); "Le congrès a rejetés les formules socialistes, mais il n'a pas rejetés les socialistes." (Dubief); "Résolument hostile au nationalisme et à l'antipatriotisme, notre parti se déclare ardemment et résolument patriote. ... Nous plaçons le devoir militaire au dessus de toute contestation. ..." (Déclaration du Parti, Oct. 13, 1907.)

[13] *L'Echo*, Oct. 22, 1907, published a long letter from Delpech, explaining that there had been nothing equivocal about the vote of the Congress: "Sans dissimuler leur réprobation indignée contre les anarchistes négateurs de la patrie et provocateurs de guerre civile, quelques uns estimaient qu'il fallait, malgré tout, user de ménagement à l'égard de groupes politiques dont le concours nous etait nécessaire dans plusieures circonscriptions."

[14] *Le Matin*, Oct. 7, 1907: "Chaque dimanche depuis quelques semaines rappelle ces jours fériés de la Révolution où les citoyens se rassemblaient pour célébrer sur les places des villes et des villages l'amour de la nation." *Le Temps*, Oct. 15, 1907: "Depuis quelque temps il n'est plus guère de discours sans un couplet en l'honneur de la patrie."

[15] *L'Humanité*, Oct. 16, 1907.

[16] *L'Aurore*, Oct. 20, 1907, reported a meeting which had taken place between Brousse (dep. Paris), Breton (Cher), Varenne (Puy-de-Dôme), Pastre (Gard), Lassalle (Ardennes), Veber and Rozier (Seine), Brunet, Heppenheimer, Paris, Deslandres, and Rauvier (Municipal Councillors), in which these Socialists had decided to dissociate themselves from the partisans of Hervé. Reports of similar language came from Palines where Bouveri, mayor and deputy of Montceau-les-Mines, had been lecturing.

[17] Adrien Dansette, *Histoire religieuse de la France contemporaine* (Paris: 1951), II, 573.

[18] *J.O.C.*, June 28, 1907.

[19] *Ibid.*: *Jules Delahaye*: Je constate que vous allez à droite. (Exclamations)
  Clemenceau: Je reste où je suis. Si j'avais abandonné une seule de mes idées, je le dirais hautement.
  Laurent Bougère: Mais vous en avez pris quelques-unes des nôtres. (Exclamations à gauche et au centre) Vous êtes devenu réactionnaire. (Bruit)

[20] Jaurès, *J.O.C.*, April 6, 1908; Pelletan, *Dépêche*, May 30, 1908.

[21] July 22, 1907.

[22] Pelletan, *Dépêche*, Oct. 17, 1906: "Une question politique capitale se pose pour l'avenir de notre démocratie. Allons-nous dévorer pour les budgets de guerre les sommes promises pour les réformes sociales?"

[23] Robert E. Sherwood, *Roosevelt and Hopkins* (New York: 1948–1950), makes this very clear in his description of Hopkins' attitude, and the story of his unwilling change from isolationism. Marxist socialism has no reasons for pacifism except material ones. Avoidance of waste is a more convincing argument for the Marxist than any based on an ethic which must be relative and irrelevant.

[24] *Dépêche*, March 26, 1907, reported Clemenceau's arguments against the proposed release of the 1903 contingent: "La situation est telle, et cela pourrait se dire presque en tout temps dans l'état de paix armée où vit l'Europe, que l'attention du gouvernement est toujours éveillée sur l'équilibre des forces armées."

[25] John Maynard Keynes, "The Council of Four," *Essays and Sketches in Biography* (New York: 1956), p. 261.

[26] On July 28, 1908, Georges Louis, *Carnets* (Paris: 1926), I, 21, quoted him as saying: "Je crois à la guerre, je la regarde comme inévitable. Je l'ai même écrit. ... Nous ne ferons rien, nous ne devrons rien faire pour la provoquer, mais il faut nous tenir prêts à la faire. ..." See also H. W. Steed, *Through Thirty Years* (London: 1924), I, 286 (Aug. 26, 1908)

[27] On Oct. 11, 1908; cf. *Le Temps*, Oct. 12, 1908.

[28] François Goguel, *Esquisse d'un bilan de la Sociologie Electorale française* (Paris: 1951), pp. 16–19; Maurice Agulhon, *L'opinion politique dans une commune de banlieue,*" in *Etudes sur la Banliene de Paris* (Paris: 1950).

[29] *Le Temps,* May 3, 1910.

[30] Radical prime ministers were Monis, Caillaux, and Doumergue; non-Radical, Briand, Poincaré, Barthou, Ribot, and Viviani.

[31] As an attempt to show the political realities behind the labels, results can be presented in two ways:

Reactionaries	−9	Radicals	−17
Républicains de gauche	9	Independent Socialists	1
Nationalists	1	S.F.I.O.	19
Gain	1	Gain	3
Reactionaries	−9	Républicains de gauche	9
Nationalists	1	Independent Socialists	1
		S.F.I.O.	19
		Radicals	−17
Loss	−8	Gain	12

Either way, the results were hardly sensational.

[32] May 27, 1910. This is confirmed by *L'Aurore,* April 11, 1910: "Aujourd'hui, les passions politiques semblent éteintes ou, plutôt, sommeiller." But see *Le Progrès* for a different impression: "Il est très peu de circonscriptions où le scrutin n'ait pas été agité. Presque tous les sièges législatifs ont été vivement disputés. ...'"

NOTES TO CHAPTER V

First Eddies: 1906–1908

(Pages 55–68)

[1] Interview in *Le Gaulois,* March 3, 1910.

[2] Jacques Rivière et Alain-Fournier, *Correspondance, 1905–1914* (Paris: 1948), II, 25 (Jan. 26, 1907): "Je suis allé à la Chambre. ... Bafouillage intolérable. Interpellation socialiste du pauvre gâteux Vaillant, et de l'ivrogne Allemane. Puis Clemenceau avec son aisance, sa ruse, sa force. Lui, est admirable. Le reste, et même Jaurès, ça a toujours l'air d'une séance pour rire, de gens qui n'ont pas l'habitude. Et la gravité des feuilles le lendemain!"

[3] Maurice Barrès *Cahiers,* IX, 211–212: "Où est donc la volonté virile, le regard droit? La Chambre? Elle participe du délabrement général. Elle est en désarroi. Il y a au Palais Bourbon le même degré d'anarchie et de désorganisation que dans tout le pays. ...'"

[4] Robert de Jouvenel, *La République des Camarades* (Paris: 1914), pp. 16–17.

[5] Charles Maurras, *Action française,* July 28, 1910: "Aujourd'hui, nous avons affaire à une bourgeoisie dont le nationalisme, souvent antisémite, a perdu toute confiance dans la démocratie libérale."

[6] See chap. II n. 3, p. 164. But in 1906, the 18-year-old Bernanos was writing from secondary school to a priest friend of his: "Pour moi, j'admire de tout mon coeur ces vaillants de l'Action française, ces vrais fils de Gaule, avec du bon sens et de la foi, qui s'imposent gaillardement, qui se définissent sans phrases. ..." Two years later, already a *camelot,* he would be arrested in the Thalamas riots. Cf. *Georges Bernanos: Essais et Temoignages réunis par Albert Béguin* (Paris: 1949), p. 249.

[7] William C Buthman, *The Rise of Integral Nationalism in France* (New York: 1939), p. 298; Coudekerque-Lambrecht, *Léon de Montesquiou* (Paris: 1925), p. 158. See also Buthman, *op. cit.*, p. 299, for the foundation of the Nouvelle Librairie nationale by Jean Rivain. It was later carried on by Georges Valois.

[8] Jan. 21, 1905; the Marquise later founded the Association des Jeunes Filles Royalistes, which also played a useful part in proselytizing for the Cause.

[9] *L'Action française*, fascicule de 80 à 100 pages, petit in-16, paraît deux fois par mois. Paris, 143, rue d'Aboukir.

[10] *L'Honneur de Servir* (Paris: 1937), p. 17.

[11] E. Goichon, *A la mémoire d'Ernest Psichari* (Paris: 1946), p. 254.

[12] In his contribution to Béguin, *Bernanos*, 261 ff. With Guy de Bouteiller, Yves and Maxence de Colleville, Georges Bernanos, and his own brother Charles, Ernest de Malibran made up during those years a group of close friends who were also militants of the Action française.

[13] Georges Bernanos, *Le Scandale de la Vérité* (Paris: 1939) p. 44.

[14] Cf. Ernest de Malibran, in Béguin, *Bernanos*: "Au cours de l'année 1912, l'action de l'Action française semblait se ralentir, les combattants de 1911 voyaient le 'coup de force' s'estomper, nous avions l'impression d'une sorte de trêve, voire même d'être au service d'un 'arrivisme arrivé'."

[15] Julien Benda, *Un Régulier dans le Siècle* (Paris: 1938), p. 144. This is not to suggest that the Action française might have had a real chance to upset the republic in 1914, but only that it never considered trying, which might have been in the logic of their avowed principles.

[16] Preface to Gaston Riou, *Aux Ecoutes de la France qui Vient* (Paris: 1913), p. 8.

[17] Marcel Sembat, *Faites un Roi, Sinon Faites la Paix* (Paris: 1913), p. 260.

[18] Henri Massis, *Maurras et Notre Temps* (Paris: 1951) II, 211–212.

[19] Cf. Albert Thibaudet, *Barrès*, p. 281.

[20] Henri Massis, *Evocations* (Paris: 1931), p. 46. Yet Maurras could write in the *Action française*, Aug. 26, 1930: "Barrès, incarnation de notre risorgimento de 1912."

[21] Massis, *L'Honneur de Servir*, p. 81, quotes from the *Cahiers* of Barrès a note of 1911: "Je sens depuis des mois que je glisse du nationalisme au catholicisme. C'est que le nationalisme manque d'infini."

[22] Maurras, *Action française*, May 14, 15, 1927: "ce fond barrèsien avait quelque chose d'un peu fataliste et déterministe: offert à tous les peuples, ce nationalisme uniforme présentait le danger de les vouer à des mêmes heurts. Moins égalitaires, obligés à certaines distinctions essentielles, nous avons aperçu pour notre part comment l'on peut et l'on doit dédier à la France un amour de choix et de liberté, un culte de paix européenne et planétaire."

[23] *Dépêche*, Oct. 9, 1906.

[24] *Action française*, July 12, 1906.

[25] Jean Drault, *Drumont* (Paris: 1935), p. 297.

[26] Massis, *Evocations*, p. 46.

[27] The Russian economic agent in Paris, Raffalovitch, wrote to Kokovtsev, on March 5, 1909: "L'Action française dispose de sommes considérables, on quête pour elle dans les familles aristocratiques de Paris et de province." (*Abominable Vénalité*, p. 216).

[28] Drault, *Drumont*, p. 298.

[29] March 4, 1908.

[30] *J.O.C.*, March 19, 1908.

[31] March 25, 1908.

[32] *Action française*, March 30, April 1, 1908.

[33] *Action française*, March 21, 1909.

[34] In a private interview with me.

[35] Cf. the statement of Lucien Lacour who tried to attack Briand in 1911, when the latter was still prime minister: "J'ai fait longtemps de l'opposition constitutionelle,

puis j'en ai reconnu l'inutilité et la stérilité. Je suis venu à l'Action française dont la doctrine est la violence mise au service de la raison." *Action française*, March 30, 1911.

[36] J. Lemaitre, *Action française*, March 21, 1908.

[37] Jules Renard, *Correspondance* (Paris: 1928), p. 375 (Dec. 2, 1908) in a letter to his friend, Paul Cornu: "Oui, l'Action française m'arrange bien. Mais je deviens sage et je n'en crois pas un mot—et Léon Daudet non plus."

[38] *A nos Amis, à nos Abonnés* in *Oeuvres Complètes* (Paris: 1947).

[39] Rivière-Fournier, *Correspondance*, II, 206, May 24, 1908.

[40] March 30, 1908.

[41] *La Lanterne*, March 30 and June 6, 1908.

[42] Feb. 16, 1908.

[43] *L'Echo*, March 28, 1908.

[44] April 1, 1908.

[45] Bouglé, May 17, 1908: "Republicanism had better watch out."

[46] Junius, *L'Echo*, May 5, 1908. Who wrote under this pseudonym is not exactly known. Aulard, *Dépêche*, Jan 7, 1910, suggests that it was used in turn by Denys Cochin, Paul Bourget, and Jules Lemaître.

[47] Louis Dubreuilh, *L'Humanité*, May 11, 1908.

[48] May 17, 1908.

[49] Cf. *Revue Socialiste*, Aug. 15, 1912, and the *Cahiers du Cercle Proudhon*—a Syndicalist-Nationalist group. It is possible that Maurras welcomed the inability of his movement to pass from theory to practice, though he may not have done so consciously. Lucien Rebatet, *Les Décombres* (Paris: 1941), p. 30, indicates very clearly that Maurras did not know what to do when the way to power seemed to lie open before him in February, 1934, and was relieved when agitation decreased.

[50] Maurras, *Action française*, April 1, 1912, writing on a fight which had taken place when Syndicalists had booed one of Millerand's tattoos: "Qu'on le veuille ou non, le syndicalisme et le nationalisme sont les deux grandes forces qui dirigent le monde moderne. ... Expliquons le nationalisme aux syndicalistes, expliquons le syndicalisme aux nationalistes. Opérons la synthèse du patriotisme lucide et du travail organisé."

[51] *J.O.C.*, Oct. 23, 1908.

[52] July 1, 1908.

[53] Sept. 12, 1908.

[54] Sept. 13, 1908.

[55] The *Action française* had been mentioned in the Senate on April 8, 1908, during the debate on Zola; cf. *J.O.S.*, 1908, p. 585.

[56] Jaurès, *L'Humanité*, May 17, 1909: "Je ne parle pas du tapage des Camelots du Roi; ce n'est qu'une mascarade d'écoliers."

NOTES TO CHAPTER VI

The Eternal Boulangism: 1908–1910

(Pages 69–76)

[1] Jan. 3, 1909.

[2] *J.O.C.*, March 21, 1905. The Right-Wing deputy, Lasies, significantly contrasted the antipatriotism of the teachers with the patriotism of the priests, *J.O.C.*, July 3, 1905.

[3] Cf. L. Vaugeois, *Action française*, Jan. 4, 1909, in a leader which begins: "Oui: nous avons fait du chemin, un fameux chemin, en 1908. Il semble bien que tout le monde en ait, en ce moment, le sentiment," writes significantly: "Ainsi, ces 'puissances de sentiment' que Barrès en 1900 nous montrait et avec raison inertes dans les foules patriotes, les voilà, très incontestablement, qui se sont ébranlées depuis quelques mois *dans les mêmes foules patriotes*. Car il n'y a pas à le contester de bonne foi:

C'était bien *les mêmes gens* à la salle Wagram, autour de Réal del Sarte, ces jours-ci, qu'en 1906–1907, autour de Mercier ou Rochefort: or, quand la moindre allusion à Dreyfus et aux Juifs mettait toute l'assistance debout, cannes et poings levés, c'était l'émotion 'nationaliste' sans plus: celle même de 1899." He might have added "et de 1889."

⁴ Cf. *J.O.C.*, Dec. 1, 1904. The minister of education, explaining the circumstance of Thalamas' transfer from Condorcet to Charlemagne, declared that his lessons had lacked measure, that freedom of judgment was not in question, and that the very light punishment inflicted was not in any way due to clerical pressure.

⁵ Cf. *Action française*, Dec. 10, 11, 1908, and Barrès in *L'Echo*, Jan. 13, 20, 30, 1909; see also the letter of Thalamas replying to Barrès in *L'Echo* for an excellent sample of how the nationalists conducted their polemics.

⁶ Cf. Aulard's article in the *Dépêche*, Jan. 28, 1909.

⁷ Cf. *L'Aurore* and *Le Progrès*, Feb.–March, and especially the latter on Feb. 16, 21, 1909.

⁸ *L'Humanité*, March 3, 1909, commenting the *camelots'* attempt to upset the bust of Zola at Suresnes, wrote: "Il fut un temps où tous ces dilletantes du monarchisme et de la trique auraient redouté la vive colère du peuple ouvrier. ... Mais quoi! le prolétariat a été si meurtri depuis trois ans par une politique brutale, railleuse et in- intelligente, qu'il n'a plus le coeur d'intervenir pour disperser ces mascarades inso- lites."

⁹ *Abominable Vénalité*, p. 215, Raffalovitch to Kokovtsev, March 5, 1909.

¹⁰ *Le Gaulois*, May 18, 1909; on May 16, 1909, Princess Radziwill had written from Paris (*Lettres*, IV, 77): "Depuis hier tout Paris est pavoisé de drapeaux tricolores qui encadrent celui du Pape et celui de Jeanne d'Arc. L'église de Paris ayant annoncé un Triduum en faveur de la nouvelle Bienheureuse, il y a une démonstration grandiose qui prouverait qu'une certaine réaction se fait au point de vue français du pays. Il est sûr que la cause de Jeanne d'Arc a réveillé beaucoup le sentiment patriotique." It was perhaps rather the revived patriotic sentiment that furthered the cause of Jeanne d'Arc!

¹¹ But its field of influence was as ever restricted; cf. Vaugeois, *Action française*, Aug. 16, 1909: "Oui, c'est un fait: le bon grain du Nationalisme intégral aura levé en 1909, fort et dru, *sur les terrains divers où il aura pu etre semé*." (Italics mine.)

¹² Cf. *J.O.S.*, March 25, 1910; *J.O.C.*, Nov. 9, 1910. In *J.O.C.* 1910, p. 955, are such exchanges as: D. Delahaye: Vous avez deux patries, vous, la Judée et la France! P. Strauss: Le Christ était juif! Gaudin de Villaine: Non, ce n'était pas un juif, c'était un Galiléen!

¹³ Cf. Léon Daudet, *Action française*, Oct. 15, 1909.

¹⁴ *L'Eclair*, Sept. 13, 1909.

¹⁵ In a speech at Gacé, reported by *Le Temps*, Aug. 24, 1909.

¹⁶ Cf. *Le Temps*, March 8, 1910, for the electoral manifesto of Adolphe Carnot's "Alliance Républicaine Démocratique." The moderates dissociated themselves from the "nationalists" the more insistently as their programs and aims appeared to differ so little. Concerning this, see Friedrich Hertz, *Nationality in History and Politics* (London: 1944), p. 35, which leads one to realize the basic difference between them: "The typical nationalist attitude . . . is to assume that national power and prestige are the best keys to all the treasures of the world, and that a strong State alone can solve the social problems and secure the best possible conditions for the development of national civilization." This helps point out why conservative and nationalist pro- grams cannot really be one: the conservatives aiming at the conservation of states liberties, privileges, situations; the nationalists aiming rather at the creation of new ones, "with prestige and power as the supreme goals." But it also shows why the superficial observer, at a time when both moderates and nationalists emphasized the importance of strong government and national prestige, could not see much difference between their respective programs.

¹⁷ *Action française*, Oct., 1910; cf. Coudekerque-Lambrecht, *Léon de Montesquiou* (Paris: 1925), p. 503.

[18] *L'Echo,* March 2, 1909.

[19] March 20 to 28, 1910.

[20] The year 1926 saw the publication of the Papal Decree of 1914 which put on the Index several works of Maurras, and also the newspaper. But it was not until 1937 that the Royal Pretender announced that neither the methods nor the teachings of the offending movement represented the true royal tradition. After proper submission, the Papal ban was conveniently raised in 1939.

[21] Although the *Dépêche* was moved to comment: "Non seulement M. Maurras a coupé en deux un parti qui n'était déja pas très puissant quand il était uni, mais encore, dans sa première rencontre avec le prince, il a été personellement humilié, rejeté, presque excommunié." But this was on January 4; four months later Maurras had reaffirmed his strength.

[22] May 9, 1910. The nationalists were Laguerre, Ernest Roche, and Castelin. The latter had won by 9,357 votes to 8,277.

[23] Cf. Jacques Piou, *Albert de Mun* (Paris: 1925), p. 292.

[24] *L'Eclair,* July 15, 1910. But he added: "Ce n'est pas tout, c'est même peu, que la restauration d'une foi qui avait tristement vacillé."

[25] *Action française,* July 30, 1910.

[26] The celebration of the twenty-fifth anniversary of his literary career would soon make this even more apparent. It took place on April 24, 1911 (*Revue Universelle,* Jan., 1937) at a great dinner during which he was presented with a memorial album containing signatures of men as wide apart as Anatole France and Jules Lemaître, Raymond de Tailhède and Desrousseaux, the Hellenist, better known as the Socialist deputy and writer, Bracke.

[27] In his *Faites un Roi* (Paris: 1913).

[28] Joseph Denais was a friend of Marc Sangnier. Jean Drault, *Drumont* (Paris: 1935), p. 299, writes of the change: "A la nouvelle de cette vente, un homme entra dans la petite rédaction en coup de vent, sans chapeau. C'était l'abbé Cantenot, attérré, affolé: 'Denais! ... criait-il, Denais! Vous allez avoir Joseph Denais avec sa rédaction du *Peuple français?* Eh bien! mes enfants! Vous allez en avoir une belle collection de sacristains!"

[29] Nov. 10, 1910: "Aujourd'hui, comme hier, tous les bons républicains finiront par se trouver réunis autour du drapeau de la République. ... Boulangisme, nationalisme, syndicalisme, trois formes de la démagogie."

[30] Vaugeois on Sept. 30, 1910.

NOTES TO CHAPTER VII

The Intellectual Front: 1910–1911

(Pages 77–84)

[1] Debate on "Les Origines Diplomatiques de la Guerre de 1870," in *J.O.C.,* Jan. 16, 1911.

[2] The government had 346 votes and a safe majority, but it took heed.

[3] *J. O., Décrets,* Feb. 9, 1911.

[4] Modeste-Leroy, *J.O.C.,* Jan 16, 1911.

[5] Jan. 26, 1911.

[6] *J.O.C.,* Jan. 13, 1911.

[7] *Action française,* Feb. 17–March 4, 1911.

[8] Feb. 20, 1911.

[9] March 12, 1911.

[10] March 14, 1911.

[11] March 17, 1911.

[12] March 29, 1911.

[13] *Dépêche*, April 17, 1911: "C'est la première prise sur les avantgardes ouvriéres et democratiques depuis que Drumont, il y a un quart de siècle, importa d'Allemagne et d'Autriche cette doctrine de haine et de réaction." See also Sembat in *L'Humanité*, April 26, 1911: "L'antisemitisme est fort à la mode."

[14] As Maurras once said during his quarrel with Larègle (*Action française*, Jan. 4, 1911), when Larègle and Judet had declared "l'antisémitisme n'est pas un programme": "Il sera temps, un de ces jours, de montrer que, bien au contraire, c'est en fonction du programme antisémite que tout le reste du programme nationaliste et monarchiste pourra passer de la conception à l'éxécution."

[15] The words of Lucien Lacour, quoted in the *Action française*, March 30, 1911.

[16] Cf. *Le Progrès*, May 25, 1911, *Dépêche* throughout May and June.

[17] Cf. Jean Maxe, *L'Echo*, April 7, 1909; Barrès, *ibid.*, June 24, 1909

[18] Henri Massis, *L'Honneur de Servir* (Paris: 1937), p. 155.

[19] Henri Massis, *Evocations* (Paris: 1931), p. 87; also Raïssa Maritain, *We Have Been Friends Together* (New York: 1941), p. 83: "With Péguy, Sorel, and Ernest Psichari, we came early to be sure of having seats. Henri Focillon, Jean Marx, Masson-Oursel, and the poetess Anna de Noailles were also regularly present." Charles Morgan, *Liberties of the Mind* (London: 1951), has an extremely interesting essay on Bergson and the Maritains, which gives the reader an impression of the place which Bergson filled in the thought and the thought-development of that time. That many of Bergson's admirers went on beyond what they had got from him, the philosopher would have been the first to think it a justification of his work.

[20] Agathon, *Esprit de la Nouvelle Sorbonne* (Paris: 1911), pp. 94–95, 307.

[21] *L'Opinion*, Nov. 12, 1910.

[22] *La Patrie*, April 4, 1911.

[23] *Le Progrès*, June 30, 1911.

[24] *Le Temps*, June 16, 1911.

[25] Massis, *Evocations*, p. 126: the Ligue was not approved by everybody: Drumont attacked it, Maurras refused to join, Aulard who called it "Ligue des fils de famille" commented: "On a déjà recruté un escadron de 120 membres de l'Institut montés sur leurs vieux dadas: le bruit des plumes se mêle au cliquetis des épées de nacre. Lemaître porte, en guise de drapeau, sa veste encore une fois retournée. Richepin, drapé dans sa pourpre d'ancien gueux enrichi, joue l'imperator. A quand la revue, ou plutôt la procession, de la Ligue!"

[26] *Henri Bazire, A Memoir*, preface by G. Goyau (Paris: 1922); see also the story of the Sillon and the Action fraçaise in Adrien Dansette, *Histoire religieuse* (Paris: 1951), II.

[27] Massis, *L'Honneur de Servir* (Paris: 1937), p. 17.

[28] *L'Eclair*, Jan. 26 and March 1, 1912. On March 1, Louis Gillet had written: "Savez-vous que nous sommes probablement en train d'assister à une renaissance littéraire chrétienne? Paul Claudel, Francis Jammes, Charles Péguy, je ne sais ce que ces noms disent au grand public: mais il se passe de ce coté-là quelque chose d'important. ... Je me demande parfois si nous ne sommes pas à la veille d'un de ces coups de théatre, ou plutôt si tout n'est pas fait déjà dans la coulisse, et s'il n'y manque autre chose qu'une consécration et une publicité, qui ne sont plus qu'une question d'heures." A year later, Gaston Riou expressed the same feeling: "Notre époque a beau affecter l'incroyance ... elle est religieuse en secret. On le verra bien quand un nouveau Augustin aura l'humilité sublime de lui conter tout haut le pélérinage de son ame." (*Aux Ecoutes de la France qui Vient* (Paris: 1913), p. 88). What would he have made of Psichari's posthumously published *Voyage du Centurion?*

[29] Dansette, *Histoire religieuse*, II, 474.

[30] Daniel Halévy, *Visites aux Paysans du Centre* (Paris: 1935), p. 44. The visit was made in 1910.

[31] Perhaps as a result of Action française intrigue, but of this there is no proof.

[32] Halévy, *Visites*, pp. 67, 69.

NOTES TO CHAPTER VIII

[1] *B.D.* III, 95, June 13, 1905; Oron James Hale, *Germany and the Diplomatic Revolution* (Philadelphia: 1931), p. 162.

[2] *Daily Telegraph*, Sept. 30, 1905.

[3] *Le Matin*, Oct. 6, 7, 8, 17, 1905; *L'Echo*, Oct. 7, 14, 24, 25, 26, 1905; cf. the discussion of this campaign and its motives in Hale, *op. cit.*, chap. viii.

[4] Cf. *ibid.*, p. 187; *Berliner Tageblatt*, July 29, Aug. 2, 1905; *Berliner Post*, July 30, 1905; *Berliner Neueste Nachrichten*, Aug. 10, 12, 1905.

[5] Camille Sabatier, *Dépêche*, Jan. 26, 1906: "L'Allemagne est en armes sur nos frontières et le monde entier redoute une conflagration." *L'Echo*, Jan. 31, 1906: "Quoi qu'on pense, l'heure est grave. ... Ne nous illusionons pas, et songeons aux choses de guerre. C'est une utile précaution."

[6] Cf. *Le Temps*, April 2, 1906; Jan. 1, 17, 1907; Nov. 13, 1908: *La Dépêche*, April 6, 1906; Jan. 7, May 21, 1907: *Le Gaulois*, March 21, 1907: *L'Echo*, June 9, 1908; Feb. 28, 1910: *Le Matin*, March 26, 1911: "Barodet" in *J.O.C.*, May 6, 1906: J Delahaye in *J.O.C.*, June 18, 1909, p. 1529.

[7] Cf. Jean Frontière, *Dépêche*, July 24, 1907; *J.O.C.*, Nov. 19, 1906.

[8] *Le Matin*, Nov. 20, 1906, reprints the interview from the previous day's *Berliner Tageblatt*.

[9] Georges Louis, *Carnets* (Paris: 1926), I, 21.

[10] *G.P.* XXI, part 2, 559; Radolin to Bülow, Paris, Feb. 22, 1907.

[11] *G.P.* XXI, part 2, 571.

[12] Philip Noel-Baker, *The Private Manufacture of Armaments* (London: 1936), p. 374. An article in the *Frankfurter Illustrierte Zeitung* (April 21, 1913), quoted in *ibid.*, p. 377, gives an excellent account of this system and shows incidentally that not everybody was blind to its workings, although apparently enough people were for enough of the time to allow it to continue: "A French newspaper announces that France plans a new armament plant; the German jingo press seizes the false report with joy, and demands threateningly if the German war leaders are asleep. Several days later appears the announcement that Germany, naturally, will arm herself to the full extent of her abilities. . . . This bullet flies back to the French press, which now naturally demands adequate French armament . . . and after a while the leading statesmen of France and Germany make declarations to the effect that months and months earlier they had planned the increased armaments." For a similar comment, cf. *Lettres de la Princesse Radziwill* (Bologna: 1934) IV, 227, March 13, 1913.

[13] P. 377.

[14] *La Petite République*, March 23, 1907. The General contested the published text: "Les mêmes causes ou des pretextes nouveaux peuvent ramener la même situation. La guerre se fera." He claimed he had said "Les mêmes causes peuvent amener les mêmes effets. La guerre peut se faire." See also *Le Temps*, March 26 and 28, 1907.

[15] *J.O.C.*, March 27, 1907.

[16] March 28, 1907.

[17] *Le Petit Parisien*, Aug. 28, 1907: "Le mot détente est évidemment celui qui se présente d'abord à l'esprit pour qualifier l'état actual des relations franco-allemandes."

[18] This brought about the resignation of Freycinet from the presidency of the Senate army commission.

[19] Those who consider the relatively small credits granted at this time for the development of gymnastic societies and rifle clubs as being indicative of a warlike policy, may well be wrong. These credits were increased by over eighty thousand francs in 1908, and by another twenty-five thousand in 1909, but it is possible that

many saw, as did Messimy, in the development of these paramilitary organizations the promise of a further shortening of the period of military service; cf. Messimy, *J.O.C.*, Nov. 24, 1909. It would be interesting to know how far such expressions of hope were merely lip-service paid to an accepted theme.

[20] Feb. 12, 1908; cf. *Dépêche*, Feb. 16, 1908. Just how unexpectedly far they went, and how close to French hearts, was shown by an incident that took place when the second Briand cabinet sought the Chamber's approval on Nov. 9, 1910 (*J.O.C.*, p. 2725). Louis Laferre, who had been included in the cabinet probably more in order to avoid dangerous Right-Wing support than to attract that of the Left (he was a high Masonic dignitary), listened patiently to the violent attacks being made against him. But when the nationalist Driant accused him of supporting a motion for the forgetting of Alsace-Lorraine he jumped up to reply: "Je proteste avec indignation. ... Jamais, à aucun moment ... la franc-maçonnerie française n'a perdu le souvenir des provinces perdues. Nous nous glorifions de compter au sein de cette grande assemblée des Franc-Maçons qui n'ont pas renoncé à leurs espérances patriotiques." (Très bien! très bien! à gauche).

[21] Cf. Gen. Langlois, *Le Temps*, Dec. 19, 1908, and *J.O.S.*, 1908, p. 1292; Jean des Gaules, *Dépêche*, Nov. 11, 1908. *La Libre Parole*, Nov. 5, 1908, shows the scene in a different aspect: "Les nouvelles complications suscitées par l'Allemagne, au sujet de l'incident des déserteurs de Casablanca, ont causé une grosse émotion hier, dans les couloirs du Palais Bourbon. On se serait cru revenu aux jours de la démission de M. Delcassé où on craignait d'être à deux doigts de la guerre."

[22] *Aussenpolitik*, I, 1171.

[23] *Abominable Vénalité*, p. 219, March 29, 1909. Raffalovitch, who has attended the annual banquet of the economic and financial press association, presided by Caillaux, Ruau, and Viviani, at which the governors of the Banque de France and the Crédit Foncier were also present, writes to Kokovtsev: he reports "L'impression de profond soulagement qu'ont eprouvée et exprimée les interlocuteurs avec lesquels l'hasard de la soirée m'a mis en contact: ministres, publicistes, députés ou sénateurs. On a reconnu l'esprit de sacrifice de la Russie, mais on s'est réjoui de voir l'issue pacifique d'une aventure dans laquelle la France ne se serait engagée qu'à contre-coeur." *G.P.*, XXIX, 5, March 30, 1909.

[24] *Ibid.*, Nelidov to Izvolsky, April 1, 1909; Siebert, *Diplomatische Aktenstücke zur Geschichte der Ententepolitik der Vorkriegsjahre*, 1921, quoted by B. E. Schmitt, "Triple Alliance and Triple Entente," *American Historical Review*, XXIX (1924), 449–473. See also Luigi Albertini, *Origins of the War of 1914* (London: 1952), I, 293–294.

[25] Such as Lt. Col. Rousset, *Le Gaulois*, July 1, 1909.

[26] July 22, 1909, with reference to the signature of the short-lived Franco-German Morocco Agreement.

[27] *J.O.C.*, Dec. 23, 1909, especially the speech of Millevoye, p. 3706 ff. On some sides this impossibility stemmed from a refusal to do so. Cf. Delafosse, *Le Gaulois*, April 3, 1905 and *L'Echo*, July 1, 1905; Millevoye, *Patrie*, April 1, 1911; Habert, *Patrie*, April 2, 1911. The yearning for the lost provinces, though never by itself sufficient to cause trouble, was shared and expressed by men in responsible positions: Poincaré, Clemenceau, Pichon, Paléologue, Georges Louis, Louis Barthou, Jean Jaurès, all expressed it openly, and sometimes on official occasions. Barrès could quote and make his own the words of Jaurès: "L'Alsace et la Lorraine sont comme ces arbres qu'on peut séparer par une muraille de la forêt, mais qui par les racines profondes vont rejoindre sous la muraille de l'enclos les racines de la forêt primitive." As for Barthou, he seemed capable of expressing his feelings even when his personal position made such statements somewhat indiscreet. The German ambassador, Von Schoen, has recorded a conversation in which he told Barthou his feeling that the current nationalist agitation was a pity and a waste for both sides. Could not France and Germany be friends? Barthou, then prime minister, replied: "Rendez-nous l'Alsace-Lorraine, alors nous

serons les meilleurs amis de la terre." Schoen was shocked; cf. Wilhelm von Schoen, *Mémoires* (Paris: 1922), pp. 219–220. The words of Jaurès were quoted by Barrès in a speech at Metz, Aug. 15, 1911 (ed. Emile-Paul, pp. 12–13). On the circumstances of its making, cf. *L'Ame française et la Guerre*, I, 49–54 (also ed. Emile-Paul). Cf. also Victor Giraud, *Barrès* (Paris: 1922), p. 104.

[28] Cf. Messimy, in his election address of 1914, *Barodet* (1914), p. 15.

[29] *Barodet* (1910), pp. 1–85; *J.O.C.*, Oct. 25, 1910.

[30] *L'Humanité*, Aug. 16, 1910.

[31] *L'Action française*, Jan. 9, March 5, 1911.

[32] *L'Aurore*, Jan. 14, 1911: "La paix si tout le monde y consent. Mais la paix armée, tout ce qu'il y a de plus armé, c'est aujourd'hui la vraie paix." (Maxime Vuillaume.)

[33] *J.O.C.*, Jan 13, 1911, p. 39.

[34] *J.O.S.*, March 31, 1911, p. 331, in the debate on the Naval building program:

Flaissières: Je m'élève contre cette sorte de folie intense des armements à outrance qui sévit sur toutes les nations. ...

Tillaye: Vous avez sans doute lu le discours du chancelier allemand? (Rires approbatifs.)

[35] The generalissimo-designate, General Michel, friendly towards the Left and on good terms with Jaurès himself, inclined decidedly toward a fuller utilization of reserve troops. The showdown came at a bad moment for Michel—the new minister of war was Messimy, himself a product of the École supérieure de Guerre, surrounded by "Young Turks" and a believer in their theories. "Ce fut une véritable levée des boucliers," writes Joseph Jacques Joffre, *Mémoires* (Paris: 1932), I, 10. No holds were barred, and it seems likely that Messimy or his friends did not hesitate to feed the press campaign against Michel with secret information. The general was removed on July 21 to be replaced by Joffre, a moderate supporter of the new theories.

[36] *J.O.C.*, June 23, 1911. Among the majority were Briand, Augagneur, Barthou, Deschanel, Jonnart, Klotz, Maginot, Millerand, Painlevé, Violette. Many Socialists abstained.

[37] Cf. Admiral Bienaimé, *Libre Parole*, July 3, 1911, and Driant, *J.O.C.*, June 30, 1911.

[38] *J.O.C.*, June 23, 1911, p. 2554: "Donc, l'incident est clos. [He refers to the discussion.] Tout le monde s'entend. Faut-il voter un ordre du jour de confiance? Se contentera-t-on de l'ordre du jour pur et simple? On n'en sait trop rien; on hésite, on vote, et le gouvernement est par terre sur cette grave question. La Chambre est toute étonnée d'avoir mis le gouvernement en minorité; et elle avait d'autant plus le droit d'en être étonnée, qu'elle ne l'avait pas mis en minorité du tout, ainsi qu'il résulte des déclarations ultérieures de plusieurs de nos collègues."

[39] *J.O.C.*, June 30, 1911.

NOTES TO CHAPTER IX

THE TURNING POINT: 1911–1912

(Pages 93–105)

[1] In his article on the fall of Delcassé, *Revue des Deux Mondes*, Jan., 1933, Barrère leads us to think that French diplomacy was not exactly conciliation-minded. Of the German attitude at Algéçiras he writes: "Une attitude conciliante eut impressioné favorablement les puissances. Elle nous aurait sérieusement embarrassés dans les fins que poursuivait la diplomatie française."

[2] *J.O.S.*, Dec. 24, 1907. This should be read in conjunction with Ribot's statement in the debate on Morocco, *J.O.C.*, Nov. 12, 1907: C'est à nous de faire comprendre à l'opinion que nous ne sommes pas à Casablanca pour notre plaisir ... que nous y

sommes pour remplir un devoir et que, par conséquent, nous ne nous irons que lorsque nous aurons rempli ce devoir complètement; et ce devoir consiste à assurer une sécurité assez grande pour que les Européens soient en sureté et qu'on puisse reprendre les travaux du chemin de fer." [Approbation.]

[3] Daniel Halévy, *Décadence de la Liberté* (Paris: 1931), p. 113.

[4] Cf. A. de Tarde, *Le Maroc, École d'Energie* (Paris: 1929), p. 28: "Le champ par excellence de l'énergie, du rajeunissement, et de la fécondité."

[5] *J.O.C.*, Jan. 24, 1908. Also Delafosse, *J.O.C.*, Jan. 20, 1909: "L'Afrique, aux jours de péril, peut mettre à notre dispositions des contingents énormes de soldats incomparables, qui rétabliront l'équilibre des forces et qui assureront notre salut." Barrès notes in his *Cahiers*, IX, 173–174, Sept., 1911: "Dans l'Afrique du Nord c'est une civilization que l'on peut fonder, et qui viendra doubler la masse de la France. Par ses soldats ... nous restituons notre rang de puissance de premier ordre en Europe. C'est modifier, c'est rétablir en notre faveur, l'équilibre éuropéen."

[6] Cf. *L'Echo*, Jan 25 and 26, 1908.

[7] Jan. 26, 1908. *Le Temps*, Jan. 27, 1908, admitting the persistence of such feelings, commented: "Le Berliner Tageblatt exagère en disant que c'est à cela surtout qu'est dû le succès de M. Delcassé. C'est son accent patriotique qui a valu à l'ancien ministre des affaires étrangères les applaudissements de toute la Chambre."

[8] *J.O.S.*, June 24, 1909, p. 509 ff. Charles Riou, quoting the Rapporteur Général de la Commission des Finances, Raymond Poincaré: "L'expédition du Maroc nous revient ... à l'heure actuelle à 58 ou 59 millions. Or, comme il est certain ... que notre action peut devenir d'un moment à l'autre plus vive ... il faut concevoir qu'à ces 58 ou 59 millions viendront s'ajouter autant de millions qu'on a déjà dépensés—car ils sont dépensés."

[9] G. Chaigne, deputy of the Gironde, *L'Aurore*, Jan. 1, 1910.

[10] *J.O.C.*, Feb. 21, 1910.

[11] *J.O.C.*, Jan. 12, 1911: "Nous sommes simplement allés militairement au Maroc à un moment donné parce qu'il le fallait pour nous y faire respecter."

[12] Cf. "Le Péril," *L'Aurore*, May 9, 1911; *J.O.S.*, April 6, 7, 1911; *J.O.C.*, June 16, 1911, when Jaurès gave warning of the danger implicit in the Fez expedition, and in the project for a Franco-Spanish partition of Morocco.

[13] Jean des Gaules, *Dépêche*, April 24, May 23, 1911.

[14] Joseph Jacques Joffre, *Mémoires* (Paris: 1932), I, 15–16: "Je me souviens d'une entrevue que j'eus au début d'août avec M. Caillaux en présence de M. Fallières. Le président du Conseil me posa à brûle pourpoint cette question: 'Général ... avons-nous 70% de chances de victoire si la situation nous accule à la guerre?' J'étais assez embarrassé pour répondre. Je finis par dire: 'Non, je ne considère pas que nous les ayons.' 'C'est bien, répondit Caillaux; alors nous négocierons.' "

[15] Paul Cambon, *Correspondance* (Paris: 1940–1946), II, 345 ff.; cf. also *Lettres de la Princesse Radziwill*, (Bologna: 1934), IV, 153, 161, 245; and for evidence as to how long this resentment appears to have been sustained, cf. *ibid.*, p. 164, Oct. 24, 1911; pp. 186–187, May 17, 1912; p. 188, May 25–26, 1912 (esp.); p. 195, Aug. 9–13, 1912; p. 214, Dec. 22, 1912; p. 230, May 6–10, 1913.

[16] Cambon, *Correspondance*, III, 11–12, letter to Xavier Charmes, Feb. 11, 1912.

[17] Cf. *L'Aurore*, July 3, 1911.

[18] July 2, 7, 1911.

[19] *L'Echo*, July 5, 1911; *Libre Parole*, July 6, 1911; *Action Française*, July 3, 1911.

[20] *J.O.C.*, Jan. 31, 1913, p. 128.

[21] July 15, 1911.

[22] Junius, *L'Echo*, July 28, 1911.

[23] *Le Temps*, Aug. 16, 1911.

[24] Aug. 27, 1911.

[25] Aug 24, 1911; cf. Georges Thiébaud, *Libre Parole*, Sept. 1, 1911.

[26] Sept. 6, 1911.

[27] J. Hedeman, Sept. 14, 1911.

[28] *Le Temps*, Sept. 17, 1911.

[29] For humbler reactions, and the general certainty of coming war, cf. in *Le Temps*, "Lettres de Province," Oct. 4, 1911, and "Resurrection Nationale," Feb. 19, 1912.

[30] *L'Aurore*, Sept. 18, 1911.

[31] *Action française*, Sept. 19, 1911.

[32] Oct. 6, 1911.

[33] Letter dated Nov. 23, 1911, in the *Correspondance de l'Union pour la Vérité*, Feb. 1, 1912. A similar point is made in an exchange that took place in March, 1913, a little over a year later. Lord Northcliffe writes to Dawson, editor of the *Times*, from Paris that "Europe is getting on a war footing," and asks for more news in the paper. Dawson replies: "It seems to me that the supreme danger at the moment is that the revival in France which everyone admires, may degenerate into an aggressive jingoism which will alienate this country altogether." Northcliffe's reply was not very different from that which appeared in the *Correspondance*: "I do not see any signs of chauvinism in France, only—no more squeezing, no more knife at the throat." *History of the Times* (London: 1952), vol. 4, part I, pp. 97–99.

[34] P. Richard, Oct. 13, 1911.

[35] On the contrary, Joseph Caillaux, *Mémoires* (Paris: 1943), II, 152: "Au lende-main de la signature du traité du 4 novembre, 1911, les journalistes, se pressant dans le bureau de la presse du ministère des Affaires Etrangères, recueillirent de la bouche du chef ou du sous-chef de service—je ne veux pas préciser—les paroles suivantes: 'Oui, c'est la paix. ... Mais, comme il est fâcheux que nous ayons eu un homme d'affaires à la tête du gouvernement. C'était la guerre qu'il nous fallait. Jamais nous ne trouverons une occasion aussi favorable.' "

[36] Dec. 7, 1911, it published a letter from Jean Izoulet, professor of Social Philos-ophy at the Collège de France: "Est-il possible de croire que de tels conflits se resou-dront pacifiquement? ... Garde à vous!"

[37] *J.O.C.*, Dec. 14, 1911.

[38] Jacques Piou, *Albert de Mun* (Paris: 1925), p. 298: "A la nouvelle d'Agadir, le premier mouvement d'Albert de Mun fut un élan d'espoir ... il crut entendre l'appel aux armes et son coeur battit. ... Les communications qu'il reçut à la Commission des Affaires Extérieures—il ne sut pas tout—ébranlèrent sa confiance en notre prépa-ration militaire et calmèrent ses patriotiques impatiences. ... Jusqu'à Agadir il avait désiré la guerre sans y croire: après Agadir, il y crût sans la désirer."

[39] Dec. 18, 1911.

[40] Dec. 26, 1911.

[41] *L'Eclair*, Dec. 28, 1911.

[42] *Libre Parole*, Dec. 28, 1911. Cf. the report of the German military attaché, *G.P.*, XXXI, Feb. 19, 1912: "There is a belief that war is inevitable; [and this is] one of the reasons for the general nervousness."

[43] *D.D.F.*, 3e série, I, 65, Crozier to de Selves, No. 9, 1911.

[44] Cf. *D.D.F.*, 3e série, I, 343 ff., Dec. 16, 1911; and II, 456, Jan. 1, 1912. On Jan. 7, 1912, *La Libre Parole* asked: "Aurons-nous la guerre au printemps? ... Il serait puéril de la prédire. Mais l'heure décisive approche. Le monde ressent l'ébranlement pré-curseur des grandes commotions. Fremuerant gentes."

[45] *L.N.*, I, 194, Feb. 15, 1912: "On s'attend dans les sphères militaires d'ici à de nouvelles complications internationales au printemps, et le département de la guerre continue à se préparer activement à des opérations militaires dans un prochain avenir."

[46] *G.P.*, XXXI, 389, dispatch of Feb. 19, 1912.

[47] Already on Sept. 7, 1908, the young Normalien, Henri Franck, was writing to a friend: "C'est à la trouée de Belfort que se jouera toute la liberté du monde, et le plus tôt sera le mieux." Not that he desired it, except as part of his despair: "J'ai peur ... qu'il y ait dans un mois, dans six mois, dans un an, la guerre. ... C'est bien,

n'est-ce pas, ce qui n'est douteux pour personne. C'est horrible." Henri Franck, *Lettres à Quelques Amis* (Paris: 1926), p. 130. The whole letter is to the point. Henri Massis, *La Guerre de Trente Ans* (Paris: 1940, p. 4 ff.), suggests that it was written under the impression of the Casablanca incidents, but they took place on September 25, and the letter dates from the 7th.

[48] *J.O.S.*, Feb. 8, 1912, p. 183.

[49] *J.O.S.*, Feb. 7, 1912, p. 167. See also the conclusion, p. 174: "Fortifions donc notre armée de plus en plus. Consentons pour elle tous les sacrifices nécessaires. ... C'est le moyen, l'unique moyen, d'entreprendre une guerre heureuse."

[50] *J.O.S.*, Jan 9, 1912, Huguet, senator of the Pas-de-Calais, Doyen d'Age.

[51] *J.O.S.*, Jan. 12, 1912, p. 7.

[52] Albert de Mun, *L'Echo*, Jan. 12, 1912: "Depuis six mois il s'est fait un changement dans ce pays, un changement profond dont il a conscience. ... Tout à coup, ce fut un brusque réveil. Le coup d'Agadir avait frappé, comme la baguette magique, le coeur de la France engourdie. ... Vous souvenez-vous? Cet été, du milieu de l'angoisse qui nous etreignait, quelle joie soudaine, et chez nous autres, les vieux, quel orgueil rajeuni! Et vous devinez bien ce que je pense, au fond du coeur: vous le pensez aussi. Jamais heure ne fut si propice! La brutalité germanique avait mis tout le monde à nos cotés! La nations était prête! Au lieu de cela. ... Ah! il faut enfermer cette douleur. Il faut l'enfermer, mais il faut en garder la mémoire. ..."

[53] *Le Progrès*, Jan 14, 1912.

[54] *L'Eclair*, March 9, 1912; see also Dammour, *J.O.C.*, June 14, 1912.

[55] *Tableau politique* (1913), p. 492.

[56] *J.O.C.*, Jan. 16, 1912, the new governmental declaration.

[57] *L'Appel au Soldat* (1926), p. 58.

[58] This compares interestingly with the speech of Caillaux at Saint-Calais on which *Le Progrès* (Nov. 6, 1911) commented: "Ce qui frappe ... dans le discours de Saint-Calais, c'est une tonalité générale qu'on pourrait qualifier d'autoritaire et qui indique chez M. le Président du Conseil la passion de la hiérarchie et de la discipline."

[59] *J.O.C.*, Jan. 16 1912.

[60] Jan. 24, 1911. Appeasement referred, of course, to faction at home, not to foreign policy.

[61] *D.D.F.*, 3e série, I, 554.

[62] The tone of the Chamber was warlike. See *J.O.C.*, Jan. 22, 1912, 39 ff.

[63] *L'Echo*, Jan. 23, 1912.

[64] Mrs. Vernon Lee quotes this letter from a French friend: "Le nationalisme français est un mouvement de défense. Un voisin formidable nous menace de nous vassaliser, de vassaliser nos savants comme nos artistes, nos industriels comme nos homme d'Etat." See n. 33 and her letter in *Correspondance de l'Union pour la Vérité*, p. 235.

[65] Among other acts, he submitted the first project for a law on the organization of military aviation. See *Le Temps*, March 6, 28, 1912. He also set up a reserve brigade in West Africa to furnish relief for the Senegalese troops in Algeria and Morocco, and increased the number of Senegalese stationed in North Africa. See André Chéradame, *La Crise Française* (Paris: 1912), p. 563.

[66] *D.D.F.*, 3e série, II, 48; on Feb. 17, 1912 the French military attaché in Berlin wrote to Delcassé, then minister of marine: "Dans les milieux gouvernementaux on souhaiterait pouvoir s'entendre avec nous, mais on est hanté par l'idée que la France désire la guerre."

[67] *Ibid.*, II, 263; on March 27, 1912, in a dispatch from Foreign Minister Poincaré to Jules Cambon in Berlin: "[Le gouvernement allemand] semble poursuivre avec une obstination inlassable un rapprochement que, seule, une réparation complète du passé rendrait possible."

[68] *G.P.*, XXXI, 385–386, Paris, Feb. 9, 1912: "Es herrscht zurzeit selbst in nicht nationalisten parlamentarischen Kreisen ein starker Chauvinismus der sichtlich durch

die französisch-italienische Zwischenfälle und jetzt wieder durch die Senats Debatten über das Marokko Abkommen neu aufgepeitscht wurde und einen Grad erreicht hat, wie er seit langer Zeit nicht mehr bestand." Cf. *J.O.S.*, Feb. 8, 1912; Paris press of March 20, 1912 on the subject of the Kaiser's visit to the French embassy in Berlin; H. Burgnet in *Le Patriote*, April 6, 1912.

[69] Wilhelm von Schoen, *Mémoires* (Paris: 1922), p. 184, considers it was a minority that kept stoking the fires on national resentment: "En aucun pays mieux qu'en France ne se vérifia la maxime qu'une minorité active peut entrainer une masse indolente."

[70] Feb. 17, 1912; cf. *L'Aurore*, Feb. 19, 1912; *Le Petit Parisien*, Feb. 18, 1912; *La Revue Hebdomadaire*, March 8, 1912.

[71] *L'Aurore*, March 9, 1912.

[72] March 11, 1912. To him it was "le vivifiant présage d'un renouveau patriotique."

[73] *La Libre Parole*, March 11, 1912. *L'Echo*, March 13, 1912 wrote: "M. Poincaré s'était dit-on juré de réveiller l'esprit militaire en France. Il y a réussi."

[74] *Le Temps*, March 22, 1912. *Le Petit Journal*, March 13, 1912, carried the story of an antimilitarist being manhandled in Belleville, a working-class quarter, for having shouted Hervéist slogans. Cf. Chéradame, *Crise française*, p. 671.

[75] Cf. *L'Opinion*, March 16, 1912.

[76] Dupuy-Mazuel, *L'Eclair*, Feb. 22, 1912; A. Gaucher, *Action française*, Feb. 23, 1912.

[77] Cf. Henriot's investigation; E. Ripault in the *Hebdomadaire*, March 8, 1912; R. Veyssié in *Renaissance Contemporaine*, May 10, 1912.

[78] Etienne obtained 208 votes against Deschanel's 292.

[79] Cf. *L'Aurore*, May 24, 25, 1912.

[80] Mistral, *J.O.C.*, Jan. 16, 1912, p. 15; *Le Progrès*, May 25, 1912.

[81] Etienne Rey, *La renaissance de l'Orgueil français* (Paris: 1912), p. 137. Cf. the comments of Charles Maurras in *Kiel et Tanger* (Paris: 1928), pp. 185–186.

[82] *Ibid.*, p. 187, but his comment was a disapproving one, see p. 179 ff.

[83] *J.O.C.*, May 24, 1912.

[84] *D.D.F.*, 3e série, III, 59, Colonel Pellé to Millerand, May 26, 1912: "Pour la masse [des Allemands] il semblerait que notre enthousiasme pour l'aviation militaire et les manifestations répétées de certains personnages au nationalisme encombrant aient révélé notre inapaisable désir de la révanche. Je constate simplement des faits. Je suis convaincu plus que personne que le réveil des sentiments patriotiques en France, dans ces derniers temps, est un bien immense pour notre pays. ... Ce qui est à regretter, c'est que le patriotisme soit exploité tapageusement chez nous par certains journaux, par certains hommes, par certains partis."

[85] *D.D.F.*, 3e série, III, 87, Poincaré to J. Cambon, June 3, 1912: "Le Gouvernement de la République ne saurait. ... décider aujourd'hui s'il se fera représenter ou non, l'an prochain, aux fêtes de Kiel, alors que l'opinion dans les deux pays est encore sous l'influence des incidents de l'an dernier."

[86] Cf. Jean Frollo, *Petit Parisien*, April 28, 1912; *J.O.C.*, June 18, 1912, p. 1537; Raymond Poincaré, *Au Service de la France* (Paris: 1926), II, 79: on July 24, 1912, Fallières, inaugurating the Musée du Souvenir at the École Spéciale Militaire, made this clear: "Disons-le bien haut, jamais l'armée n'a été plus près du coeur de la France."

[87] Aulard, *Dépêche*, June 25, 1912: "Il me semble que nous autres pacifistes français, nous ne devons pas être les derniers à provoquer un movement d'opinion pour l'amélioration. ... de la force défensive de notre nation. La guerre sortirait sûrement de notre négligence à nous fortifier contre la récente menace de l'Allemagne. Travailler à rendre plus efficace notre système de defense, c'est travailler à rendre la paix, je ne dis pas certaine, mais plus probable ou moins improbable."

[88] *Le Temps*, Aug. 11, 1912; *Dépêche*, Aug. 12, 1912; for outside comment on the German fleet's salute, cf. *Lettres de la Princesse Radziwill*, IV, 195.

[89] *D.D.F.*, 3ᵉ série, III, 523 n. 1: the decision was made on Sept. 6, and the fleet left Brest on October 16. There is an interesting dispatch on the subject from Cambon to Poincaré, dated Sept. 19. *Lettres de la Princesse Radziwill*, IV, 199 (Sept. 22–26, 1912): "La concentration de la France dans la Méditerranée empêche de dormir toute la presse allemande, et le ton qu'elle a pris n'est pas fait pour donner du calme à l'Europe." For British side, cf. Ernest Hewellyn Woodward, *Britain and the German Navy* (London: 1935), p. 380 ff.

[90] Gabriel Hanotaux, *Etudes Diplomatiques* (Paris: n.d.), II, 29, June 1, 1912: "Le panchauvinisme règne; les passions aveugles qu'il engendre sont les plus redoutables."

[91] Jacques Bainville, *Le Coup d'Agadir* (Paris: 1913), p. 40, quotes an article of his own of Sept. 24, 1912. Cf. *ibid.*, p. 72, the letter of Jules Destrée, Socialist deputy of Charleroi in Belgium, to his King: "Nous la sentons chaque jour approcher comme un fleau terrible, la guerre entre nos voisins du Sud et de l'Est. ..." See also *L'Action Nationale* of Nov. and Dec., 1912, for the articles of Charles Andler.

[92] Jean Variot, *Propos de Georges Sorel* (Paris: 1935), pp. 27–28: "... la guerre, il faudra bien la faire un de ces jours. Et alors, ce ne sera tout de même pas avec les bavardages socialistes qu'on fera face aux événements. Ce sera avec les principes du nationalisme." (Dec. 11, 1912) Sorel had long been known in a restricted circle, and his *Réflexions sur la Violence* had in 1906, but more notably 1908, caused some stir. Cf. *Le Matin*, May 18, 1908; *L'Echo*, Jan. 4, 1910, for a long article on him by A.-E. Sorel; G. de Macière, "Aux Armes les Bourgeois," *Le Gaulois*, Jan. 11, 1910. Yet the name did not really become known until Jan., 1910, when Paul Bourget declared that the *Réflexions* had inspired his latest play, *Barricade*. After this, Sorel served more than ever as a bridge between Syndicalist and nationalist theories of violence; cf. *L'Action française*, Aug. 22, 1909, and *Revue Socialiste*, Aug. 15, 1912. For an important qualification of this, cf. Edouard Dolléans, *Proudhon* (Paris: 1948), p. 491: "Si G. Sorel recontrait des militants syndicalistes, il n'était pas lu par eux. Victor Griffuelhes protestait toujours quand on lui parlait de l'influence sorélienne—'Je lis surtout Alexandre Dumas.' "

[93] *G.P.*, XXXI, 413, Sept. 25, 1912.

[94] *A.A.*, V, 103, for the Belgian foreign office circular of Oct. 28, 1912, giving the extract of a Paris report of Oct. 1, 1912.

[95] Cf. Millerand's speech at the banquet of the military press of March 6, 1912, quoted in *La Patrie* the following day: "Certes, l'opinion est la grande maîtresse, mais il faut que la presse fasse l'éducation de l'opinion. ..."

[96] Charles Antoine Micaud's introduction to *The French Right and Nazi Germany* (Durham, N.C.: 1943), comes to a similar conclusion for the press of a later period.

[97] *L.N.*, I, 372, Dec. 18, 1912: "Ce n'est plus l'idée que la France peut se voir imposer la guerre pour les intérêts étrangers que j'aurai à combattre, mais plutôt la crainte que nous ne soyons pas trop passifs dans une question touchant la situation et le prestige de toute l'entente."

[98] *D.D.F.*, 3ᵉ série, IV, 482; Poincaré to G. Louis, Nov. 16, 1912: "Je sais qu'en 1908–09 M. Isvolsky a cru pouvoir attribuer les échecs de sa politique aux hésitations de la France. Je tiens essentiellement à ce que des reproches de cette sorte ne puissent pas nous être adressés, et à ce qu'on ne nous prête pas des responsabilités qui ne sont pas les nôtres."

[99] Jules Isaac, *Origines de la Guerre* (Paris: 1933), p. 43: "Victoire de la France sur l'Allemagne, écrivait Albert Malet, présage d'autres victoires, laissait-il entendre, et combien en France pensaient comme lui, sans que 'l'abominable vénalité de la presse' y fut pour rien."

[100] *G.P.*, XXXI, 414 ff., Nov. 11, 1912.

[101] Alfred Capus, *Les Moeurs du Temps* (Paris: 1912).

[102] *Tableau Politique* (Paris: 1913).

[103] *Action française*, Dec. 26, 1912.

[104] *G.P.*, XXXI, 399, March 22, 1912.

[105] In April, Poincaré had recalled Paul Cambon to Paris for talks. On his return to London, this latter informed the foreign office of the premier's conviction that war with Germany was inevitable. Cf. Sir Arthur Nicolson's memorandum to Grey on his conversation with Cambon on April 15, 1912, in Harold Nicolson, *Lord Carnock* (London: 1930), pp. 367–369. See also *J.O.S.*, Dec. 21, 1912, p. 1586: "Comte de Tréveneuc: Il n'est un secret pour personne que, dans les circonstances à prévoir pour la guerre de demain, nous n'aurons à envisager qu'un seul adversaire."

NOTES TO CHAPTER X

OF HEROES AND HERO-WORSHIP: 1912–1913

(Pages 106–119)

[1] *La Libre Parole*, Dec. 6, 1911.
[2] Cf. *ibid.*, "lorsqu'il s'agit, comme maintenant, d'un réveil général du patriotisme."
[3] *Ibid.*, Dec. 13, 1911.
[4] *Libre Parole*, May 8, 1912.
[5] Emile Henriot, *A Quoi Rêvent les Jeunes Gens* (Paris: 1913), p. 39, Georges Duhamel: "Il y a là tous les signes d'un renouveau." P. 47, Jacques Copeau: "Je crois que chaque jeune homme aujourd'hui est soutenu, inspiré par le sentiment profond de 'préparer quelque chose,' de collaborer ... à quelque chose de plus important que la gloire personelle, et qui est le relèvement de notre grandeur nationale." Pp. 86–87, Jacques Boulenger: "Je suis fâché que le mot 'nationalisme' ait pris un sens singulier par l'emploi qu'on en a fait dans les batailles électorales, car c'est lui qui serait la meilleure dénomination de la principale école d'aujourd'hui, de l'école qui représentera certainement plus tard le mouvement littéraire de notre époque." P. 121, Emile Henriot: "Il nous a été donné d'assister au cours de l'été dernier à un magnifique mouvement d'opinion publique en France, qui n'a été rien de moins que le réveil de la conscience nationale et de la notion de patrie."
[6] G. Rozet, *L'Eclair*, Sept. 15, 1911; for the connection between sport and the patriotic revival see also John Edward Courtenay Bodley, "The Decay of Idealism in France," in *Cardinal Manning and Other Essays* (London: 1912), p. 138 ff.; Victor Marguerite, *Le Goût de l'Energie* (Paris: 1912); *G.P.*, XXI, 2, p. 544.
[7] Pierre Mille, *Dépêche*, Feb. 2, 1912.
[8] Alfred de Tarde, *Le Maroc* (Paris: 1929), p. 26.
[9] Jacques Bardoux commented in *L'Opinion*, Dec. 28, 1912: "The year ends well for France. She moves once more in the martial atmosphere which recalls her glories and her hopes. She is united. She is calm. She is ready."
[10] *J.O.S.*, April 6, 1911, pp. 384–385:
Lamarzelle: ... pour éviter la guerre, il faut entretenir dans le pays. ...
Un senateur à droite: L'Union!
Lamarzelle: ... non seulement le sentiment patriotique, mais aussi le sentiment guerrier, le seul support du patriotisme et sans lequel celui-ci ne peut pas longtemps exister.
Flaissières: C'est le retour à la barbarie! Si vous voulez la paix, préparez la paix, d'abord!
J. Delahaye: Vous préférez, vous, la guerre entre citoyens, la guerre civile!
Lamarzelle: M. Flaissières, j'ai dit qu'il fallait entretenir dans un peuple le sentiment guerrier pour cette raison que je suis patriote et qu'aucune patrie ne peut se former, se conserver et durer qu'à la condition d'entretenir toujours dans la nation le sentiment guerrier ... dans l'état actuel du monde, il faut voiler les horreurs de la guerre par ses grandeurs, par ses sacrifices, par ses gloires."

[11] Agathon, *Les jeunes gens d'aujourd'hui* (Paris: 1913) *passim.*

[12] Sept. 17, 1911.

[13] Henri Massis, *Evocations* (Paris: 1931), p. 215: "Quel ascendant, quelle supériorité n'allait-il pas prendre aussitôt, ce magnifique garçon qui, seul d'entre nous avait vu le visage de la gloire! Car les Français, en ce temps-là n'avaient pas tous une blessure de guerre, des citations, ou la croix. L'héroïsme était chose plus rare, et plus rares aussi les honneurs qui en recompensaient le singulier mérite."

[14] *L'Eclair*, Jan. 30, 1912.

[15] Henri Franck, *N.R.F.*, Nov., 1911; *L'Aurore*, Jan. 17, 1912; *Le Progrès*, Jan. 26, 1912; *Lettres de la Princesse Radziwill* (Bologna: 1934), IV, pp. 155, 156, 174. Cf. Maurice Barrès, "Le Tombeau de l'Empereur," *L'Appel au Soldat* (Paris: 1926).

[16] *Le Rappel*, July 1, 2, 1912; Leon Daudet, *Action française*, July 3, 1912; *La Guerre Sociale*, same date: "Pas une voix ne s'éleva au quartier latin pour répondre aux camelots du roi, pas une contre-manifestation ne s'organisa pour les faire taire."

[17] *J.O.C.*, June 11, 1912.

[18] *Les jeunes gens d'aujourd'hui* (Paris: 1913), p. II. Allard, *L'Humanité*, May 2, 1912: "Bien entendu, il ne s'agit que de la jeunesse bourgeoise." E. Faguet in his conclusion to an "Enquête sur la Jeunesse" in the *Revue Hebdomadaire*, July 20, 1912: "Toute la jeunesse bourgeoise est en retard sur la jeunesse philosophe et littéraire, sur la jeunesse penseuse, et n'arrivera que plus tard, si elle peut y arriver, au point où est, dès à présent celle-ci."

[19] *Les jeunes gens d'aujourd'hui*, p. V. Pierre Désanges and L. Mériga, *La vie de Jean Jaurès* (Paris: 1924), p. 203: "Il n'était pas interdit de croire que l'influence d'une telle enquête importait autant que son exactitude."

[20] Jules Romains, writing more than twenty years after these events, has yet given us an excellent picture of the temper of the times and (in *Les Hommes de Bonne Volonté*, XIII, 125) a penetrating commentary on these investigations. It was Jerphanion who commented to Jallez: "Je veux bien que l'enquête ait été menée d'une façon très tendancieuse. Mais en admettant même qu'il soit scandaleusement abusif de présenter ce choeur trop bien reglé de jeunes gens comme l'expression de la jeunesse d'aujourd'hui, il constitue pourtant un témoignage; il est l'indice—plus ou moins truqué—de quelque chose; il faut refléchir. ... Et je veux bien que ça soit l'effet de deux ou trois influences, toujours les mêmes, qui se sont répandues ici et là; mais l'inquiétant est alors que ces influences se soient si diversement répandues, et qu'elles aient été si docilement subies; au point qu'on a l'impression d'entendre la même leçon vingt fois répétée. ..." See also the reply of Jallez, *ibid.*, p. 130.

[21] Henri Massis, *L'Honneur de Servir* (Paris: 1937), p. 11.

[22] Cf. *ibid.*, p. 145 ff. The words of Paul-Boncour are worth quoting in part: "En l'espace de dix ans, un mouvement de désaffection pour beaucoup de choses que nous aimons et que nous voulons défendre, a gagné une partie de la jeunesse. Ce sont les mêmes milieux, les milieux des écoles et des universitaires où nous recrutions pour la démocratie et pour le socialisme qui, à l'heure actuelle, fournissent à l'Eglise et à la réaction ses plus précieuses recrues."

[23] For a view of Romain Rolland as representative of his generation at this time, see Gaston Riou, *Aux Ecoutes de la France qui Vient* (Paris: 1913), p. 286.

[24] Massis, *L'Honneur de Servir*, pp. 154–155: "Quand nous avons eu l'âge de refléchir, nous avons vu un régiment français en révolte, des grèves éclatant sur tous les points; nous avons vu la France en désarroi, déchirée, douloureuse, incertaine de son destin; nous avons subi Agadir, nous avons vu la guerre s'allumer en Europe, et partout les peuples s'armer, les nationalités s'éxaspérer, la fièvre belliqueuse gagner de proche en proche. ... En face de l'Idée, nous avons appris à connaître la Force." What would he say today?

[25] *Ibid.*, p. 148, and Ernest Psichari, *Lettres du Centurion* (Paris: 1947), pp. 180 ff.

[26] Joseph Caillaux, *Mémoires* (Paris: 1947), III, 90. Georges Dupin, *M. Poincaré et la Guerre de 1914; études sur les responsabilités* (Paris: 1935), pp. 101–102, quotes

Poincaré writing in the *Revue de l'Université de Paris*, Oct., 1920: "In my years at school . . . I saw no other reason for my generation to live than the hope of recovering our lost provinces." On the importance of this, see the discussion in Gordon Wright, *Raymond Poincaré and the Presidency* (Stanford: 1942), p. 129 n. 99. The fact that Poincaré appears to have made efforts to suppress it, indicates a certain embarrassment over this passage, but not necessarily guilt.

27 *L'Humanité*, Jan. 14, 1913: "Telle est la force de pénétration du bluff et du mensonge, que cette campagne de démagogie [of the Right-Wing press in favor of Millerand] a pénétré les couches populaires." In other circles the same idea was mooted; cf. *Lettres de la Princesse Radziwill* (Bologna: 1934), IV, 204, Feb. 4, 1912.

28 *J.O.S.*, Feb. 16, 1905. Among those in favor had been Charles Dupuy, Clemenceau, Freycinet, Mascuraud, Pams, and Rouvier.

29 *J.O.C.*, March 17, 1905. Andrieux, Archdeacon, G. Berry, G. Cavaignac, C. Bos, Couyba, Dansette, J. Delafosse, Delcassé, Deschanel, Etienne, Gauthier de Clagny, Klotz, Lafferre, de Lannessan, M. Binder, de Maussabré, Millerand, Millevoye, Louis Passy, Siegfried, Vazeille, had all voted in favor of the law.

30 On Sept. 28, 1908, Berteaux, then president of the army commission, former minister of war, stressed after maneuvers "la conviction que l'armée de la loi de deux ans est supérieure à sa devancière, et qu'elle peut se considérer comme l'égale des meilleures armées du monde. La République française peut se reposer sur son armée." A year later *Le Progrès* Sept. 9, 1909, commented on the autumn maneuvers: "Le service de deux ans a fait ses preuves. Elles sont concluantes. Les avis sont unanimes."

31 *J.O.S.*, June 17, 1911, p. 761: D. Delahaye: "Il faudra la réformer, cette loi de deux ans; il faut y préparer l'opinion publique."

32 Nov. 15, 1911.

33 General Zurlinden, *Le Gaulois*, Jan 26, 1909, was typical of a school excellently described in *L'Histoire de l'Armée*: "Je fais des voeux pour que notre vaillante infanterie conserve ses glorieuses traditions d'accourir au combat, d'attaquer toutes les fois que des ordres précis ne s'y opposent pas; qu'elle se laisse aller à ses admirables aptitudes pour l'attaque; qu'elle se laisse aller à l'impulsion du sang gaulois qui coule dans les veines de ses soldats, à l'entrain, à l'elan de notre race, qui n'a jamais connu qu'un seul cri de guerre: En avant!"

34 "Vers le service de trois ans," May 27; "Un appel au pays," May 28.

35 Cf. General Cherfils, "Pour les Trois Ans," *Libre Parole*, June 9, 1912; *L'Aurore*, May 30, 1912.

36 *J.O.C.*, June 18, 1912, p. 1535, Driant: "Le service de trois ans seul peut remettre la France en état de reprendre sa place en Europe." But he adds: "Je ne proposerai pas le retour au service de trois ans, parce que ce serait parler pour parler, parce que le pays, la Chambre, ne comprendraient pas, parce que l'heure n'est pas encore venue."

37 J. Reinach, *J.O.C.*, Dec. 20, 1912, p. 3340: "Nous n'en parlons que pour la cavalerie. C'est pour la cavalerie seulement. ..."

38 *Le Progrès*, Dec. 22, 1912: "Le ministre de la guerre n'a pas protesté; il a même laissé entendre qu'il était favorable au projet. ... Ainsi le pays est averti: on prépare une modification à la loi de deux ans."

39 Joseph Caillaux, *Mémoires*, III, 25–26.

40 Jacques Piou, *Albert de Mun* (Paris: 1925), p. 313; Caillaux, *Mémoires*, III, 24, recounts a conversation with Jacques Piou in 1916: "Poincaré ... c'est M. de Mun qui nous a entraînés ... en nous promettant le service de trois ans." Caillaux remarks that, officially, this was only introduced in reply to German measures that occurred *after* Poincaré's election. "Ce n'est pas vrai," replies Piou. "Mun nous a parlé du voyage en Russie de Poincaré. Que s'est-il passé de juste là-bas? ... En tout cas, Mun nous a dit que le service de trois ans était indispensable et que, seule, la présence de Poincaré à l'Elysée assurerait le dépôt et le vote de la loi."

41 Charles Maurras, *Pour un Jeune Français* (Paris: 1949), p. 130.

[42] As shown by this extract from a private letter from Maurras to Massis, about the latter's book, *Maurras et Notre Temps*: "C'était vers la fin de 1911. Je restais souvent fort tard au journal à la Chaussée d'Antin, lorsque j'y faisais toute la revue de la presse et toute la chronique de la Ligue, y compris le fameux 'talisman.' Il ne restait que les camelots de garde. Vers 11.30 on me fait passer la carte de Barrès. Je cours l'introduire, il me dit qu'il me savait là et il avait voulu me voir seul. Air discret. Air mystérieux. Une figure que je lui vis rarement. 'Je viens de dîner chez Paillard (en face) avec Poincaré. ...' Il avait l'air de demander si j'allais lui demander de le faire monter ou de descendre moi-même. ... Alors nous causâmes un moment de choses et d'autres et il se détendit. ... Il est parfaitement possible que Poincaré lui ait demandé cette demi-démarche, car il avait été attiré d'assez bonne heure par notre mouvement. Lorsque, en 1915, je fus amené à lui écrire pour lui donner un conseil de mon correspondant, il me répondit par retour du courrier, en me proposant un rendez-vous à l'Elysée, rendez-vous où j'acceptais d'aller."

[43] Wilhelm Von Schoen, *Mémoires* (Paris: 1922), p. 208; American Embassy in Paris, Correspondence, 1913 (Dept. of State class. 800, Jan. 20, 1913), Ambassador Herrick's dispatch; *Dépêche*, Jan. 18, 22, 1913, and article of Jaurès in *ibid.*; *Le Progrès*, Jan. 19, 1913. *J. O. Assemblée Nationale*, Jan. 17, 1913, p. 2:

> President: "M. Raymond Poincaré ayant obtenu la majorité absolue des suffrages. ..."
> Voix à gauche: Avec la droite! (Oui! oui! à droite)
> Brager de la Ville-Moysan: Eh bien, oui, nous l'avons nommé malgré vous!

[44] Cf. P. Le Breton in his Senate speech of May 13, 1913, and letter to *L'Homme Libre*, March 14, 1914.

[45] Feb. 28, 1913: "... ce sont en effet les mêmes gens et la même agitation que nous avons connu à l'époque nationaliste. ... C'est à la faveur de la confusion proportionelle que le mouvement a commencé ... a envahi Paris, qui offre en général une minime résistance aux poussées de cet ordre. Il y a donc, à cette heure, un parti national, où figurent tous les militants de la droite, et une presse nationale, seule détentrice de la vraie doctrine republicaine et patriotique, telle que la conçoivent les royalistes. ... Les péripéties de l'élection présidentielle, considérées sous ce nouveau jour, s'éclairent pleinement. Ce fut la première grande manoeuvre du parti national."

[46] Jan. 18, 1913.

[47] Caillaux, *Mémoires*, III, pp. 38, 50.

[48] Cf. Eber Malcolm Carroll, *French Public Opinion and Foreign Affairs* (New York: 1931), p. 266 ff.; J. Herbette in *Le Siècle*, Nov. 9, 1912; Bérenger in *L'Action*, Nov. 13, 1912.

[49] *France de Bordeaux et du Sud-Ouest*, Aug. 16, 1913; *Berliner Tageblatt* Nov. 12, 1912; *G.P.*, XXXIX, 188–189, April 29, 1913; quoted by Carroll in *French Public Opinion*, p. 277.

[50] *L. N.*, II, 15; Isvolsky's account dated Jan. 29, 1913, of his conversation with the newly elected president, is disputed by Poincaré in his memoirs, *Au Service de la France* (Paris: n.d.), III, chap. 4. While denying specifically a number of statements attributed to him, Poincaré makes no mention of the passage quoted, which may indicate that it was not an incorrect presentation of his views.

[51] Cf. Joseph Joffre, *Mémoires* (Paris: 1932), I, 53; also *D.D.F.*, 3e série, V, 303. On Jan. 20, 1913, the French Military attaché in Berlin advised his superiors of the coming of a new military law. This was twice confirmed by Cambon, on Jan. 24 in a dispatch received in Paris on Jan. 26, and again on Jan. 28 (after the Reichstag statement) in a dispatch received in Paris on Jan. 31, 1913. Serret, the military attaché, also wrote again to the minister of war (now Etienne) on Jan. 31, 1913. Cambon's dispatch of April 13, 1913, was intended to explain that the idea of the German supplementary effort stemmed back at least to the Allied successes in the Balkan wars, possibly even further, and that it was in no way influenced by French politics at home; *ibid.*, VI, pp. 346–348.

⁵² Bazire, *Libre Parole*, Jan. 29, 1913: "Ce n'est pas tant à [Poincaré que les accla-mations de la foule] s'adressent, qu'au drapeau dont il tient la hampe."

⁵³ Who, on Sept. 30, 1912, had published *Lettre Aux Jeunes France* and who preached a Protestant offensive, which would accord with the general renascence of idealism and patriotism. Cf. his speech to the Congrès National des Unions Chré-tiennes at Nantes on Nov. 1, 1912.

⁵⁴ Cf. *Revue Bleue*, Jan. 11, 1913; E. Herriot, *Le Journal*, Feb. 6 1913.

⁵⁵ Feb. 7, 1913.

⁵⁶ *Les jeunes gens d'aujourd'hui*, p. 34 ff.

⁵⁷ *Revue des Français*, April 25, 1912.

⁵⁸ *Le Progrès*, March 19, 20, 1912.

⁵⁹ *L'Echo*, Jan. 2, 1912.

⁶⁰ *J.O.S.*, Jan. 14, 1913.

⁶¹ *Le Matin*, Aug. 30, 1909; *Le Progrès*, Aug. 29, 1909; *Action française*, Sept. 2, 1908.

⁶² Cf. *Le Temps*, Nov. 29, 1909.

⁶³ E. Fournière, *Dépêche*, Feb. 10, 1913.

⁶⁴ A. Brisson, Feb. 24, 1913.

⁶⁵ Jan. 2, 1913.

⁶⁶ *G.P.*, IXL, p. 190 n. 2; *A.A.*, IV, 148.

⁶⁷ *B.D.*, X, part 2, 674–675.

⁶⁸ Harold Nicolson, *Lord Carnock* (London: 1930), pp. 397–398, Feb. 24, 1913.

⁶⁹ *L.N.*, II, 304.

⁷⁰ *Le Temps*, Feb. 21, 1913; *L'Humanité*, Feb. 24, 1913; cf. Sembat, *ibid.*, Feb. 19, 1913.

⁷¹ Cf. *Dépêche*, Feb. 23, 25, March 17, 1913.

⁷² *D.D.F.*, 3ᵉ série, V, Feb. 27, March 1, 5, 8, 1913.

⁷³ *G.P.*, IXL, 163, March 1, 1913.

⁷⁴ *A.A.*, VI, 275 ff., March 3, 1913.

⁷⁵ *Times*, March 3, 1913.

⁷⁶ *J.O.C.*, March 6, 1913, pp. 815 ff.; cf. *L.N.*, II, 43.

⁷⁷ *L'Eclair*, March 14, 1913.

⁷⁸ *L'Humanité*, March 8, 1913.

⁷⁹ *L'Aurore*, March 13, 1913, published the letter of a large number of them. Among the signatories were Anatole France, Louis Havet, Michel Bréal (all of the Institut), Meillet, Langevin, Seignobos, Ch. Andler, G. Séailles, Bouglé, Brunschwicq, Durk-heim, G. Bourgin, P. Caron, Paul Dupuy, Lucien Herr, Chartier (Alain), Felicien Challaye, Gautrot, and many others.

⁸⁰ *Les jeunes gens d'aujourd'hui* (Paris: 1913), p. 28 ff.; it is worth remembering that of 192 men appointed to diplomatic and consular vacancies between 1907 and 1927, a total of 153 held diplomas from the Ecole libre des sciences politiques. G. W. Sharp, *The French Civil Service* (New York: 1931), p. 112, quoted by R. D. Challener, "The French Foreign Office," in Gordon A. Craig and Felix Gilbert, *The Diplomats* (Prince-ton: 1953), p. 63.

⁸¹ Within a week the teachers were blamed by Messimy in the general council of the neighboring department of the Ain, by an order of the day of the departmental assembly at Chambéry, by open letters in *Le Temps* from Pugliesi-Conti, deputy from Corsica, and General Fory, O.C. 16th Army Corps, and finally in a Cabinet council of August 28.

⁸² *G.P.*, IXL, 187: "Der französische Chauvinismus habe sich ... in so vielgestaltiger und bedeutsamer Form bemerkbar gemacht, dass wir nicht umhin könnten, ihn als ein zur Beruhigung nicht beitragendes Symptom in Rechnung zu stellen." Paléologue was working hard on the new foreign minister, Jonnart. On March 2, 1913, he argued for three hours to convince him that war was imminent and that the Three-Year Law must be passed without delay to enable France to face it. See his article, "Sur le Chemin de la Guerre Mondiale," *Revue des Deux Mondes*, Oct., 1933.

[83] Cf. Jean Variot, *Propos de Georges Sorel*, p. 44; as Sorel said, "On n'avertit pas les peuples avec des revues qui tirent à cinq cents exemplaires."

[84] *Le Progrès*, March 9, 1913; *Vie Ouvrière*, March 20, 1913.

[85] *L'Humanité*, March 25, 1913; *Le Matin*, April 9, 1913; cf. Charles Andler, *Lucien Herr* (Paris: 1932), p. 180; Charles Péguy, *L'Argent (suite)* (Paris: 1932), p. 240 ff.

[86] Paul Passy, *Espoir du Monde*, April, 1913; *Vie Ouvrière*, May 20, 1913.

[87] *J.O.S.*, May 22, 1913, p. 591: Lamarzelle: "Cette propagande antimilitariste et antipatriotique dans les régiments, je n'étonnerai personne en disant qu'elle a augmenté dans des proportions considérables, depuis que le Gouvernement a déposé son projet de loi sur le retablissement du service de trois ans." Larère: "C'était fatal."

[88] *J.O.C.*, May 23, 1913, p. 1536.

[89] *J.O.C.*, May 23, 1913, p. 1531 ff.

[90] *L'Humanité*, May 26, 1913.

NOTES TO CHAPTER XI

The Debate: 1913

(Pages 120–128)

[1] *L'Echo*, Sept. 19, Oct. 10, Nov. 1, 23, 1913.

[2] *Questions de critique militaire et d'actualité*, 5e série, 255 ff.; *Le Temps*, Feb. 23, 1912; *Le Figaro*, Nov. 18, 1912.

[3] *J.O.C.*, Dec. 3, 1912.

[4] *Annales*, Dec. 15, 1912: Georges Michon, *La Préparation à la Guerre* (Paris: 1935), p. 104.

[5] *Ibid.*, 23 ff.

[6] Cf. Jaurès, *J.O.C.*, April 6, 1911; also the very interesting interpellation of Henri Michel on the Naval Estimates, *J.O.C.*, Nov. 19, 1906, for the glimpse it affords of the big companies milking both government and taxpayer in shipbuilding contracts, combining illegally to fix their bids and prices, putting pressure on administration and press to advance their own interests. See also Allard, *J.O.C* , Nov. 21, 1906.

[7] Anatole France, "L'Orme du Mail," in *Histoire Contemporaine* (Paris: 1948), p. 123.

[8] "Rien ne blesse autant les gens indécis que de s'entendre traiter d'antipatriotes."

[9] This may explain in part the result of the elections of 1914.

[10] Maurice Reclus, *Le Péguy Que J'ai Connu* (Paris: 1951), p. 114. For Péguy himself, cf. Eugen Weber, "A Persistent Prophet—Péguy," *The French Review* (April: 1954).

[11] Jérome et Jean Tharaud, *Pour les Fidèles de Péguy* (Paris: 1949), explain that the reconciliation took place when Millerand, as minister of war, led the fight for the Three-Year Law. Of course, during Millerand's ministry this had not yet been seriously mooted.

[12] Reclus, *op. cit.*, p. 115.

[13] *Ibid.*, p. 117.

[14] Jean Variot, *Propos de Georges Sorel* (1935), p. 258. But Sorel himself was a peculiarly individualistic sort of "nationalist"; thus, on Oct. 13, 1912, in a letter to Edouard Dolléans which the latter quotes in his book, *Proudhon*, p. 500, Sorel rejected the "traditionalism" of the Action française and went on to write: "Si donc votre collaborateur a voulu insinuer que je marche à la suite de Maurras, il a commis une grossière erreur." Similarly we know that he left *L'Indépendance* "quand *l'Indépendance* est devenue une revue pour pipelets nationalistes."

[15] *Action française*, April 14, 1910. Sorel wrote: "Dans vingt ans le nom de Péguy sera inséparable de la renaissance du patriotisme en France."

[16] Henri Massis, *Maurras et Notre Temps* (Paris: 1951), II, pp. 192, 194. Yet he was ready to charge Maurras and all his crew on behalf of his loyalties. When the works of Bergson were put on the Index and the philosopher became a target for anti-Semitic attacks, Péguy (quoted in *Esprit*, March, 1953, p. 338) wrote him on March 2, 1914: "... moi seul ai la plume assez dure pour réduire un Maurras, moi seul ai la poigne assez lourde pour refouler à la fois les antisémites et les fanatiques. Verrais-je, pour la première fois de ma vie, se livrer et peut-être se compromettre une bataille faute que j'y sois?"

[17] *Oeuvres* (Paris: 1932), XIV, 183; the book was first published on April 22, 1913.

[18] The navigator declared that they had lost their way because of bad visibility and unexpected air currents. Cf. Raymond Poincaré *Au Service de la France*, III, 189 ff., the correspondence in *D.D.F.*, 3e série, VI, and the letter of a soldier eye-witness in *La Vie Ouvrière*, April 20, 1913; *B.D.*, X, 2, p. 696.

[19] J. J. Joffre, *Mémoires* (Paris: 1932), I, 54.

[20] Joffre merely confirmed the words of General Dubail, *Krasny Arkhiv* (1929), Vol. 34, pp. 174–175, 178. The war, it was held by many, would be decided in the first few great clashes between massed armies. Joseph Paul-Boncour, *Entre Deux Guerres* (Paris: 1945), I, p. 235, recounts an interview with Joffre in 1915, when the latter mentioned the Messimy-Boncour counterproject: "C'était intéressant ce que vous souteniez, mais voyez-vous, nous n'avions pas le temps."

[21] *Ibid.*, pp. 235–236: "C'est peut-être parce que lui le sut, et de la bouche de Poincaré, que Clemenceau prit parti pour les trois ans. Car il avait d'abord hésité."

[22] Paul Cambon to his brother, Oct. 1, 1913, *Correspondance* (Paris: 1946), III, 53; General de Castelnau told Paul that Jules had a great deal to do with the government's resolution to propose the Three-Year Law: "Le Conseil hésitait beaucoup: tes dépêches et celles de ton attaché militaire étaient lues au Conseil et communiquées au ministre de la guerre à qui elles fournissaient des arguments." *D.D.F.*, 3e série, VI, Cambon's letter to Paléologue of March 17, 1913, and dispatches of March 30 and May 6, 1913. See also on the last-named date a dispatch from Serret.

[23] Authors also revised books already published. Thus, René Pinon's *France et Allemagne*, published in Dec., 1912, reappeared with a new chapter on armaments for its fourth edition.

[24] P. Désanges and L. Mériga, *Vie de Jaurès* (Paris: 1924), p. 194; *Dépêche*, Aug. 4, 1913.

[25] Joseph Caillaux, *Mémoires* (Paris: 1947), III, 65.

[26] *D.D.F.*, 3e série, VI, 256. A secret dispatch from Pichon to Cambon and Delcassé, dated April 5, 1913, indicates that by this date the government had reason to be certain of war, and sooner rather than later. It would be interesting to know whether such information as it had in its possession was used at all in the couloirs during the debate on the Three-Year Law. Probably not.

[27] *L'Homme Libre*, June 1, 1913.

[28] *J.O.C.*, Jan. 24, 1913, p. 22: "Vous vous imaginez qu'il s'agit d'une crise de troupes. ... Et moi je vous dis qu'il ne s'agit que d'une crise de chefs." To which Jaurès replied: "Vos chefs, comment seraient-ils responsables de la défaite, puisqu'ils étaient dans les deux camps?"

[29] Cf. "L'Assiette au beurre," *L'Aurore*, Feb. 9, 1913; *J.O.C.*, Jan. 24, 1913, pp. 30–31.

[30] Defections came one each in Hte. Saône, Manche, Orne, Maine-et-Loire, Vendée; a solid vote in (E) Meuse, Meurthe-et-Moselle, Vosges, Hte. Marne, (W) Seine Inf., Calvados, Eure, Ille-et-Vilaine, Mayenne, Loire Inf.

[31] *Le Progrès*, March 16, 1913.

[32] Sixty Radical-Socialists, 78 Radicals, 69 Gauche démocratique, 29 Union républicaine, 17 Républicains socialistes, 41 Progressistes, and 30 members of the official Right. *L'Humanité*, Jan. 22, 1913, called the cabinet "Le Ministère des Gens d'Affaires."

[33] Franklin-Bouillon, *J.O.C.*, Jan. 24, 1914.

[34] Franklin-Bouillon, *J.O.C.*, March 25, 1913; G. Ponsot, deputy of the Jura, in *L'Aurore*, May 8, 1913.

[35] *J.O.C.*, June 3, 6, 11, 13, 1913. Thus Driant, p. 194: "Nous avons la conviction de servir le pays en soutenant le ministère en ce moment, et nous le soutiendrons, tant qu'il fera son devoir envers le pays, dût-il nous payer de notre appui comme l'a fait récemment M. Barthou, par une declaration pénible qu'il a dû regretter ensuite ... que la neutralité scolaire comportait l'oubli de l'enseignement des devoirs envers Dieu."

[36] *La Dépêche*, June 4, 1913; on the same day Clemenceau commented in *L'Homme Libre*, "Il faut que le français parle: cela lui donne l'illusion de l'action."

[37] *J.O.C.*, June 8, 1913, p. 2504: Rapporteur: "Mais enfin, dans l'article 18 nous ne proposons tout de même pas la guerre!" Brizon: "Non! mais vous avez l'air de la préparer avec les trois ans."

[38] L. Tissier, *J.O.C.*, June 9, 1913; Augagneur, *ibid.*, June 10, 1913, p. 1818: "Non, MM., le pays n'est pas pour la loi de trois ans. Tout le prolétariat des villes s'est déjà soulevé contre elles, et si dans les campagnes, lentes à s'émouvoir, la protestation n'est pas aujourd'hui aussi vive, attendez quelques mois. Que les bras de la charrue ne trouvent pas celui qui devait les reprendre; attendez que les feuilles d'impôt ... frappent lourdement."

[39] *J.O.S.*, June 12, 1913: "Discussion de la proposition de loi, adoptée par la Chambre des députés, tendant à permettre l'autorisation de la pêche à la ligne le 15 juin lorsque cette date tombe un dimanche."

[40] *Le Temps*, July 1; *L'Homme Libre*, July 2.

[41] *Dépêche*, June 26, 1913; *Action française*, July 1, 1913; *L'Humanité*, July 3, 1913.

[42] *L'Humanité*: loi néfaste; *La Bataille Syndicaliste*: loi inapplicable contre la volonté populaire; *La Lanterne*: loi d'état major; *Le Radical*: loi éphémère; *L'Aurore*: preuve du mensonge gouvernemental; *La Petite République*: le nécessaire devoir; *La République Française*: la chambre a répondu au sentiment de la nation; *La Libre Parole*: vote libérateur; *La Liberté*: la France s'en trouvera bien; *L'Autorité*: cette belle fille qui finit en poisson; *Le Gaulois*: telle quelle, avec ses verrues et ses défauts, la loi nouvelle vaut mieux que l'ancienne; *Le Petit Parisien*: pas moyen de faire beaucoup mieux pour concilier les intérêts particuliers avec ceux du pays; *Le Temps*: la victoire est acquise; *Les Débats*: imperfections; *Le Figaro*: heureuse journée; *L'Eclair*: imperfections ... lacunes ... [but] donne au pays la chose essentielle qu'il attendait.

[43] Cf. *Le Progrès*, July 20, 1913.

[44] *Mercure de France*, July 1, 1913.

[45] *G.P.*, IXL, 203; see also the quotation from Herbert Hoover preceding the conclusion.

[46] *J.O.C.*, July 19, 1913; cf. *L'Homme Libre*, July 16, 1913.

[47] *L'Homme Libre*, July 19 to 27; cf. *Action française*, July 16, 1913: "plus les discours de M. Poincaré imitent le ton de M. Barrès, plus les déclarations de M. Louis Barthou affectent le genre des ordres du jour de l'Action française, et moins le public peut songer à imputer à ces messieurs la responsabilité de ces retards et de ces à-coups."

[48] *France Militaire*, July 25, 1913; Boudenoot, *J.O.S.*, July 31, 1913, p. 1265 ff.; cf. *Lettres de la Princess Radziwill* (Bologna: 1934), IV, 230 (June 6–10, 1913), MM. de Barante and de Laborde who tell her: "Sans l'Allemagne, jamais on aurait obtenu le service de trois ans"; Iswolsky gives a similar opinion, *ibid.*, p. 245 (Oct. 25, 1913).

[49] *J.O.S.*, Aug. 5, 1913, p. 1311. General Bernhardi's *Germany and the Next War* was published in the spring of 1912. His writings on military matters were extremely influential.

[50] By 244 votes to 36. Herriot and Pelletan were among the 36, Combes and Sarrien abstained.

[51] *Action française*, Aug. 8, 1913: "Un pareil renvoi, mais ca serait l'effondrement de la loi! s'est écrié M. Barthou. Le vote des sénateurs a répété et confirmé son cri."

NOTES TO CHAPTER XII

THE DECISION: 1913–1914

(Pages 129–144)

[1] Junius, Aug. 23, 1913.

[2] Cf. Jean Darville in the *Cahiers du Cercle Proudhon* quoted by the *Action française*, Sept. 4, 1913, and the reply of Georges Valois, *ibid.*

[3] *Action française*, Sept. 11, 1913.

[4] Aug. 23, 1913, *Etudes Diplomatiques*, II, 393–394. In this he may have been doubly naïve.

[5] Oct. 24, 1913, *Mes Cahiers* (1929), X, 205.

[6] *Le Rappel*, Oct. 3, 1913.

[7] Franklin-Bouillon, Malvy, and Chautemps were elected vice-presidents of the executive committee.

[8] That the Barthou ministers had to go, cf. Jaurès, *Dépêche*, Jan. 1, 1914.

[9] Margins at this time were exceedingly narrow; on December 1 the government had won 291 to 270; on December 2 it lost 290 to 265. The American ambassador wrote: "one of the factors contributing to the defeat was a coterie of bankers that had not been included in the new loan negotiations; another is the resentment against the three years' military service." American Embassy in Paris, Correspondence 1913 (class. 800.2 Dec. 5, 1913).

[10] Raymond Poincaré, *Au Service de la France* (Paris: 1926), III, 339.

[11] *J.O.C.*, Dec. 3, 1913.

[12] Dec. 3, 1913.

[13] Dec. 7, 1913.

[14] Dec. 13, 1913: "L'homme éloquent et si bien doué qu'est M. Barthou n'aurait pas glissé sur cette pelure si l'unification du parti radical-socialiste n'avait rendu titubante la marche du ministère modéré."

[15] *J.O.C.*, Dec. 2, 1913, p. 3732. When the result was announced there was great applause on the Left and extreme Left.

Vaillant: A bas les trois ans!

J. Reinach: Je demande que cette interruption figure au Journal Officiel.

Driant: Vive la France!

H. Paté: Vous n'avez pas le droit de dire que le vote est dirigé contre la loi de trois ans.

Millevoye: Je demande la parole. ...

A l'extrême-gauche: Vive la République!

Barthou: Vive la France!

C. Danielou: Il faut que l'interruption de M. Vaillant soit au Journal Officiel. C'est la signification du vote.

C. Leboucq: Vive la France!

Raffin-Dugens: A bas la réaction!

Driant: Vive les trois ans!

Millevoye: Je demande la parole. ...

[16] "Non pas un homme, un sourire," E. Mounier would write twenty years later in "La Révolution contre les Mythes," *Esprit*, March, 1934, a description good also for the prewar years.

[17] Dec. 11, 1913. It is, in fact, doubtful whether Doumergue who expected war to break out from one day to the next would have lent a hand against the law. Cf. also John C. Cairns, "International Politics and the Military Mind," *Journal of Modern History*, XXV, 3 (Sept., 1953), 285 *passim*

[18] Dec. 14, 1913.

[19] Bienvenu-Martin, *J.O.S.*, Dec. 11, 1913.

[20] It is probable that Clemenceau would not have supported the new cabinet as he did, had it expressed itself differently; cf. *J.O.S.*, Dec. 16, 1913, p. 1531.

[21] *J.O.S.*, Dec. 16, 1913.

[22] *J.O.C.*, Dec. 11, 1913, p. 3747.

[23] Dec. 12, 1913.

[24] *D.D.F.*, 3ᵉ série, VIII, 247, Klobukowski to Pichon, Brussels, Sept. 22, 1913.

[25] J. Cambon to Pichon, sent Nov. 22, 1913, marked "reçu direction politique, Dec. 23, 1913." (*D.D.F.*, 3ᵉ série, VIII, 653.) This was confirmed in a private letter, Nov. 30, 1913, *ibid.*, 698. Paléologue told Joffre and Castelnau; Pichon told Nisard.

[26] *L.N.*, II, 197; for a contrary view see J. Noulens, "Le Gouvernement Français à la Veille de la Guerre," *Revue des Deux Mondes*, Feb. 1913, 608–609: "Le secret fut observé avec un souci ... poussé jusqu'au risque de rendre la démarche inutile. C'est ainsi que les ministres du cabinet Doumergue qui succéda, le 10 décembre 1913, au cabinet Barthou demeurèrent dans l'ignorance des menaces de l'empereur Guillaume. Ils ne les ont connues, le fait est à peine croyable, que par la publication du Livre Jaune de 1914." But cf. *B.D.*, X, 2, p. 723, for Paléologue's discretion.

[27] *Au Service de la France*, Vol. IV, p. 55.

[28] *L'Aurore*, Jan. 3, 1914.

[29] *L'Echo*, Jan. 5, 1914.

[30] Bouglé, *Dépêche*, Jan. 12, 1914.

[31] *L'Humanité*, Jan. 29, 1914.

[32] *L'Echo*, Feb. 6, 1914; Marc Reville in *L'Aurore*, Feb. 22, 1914.

[33] *Albert de Mun* (Paris: 1925) p. 329.

[34] *Le Temps*, Feb. 28, 1914; M. Brossé in *L'Aurore*, March 11, 1914.

[35] *J.O.C.*, March 17, 1914.

[36] *L'Homme Libre*, March 18, 1914; *Le Progrès*, April 5, 1914.

[37] Bazire, *Libre Parole*, Feb. 25, 1914; cf. Brossé, *L'Aurore*, March 13, 1914: "En 1898, on pouvait se permettre d'être partisan de l'impôt sur le revenu, y compris l'impôt sur la Rente, il y avait si peu de chance que cela fût jamais! Mais en 1914, ce n'est plus la même chose. Le Sénat est à pied d'oeuvre; suivant qu'il dira oui ou non, l'impôt sera ou ne sera pas. Et beaucoup qui avaient jadis dit oui, disent maintenant non." See also *History of The Times* (London: 1952), vol. IV, part 1, pp. 160–161.

[38] *Action française*, March 26, 1914.

[39] *Revue Hebdomadaire*, April 4, 1914.

[40] Brossé, *L'Aurore*, April 11, 1914.

[41] Robert Cornilleau, *De Waldeck-Rousseau à Poincaré* (Paris: 1926), pp. 313–314: "La Fédération des Gauches ... semblait une sorte de Patrie Française, plus à gauche." In this connection, Barrès was right to comment on Déroulède's death that the great patriot died just as the ideas he had always fought for were really reviving. See *L'Echo*, July 13, 1913, and Feb. 3, 1914.

[42] *D.D.F.*, 3ᵉ série, X, 293; from the French chargé d'affaires in London, April 28, 1914.

[43] *La Libre Parole*, April 30, 1914.

[44] *Junius*, June 8, 1914.

[45] *La Lanterne*, April 30, 1914.

[46] *La Lanterne*, May 9, 1914.

[47] See the appeals of the Fédération des Gauches and of the Alliance Républicaine Démocratique, May 10, 1914.

[48] Pelletan, *Dépêche*, May 24, 1914: "Il n'y a pas de majorité de gauche possible avec le maintien de la loi de trois ans et sans la véritable réforme fiscale, inséparable de la déclaration controlée."

[49] Junius, May 14, 1914. Of course, the socialist-voting peasant was no more revolutionary in 1914 than the communist-voting peasant is today. For an excellent analysis of the peasant's attitude in this connection see André Siegfried, *Géographie Electorale de l'Ardèche sous la 3ᵉ République* (Paris: 1949).

[50] *L'Echo*, May 1, 1914.

[51] May 12, 1914.

[52] *Le Petit Parisien*, May 13, 1914; *L'Aurore*, May 21, 1914.

[53] *L'Echo*, May 14, 1914.

[54] *Dépêche*, May 22, 1914; see n. 48.

[55] Cf. *Le Temps*, April 25, 1914.

[56] Brossé, *L'Aurore*, April 30, 1914.

[57] May 3, 1914.

[58] Georges Michon, *La Préparation à la Guerre* (Paris: 1935), p. 197.

[59] *L'Humanité* and *Le Progrès*, June 7, 1914.

[60] Poincaré, *Au Service de la France*, IV, 144.

[61] René Viviani, *Réponse au Kaiser* (Paris: 1923), p. 75.

[62] Bourgeois judged the Three-Year Law essential to French security. In a letter to Charles Richet, dated May 10, 1913, he explained the basis of his attitude: "Ce serait désarmer la cause de la paix, que d'affaiblir ceux qui préparent le règne du droit." Quoted in Georges Michon, *La Préparation à la Guerre* (Paris: 1935), p. 152 n. 2. The old statesman mistrusted Viviani's intentions.

[63] Herbette commented in *L'Echo*, June 7, 1914: "C'est sur la loi de trois ans qu'à échoué la combinaison Viviani. Du coup le problème de la défense nationale qui dominait déjà notre politique extérieure, domine aussi notre politique du dedans. Une coupure se fait, plus profonde que n'importe quelles distinctions de partis: d'un coté sont ceux qui veulent réduire le service militaire, de l'autre ceux qui ne veulent pas y toucher ... il faut être pour ou contre les trois ans."

[64] *L'Echo*, June 12, 1914.

[65] *J.O.C.*, June 12, 1914, p. 2459.

[66] Not only was the success of the visit in peril but also, suggested an Austrian diplomat writing in June, 1914, the presidential office itself: the governmental crisis could lead to a presidential crisis. Cf. *Aussenpolitik*, VIII, 201.

The Russian press was anxious about the fate of the Three-Year Law and the general political situation in France. This was taken as indicating official opinion. Thus, on June 13, 1914, the French chargé d'affaires in St. Petersburg sent home an analysis of an article published that evening by the *Gazette de la Bourse*, entitled "La Russie est prête: La France doit l'être également." The article demanded that the Three-Year Law should not be touched at the very time when Russia was making ever greater sacrifices. The dispatch was received in Paris three days later. *D.D.F.*, 3e série, X, 542. Paléologue's visit to Paris at this time may have been caused by knowledge of the dissatisfaction in high Russian circles, and not only by a natural inclination toward warlike and Machiavellian meddling which Albertini ascribes to him in *The Origins of the War of 1914*, vol. I, pp. 553–555.

[67] Jacques Piou, *Albert de Mun* (Paris: 1925), p. 332, describes the mood of the Chamber after the election of 1914: "Les défenseurs des trois ans avaient la loi qu'ils voulaient et désiraient ne rien risquer; les autres craignaient de compromettre par trop de hâte leurs chances de revision. Tous d'ailleurs, fatigués de la lutte électorale, désiraient, sinon la paix, au moins une suspension d'armes."

[68] June 14, 16, 1914. This actually happened, and the Senate voted the income tax in July, 1914.

[69] *J.O.C.*, June 16, 1914.

[70] All three dated June 17, 1914.

[71] *Dépêche*, June 18, 1914.

[72] June 18, 21, 1914.

[73] Cf. *J.O.C.*, June 12, 1914, p. 2453.

[74] *L'Eclair*, July 5, 1914.

[75] *L'Homme Libre*, July 6, 1914.

[76] Adolphe Messimy, *Souvenirs* (Paris: 1937), pp. 124–125.

[77] *J.O.C.*, July 7, 1914, p. 2717.

[78] *L'Aurore*, July 17, 1914.

[79] *J.O.C.*, May 11, 1907. This had met with general approval: Charles Benoist: "C'est bien vrai." Paul Constans: "C'est comme à la Chambre."

[80] July 19, 1914.

[81] *Le Progrès*, July 19, 1914.

[82] Daniel Halévy, *Décadence de la Liberté* (Paris: 1931), pp. 78–79; Desbois and Descolas, *Correspondance* (Paris: 1921), p. 14.

[83] *Le Progrès*, July 27, 1914.

[84] *Le Progrès*, July 28, 1914.

[85] Emile Vandervelde, *Souvenirs d'un Militant Socialiste* (Paris: 1939), p. 171; Marcel Prélot, *Evolution politique du socialisme français* (Paris: 1939), p. 203.

[86] Colonel House to President Wilson from London, June 17, 1914, Charles Seymour, *The Intimate Papers of Colonel House* (London: 1926), I, 269. The Austrian ambassador seems to have had a deeper understanding of the circumstances. Cf. Szeczen writing from Paris on July 28, 1914, *Aussenpolitik*, VIII, 844–845: "Abgesehen von gewissen nationalistisch-chauvinistischen Kreisen und von militärischen Kreisen, die von Fach wegen kriegerisch gesinnt sind, wünscht, glaube ich, in Frankreich eigentlich niemand den Krieg, man hat aber in den letzten Jahren so viel vom bevorstehenden unvermeidlichen Kriege gesprochen, dass die Bevölkerung sich an diese Idee gewöhnt hat und die Möglichkeit eines kriegerischen Konfliktes mit Resignation hinnimmt."

[87] Cf. P. Vignaux, "Le Mouvement Ouvrier et la 3e République," in *Oeuvre de la 3e République* (Montreal: n.d.), p. 153.

[88] *L'Humanité*, July 31, 1914.

[89] Drumont, *La Libre Parole*, Aug. 1, 1914.

[90] *L'Echo*, Aug. 9, 1914.

[91] On Aug. 2, 1914, at a great meeting in the Salle Wagram, Vaillant declared: "En présence de l'agression, les Socialistes rempliront tout leur devoir, pour la Patrie, pour la République, et pour l'Internationale."

[92] André Gide, *Journal* (Paris: 1948), p. 648, notes on March 3, 1918, his feeling that the resistance that the *Action française* is preparing against the inevitable revolution makes that group the only alternative to socialism. "Le groupement de *l'Action française* ne vous plaît pas? Ce n'est pas que moi-même je l'estime le meilleur —mais c'est le seul!"

NOTES TO CONCLUSION

(Pages 145–160)

[1] Cf. Lieutenant Jean Taboureau's lectures at St. Maixent and St. Cyr, "Le Sophisme antipatriotique," *Spectateur Militaire*, Jan. 15, 1912; Commandant René Brenner, *Patriote Avant Tout* (1912); and review by Boissonnet, *Revue Militaire Générale*, XIII (Feb., 1913), 287–288. The case of General Michel is a good example of the nationalist attitude to nonconformity. Like every other doctrinaire, the nationalist is essentially exclusivist and intolerant of ideas and panaceas other than his own. Hence his almost inevitable inclination to authoritarianism; hence also his insistence on unity and discipline (ideally accepted by all men of good will but in fact to be imposed from above because most men are too foolish, selfish, or short-sighted to do freely the nationalist's biddings).

[2] Cf. Jean Galtier-Boissière, *Troisième République* (Paris: 1935), p. 213 ff.

[3] Speech of Oct. 20, 1912, in his *Pour la défense nationale* (1913), 106.

[4] John C. Cairns, "International Politics and the Military Mind in France," *Journal of Modern History* (Sept., 1953).

[5] Anatole France, *Histoire Contemporaine* (Paris: 1948), pp 742–743.

⁶ Even Augagneur seemed inclined to let sleeping laws lie: *J.O.C.*, June 12, 1914, p. 2453.

⁷ Frederick Schuman, *War and Diplomacy in the French Republic* (Chicago: 1931), p. 414.

⁸ The public reaction to the various crises has already been discussed in the body of the work. I have not gone into it in greater detail partly because it has been thoroughly covered by O. J. Hale, E. Anderson, and E. M. Carroll, but chiefly because the influence of these crises on the wider public was relatively slight. Their frequency and the efforts of men aware of their implications to keep them before the public eye were more important. It is notable that the new nationalism which might conceivably have sprung up in 1905 smoldered through the years of relative calm which followed and made its mark only in the years of strain and almost constant crisis, 1911–1914.

⁹ As Bainville says of the struggle of April–May, 1914, in his *Histoire de Trois Générations* (Paris: 1934), pp. 232–235: "L'ensemble de la nation n'y participait que faiblement et de loin. C'est dans les régions supérieures de l'opinion et dans les états-majors du personnel parlementaire que les deux tendances se retrouvèrent aux prises." See also my article, "Political Language and Political Realities " *Cambridge Journal*, VII (April, 1954), 408–423.

¹⁰ March 3, 1913. As Anatole France writes of the local prefect in *L'Orme du Mail*: "Il lui plaisait que les journaux du gouvernement et ceux de l'opposition, compromis les uns et les autres dans les affaires financières, eussent perdu tout crédit pour la louange ou l'injure. La feuille socialiste, seule pure, était seule violente. Mais elle était très pauvre et la peur qu'elle inspirait rejetait les esprits vers le gouvernement."

¹¹ Dufferin to Roseberry, Nov. 3, 1893, *B.D.*, II, 285–288.

¹² *A.A.*, VI (Erster Ergänzungsband), 303, Berlin, Feb. 20, 1914.

¹³ *Ibid.*, p. 317, Paris, May 8, 1914; cf. also vol. V, 261, for same document appearing in a circular from Brussels, May 16, 1914.

¹⁴ Jules Isaac, *Un débat historique* (Paris: 1933), p. 24.

¹⁵ *J.O.C.*, June 12, 1914, p. 2461.

¹⁶ Interview in *La Dépêche*, Feb. 16, 1914. Significantly enough, only shortly before this Julien Benda had put forward the idea of Bergsonism as an intellectual Boulangism (*Une philosophie pathétique* [Paris: 1913], p. 15).

BIBLIOGRAPHY

BIBLIOGRAPHY

ANY ACCOUNT OF THE SOURCES used in this study must begin with the names of MM. Siegfried, Goguel, and Lavau who have given such admirable accounts of continuity and change in French electoral geography. Their works and other publications of the *Cahiers de la Fondation Nationale des Sciences Politiques* have been of great help to me. While I find myself in agreement with their general conclusions, it may be worthwhile to point out that most of the conclusions are not relevant to this study, where only their *facts* are used as corroborative evidence. In one instance alone, M. Siegfried's classic study of political opinion in the west, have I gone so far as to use not only facts but general opinions as evidence, and I gladly acknowledge my debt to him. But the *Tableau Politique*, published in 1913, is as much a contemporary document as it is a work of scholarship, and its views deserve to be considered as evidence of contemporary opinion, politically as well as scientifically significant.

It is unfortunate that more studies are not available of political opinion in the well-defined area of this study. A number of theses for the *Diplôme d'Etudes Supérieures* of the Sorbonne have, however, been written from this point of view and deserve attention: G. Palmade, "L'Evolution de l'opinion politique dans le départment du Gers, 1848–1936"; Yves Magadur, "L'Evolution de l'opinion politique au faubourg Saint-Antoine, 1871–1914"; and, for the region around the Gare de l'Est, J. van Regermorter, "L'Evolution de l'opinion politique à Paris, 10ᵉ arrondissement, 1848–1914." They are more concerned with presenting facts than with their interpretation. A more important work, which has not yet appeared, is Professor A. Railliet's thesis, "Géographie de la France politique du Nord-Est."

During the next fifteen years other material should become available for a more thorough appreciation of this period. I wonder whether, when the archives are opened, we shall have occasion to revise judgments that, at best, can only remain partial and tentative.

Many students are dissuaded from approaching a subject less than fifty years old "because all the documents are not yet available." Will they be when the archives open? Quite apart from the willful or thoughtless losses, mislayings, destruction; quite apart from the habit (so popular in France) of ministers carting away all the papers they can at the end of their tenure of office; quite apart from the fact that much of the information is (or was) in the private archives of banks, companies, and families; will not the historian, in the end, be faced with the eternal problem of choice, of selection, of what to believe, of what to stress, of what to point out?

I look forward to reading through the prefects' reports of 1914, if they still exist when they should be made available in 1965. Although certainly there will be found in them much to interest and amuse, I doubt that they would change my present impression of the situation.

On the Moroccan affairs, particularly on events between Algeçiras and Agadir, it is more difficult to form an opinion. Certainly the events cannot be described in the splendid isolation of a monograph, if only because during this period Franco-German conversations "on Morocco" dealt largely with the Congo Basin (Hence the N'goko Sangha affair) and financial interests seem to have been as or more active than political ones. When the N'goko Sangha proposals were mentioned before a parliamentary commission, the hostility shown seems to have stemmed rather from a desire to frustrate certain financial combinations than from principial antagonism toward a Franco-German *rapprochement*.

As the earliest talks had taken place between businessmen, not diplomats, it is doubtful whether fresh documents will appear to throw light on this question. On the German side, similar factors affected the issue, and research met with similar difficulties in spite of F. W. Pick's welcome publication of the illuminating diaries of Dr. Regendanz in *Searchlight on German Africa*. It is therefore fortunate that this work is concerned rather with the effects than with the causes of these often enigmatic goings-on.

Obscure interests were continually trying to affect private and public opinion. Indeed, Austrian diplomatic dispatches from Paris and Brussels show a firm conviction that the French press and government were enfeuded to Russia. We are also fortunate to have in *L'Abominable Vénalité de la Presse* a classic collection of documents concerning such activities. First published in a series of articles in *L'Humanité* of 1923, they might well, as Georges Weill comments in his study *Le Journal*, be regarded with some suspicion: "mais le nom du principal rédacteur de ces lettres, Arthur Raffalovitch, économiste honnête et consciencieux, ne permet point de les écarter comme négligeables." If the documents have their importance, the influence on the public of the activities they disclose was, in my opinion, very slight from the point of view pertinent here.

The firm base of my work lies in a relatively small number of collections of documents, reviews, and newspapers. Concerning the last, it has not been easy to determine what periodicals would best contribute to an understanding of the subject, particularly as objective studies of the French press are hard to find. Weill's *Le Journal* offers little to our purpose, and Raymond Manévy's *Histoire de la Presse* (1945) (his *Presse de la 3ᵉ République* [1955] appeared too late to be used) begins in 1914 with a cursory chapter on prewar conditions. It is not difficult to discover the orientation of a particular publication, but it is almost impossible to discover its circulation figures. Those given by Weill in general terms concern only the very great Paris dailies; neither the *Newspaper Press Directory* nor *Willing's Press Guide* give the circulation of the newspapers they list; Manévy is vague.

Manévy does indicate however that in 1914 the sales of *Action française*, *Temps*, *Figaro*, and *Gaulois* stood between thirty and eighty thousand; *L'Autorité*, *Gazette de France*, *Libre Parole*, *Patrie*, *Soleil*, all nationalist, below twenty thousand. The Catholic *Croix* and the nationalist *Presse* passed the hundred-thousand mark; but so did the Socialist *Humanité*. Other publications of the extreme Left, like Hervé's *Bataille Syndicaliste* and Almereyda's *Bonnet Rouge*, challenged the circulation levels of *Action française* and *Figaro*. Failing further investigation, such figures must be treated with caution.

Some indication of a paper's importance may also be found in the judgment of the editors of the publication *Newspaper Press Directory* that, unlike *Willing's*, discriminated in its listings. More significant still, perhaps, is the disappearance of a number of newspapers that had drawn their readers from a public of nationalist sympathies: *La Nation*, *Le National*, *La France Militaire*, in 1908; *Le Pays* in 1911; *Le XIXᵉ Siècle* in 1912. The rebirth of this latter as *Le XXᵉ Siècle* did not apparently restore its fortunes, and the editors of the *Newspaper Press Directory* dropped it from their list of the principal political papers. It is however hard to say what the criterion for inclusion in this list may have been, since it included Bérenger's *Action*, of very limited circulation, though admittedly read in parliamentary circles, and not the *Action française*. More accurate judgment can be expected in the estimates of Arthur Raffalovitch, and some useful indications may be found in his dispatches mentioned above.

The names of those publications used methodically are given below. Those listed as "consulted" have not been read through from 1905 to 1914 as the others have. However, I have tried to cast my net as widely as I could by reading through seventeen daily newspapers and two periodicals of this time.

L'Illustration apart and needing no comment, on the Right all shades of opinion are represented from the monarchist *Gaulois* of Arthur Meyer and *l'Eclair* edited by the Bonapartist Judet, through *La Libre Parole*, grand old standard-bearer of anti-Semitic nationalism, which changes in 1910 from the hands of Drumont to those of the liberal Catholics, Denais and Bazire, to the great conservative daily *L'Echo de Paris* in which wrote de Mun, Bourget, and Barrès, as well as Delcassé's great admirer, André Mévil.

I have tried to choose newspapers representative of or with an influence on public opinion, not simply publications which, like *La Cocarde*, *L'Autorité*, or *Le Soleil* preached only to a narrow circle of the converted—a shrinking circle at that. Thus, of the purely nationalist papers I have read through only *L'Action française* because of its growing influence and lively activity.

More interesting from the viewpoint of the phenomenon to be investigated—the *Drang Nach Rechts* of individuals, parties, and classes, and the growing assertiveness of their new nationalism—were the organs of the Left and of the center, which, during the post-1898 period of the bloc, had sided with it. The first point to note concerning this is that the great organs of the "independent," "popular," or "center" press belonged to men or groups whose economic interests carried them to the Right, and whose political easement from bloc on the Left to Union on the Right is a significant part of the tale. *Le Figaro* edited by Gaston Calmette is republican, conservative, and academic. *Le Matin* has two commanding personalities: the editor, Stéphane Lauzanne, another admirer of Delcassé, and the owner, Bunau-Varilla. The result is vulgar, patriotic, and somewhat reminiscent of the *Daily Express*. *Le Petit Parisien* and *Le Temps* have nothing in common but their devotion to the moderate interests of the *Alliance démocratique*, and follow its shift from the bloc to Poincaré.

To their Left, the Radical press offers the picture of growing awareness of and reaction against a danger it had thought past. *L'Aurore*, still affected by Clemenceau, though he had left it in 1906, often reflects his reactions to the growing danger of war and his uncomfortable support of the detestable Poincaré's necessary policy; so eventually does his *Homme Libre*. On the other hand *La Lanterne*, organ of Combes, stands firm against all aspects of Poincarism, while the Socialist *Humanité* fights the ominous trend with vigor and vehemence.

The only two great provincial newspapers I read were both of the Left. I thought it wisest to look far away from Paris, where the metropolitan press takes longer to penetrate and a strong local orientation already exists; and yet acquaintance with these great dailies leaves no doubt of their domination by Paris. Thus, even in the provincial capitals of Lyon and Toulouse where local tradition is strongest, the centralization of the country enforces its rule and makes the politician turn as does the sunflower toward the center of political power whence come the *mots d'ordre* for local activities.

Like myself, E. M. Carroll, whose book is discussed below, after a "rather extensive examination" of a number of provincial newspapers, concluded that they "failed to show any great difference in their reactions to foreign affairs from those of the Paris press." He adds: "Nevertheless, there is need of a more careful comparison between the Paris press and the provincial newspapers than has been possible in this study. In its absence, the latter cannot safely be neglected." The statement also applies to the present study with the important qualification that, as explained in the introduction, a study of the nationalist revival from 1905 to 1914 is more likely than Mr. Carroll's work to focus on changes mirrored in the Paris press.

I have also constulted other newspapers, like the *Lyon Républicain* that belonged to the city's Socialist mayor, Victor Augagneur, the nationalist *Patrie* of Lucien Millevoye, and most particularly the Assomptionist's *La Croix*, pattern of many local editions of the same name and a strong influence among the Catholic small *bourgeoisie*. I would have read more had I not found after a certain point that my evidence was simply repeating itself beyond the needs of reasonable corroboration.

A word of warning might be added at this point concerning the evidence of foreign publications, most of which I read *after* I had become familiar with the tone of the French press throughout these years. The accuracy of their evidence is, of course, not as important as their impression of, or their reaction to, events and changes taking place in France. To these they are fully awake by 1912, and their evidence of the new spirit is useful. Their writing becomes useless, however, when it tries to interpret public opinion in any detail as, for instance, the *Times* tried to do at the time of the Three-Year Law debate. Then it is clearly inaccurate reporting, often indicative of wishful thinking, often, too, apparently taken from the *Temps* or *L'Echo de Paris*.

In order to enter, as it were, into the skin of the period, I considered it necessary to read a great number of books not directly relevant to the subject. It seemed necessary to know not only every aspect of the background of the events under consideration, but also the circumstances of the people involved in them: the life they led or would like to lead, the books they read, the news they saw in their newspapers, and their preoccupations. Novels, biographies, pamphlets, letters, and diaries have therefore been read, some of which receive no mention in text or footnote, or have even been considered irrelevant to the bibliography, but which helped me to understand a situation or a protagonist. Lucien Rebatet's *Les Décombres* is one of these, throwing an interesting light on the later developments of the Action française and on the character of its leaders. Such works as have been listed in the bibliography are those I thought most relevant.

Interesting in this connection have been the letters, diaries, and memoirs of men who were important protagonists of my story, or close to them. Thus the letters of Paul Cambon are a mine of information easily comparable to the resources of the *Livre Noir*. The *Cahiers* of Barrès should be read together with the articles and speeches published in *Scènes et Doctrines du Nationalisme* for an understanding of the role he played in the making and development of nationalism, and of his own changes in attitude. Before 1914 the popular influence of his novels was chiefly restricted to the two trilogies of the *Culte du Moi* and the *Roman de l'Energie Nationale*. A novel like *Colette Baudoche*, though enthusiastically reviewed by Paul Bourget as early as 1909, does not appear to have been widely read before the war; its argument, like that of *Au service de l'Allemagne*, was not popular. As for his campaign to save churches from decay, that appears to have touched only narrow circles, though apparently ones which were influential enough to afford it partial success.

Little has been written *on* Barrès that a reading *of* Barrès could leave necessary: the book of Jacques Madaule is good, but like that of Professor Curtius it has little new to tell the student already acquainted with the man and his work. Even Thibaudet, who has written such a true and sparkling study of Maurras, is uninspired on the subject of Barrès. Perhaps the important thing to note is that, whereas to the great public Barrès continued to appear as the inspired troubadour of nationalism, to militant young nationalists of the Action française he soon became a back number. The confusion was never cleared up; favored by the misunderstanding of one side, which took his doctrines to be those of "nationalism," and by the respect of the other side, which sometimes placed him with Déroulède in the category of sacred relics, Barrès was able to serve as *trait d'union* between followers of different conceptions, who, by the use of a common name and by their belief in the sameness of the phenomenon or the policy therein represented, acquired a unity they otherwise might well have lacked.

The first four volumes of Poincaré's voluminous *Souvenirs*, like the memoirs of his rival, Joseph Caillaux, are full of information that has been contested and must be used with care. I have indicated in notes where different sources of evidence appear to conflict, and have only used them in conjunction with other evidence, or, unsupported, when the subject they treat does not appear to warrant falsification. The first volume of Paul-Boncour's memoirs, *Entre Deux Guerres*, is especially informative about the Three-Year Law struggle in which the author, with a rival project of his own, played an important role. For his part Maurice Paléologue, Poincaré's old schoolfellow and friend (they called each other *tu*—a practice not readily indulged in by either Poincaré or members of the *Carrière*) has published important fragments of his diaries. Their worth would be greater if the odor of later editing did not hang so heavily about their pages, but even so their interest is unusual.

The activities and personalities of the Action française, for which the best evidence is to be found in the newspaper itself and in certain works of Maurras, *Au Signe de Flore* and *Kiel et Tanger* with its successive prefaces, are chronicled by Léon Daudet and, later, by Henri Massis. Louis Dimier, who later quarreled with Maurras, is a useful witness; less so the rather self-centered Georges Valois. The nationalist revival itself receives contemporary notice and expression in the works of Agathon, Chéradame, Pilaut, Pinon, Victor Giraud, Etienne Rey, and Gaston Riou among others. The latter's *Aux Ecoutes de la France qui Vient*, excellent evidence of the spirit of the times, is best read in the first edition of 1913. Later editions have been revised and lack long passages on the ideas of the years when it was written, passages judged by the author to be out of date after the war. In a class apart I might mention authors dealing specifically with Alsace-Lorraine, especially M. Leroy, the Belgian journalist Dumont-Wilden, or Delahache, whose work, first published in 1909, was crowned by the Académie française and went into a fourth edition in 1911.

Both evidence of and fuel to the new fire lay in the crop of investigations published in reviews and books at this time. The names of Camille Mauclair, Emile Henriot, and Agathon are among the most important of these, but echoes of the prewar spirit can still be heard in two *enquêtes* of 1924—Varillon and Rambaud on *La jeune littérature*, and Maurice Vaussard on nationalism itself. The findings of such investigations, it was generally recognized, had only a limited validity and application, but they touched a lively section of the *minorité agissante* and had a propaganda value of their own.

A broader field of investigation, covered by a different method, was chosen by J. F. Scott for his study of nationalism in French education (*Patriots in the Making*, New York, 1916). This very interesting book suffers a little from the author's insistence on manuals of the 'eighties whose popularity tended to wane in prewar years. In 1902 a new tendency had appeared when the *Plans d'Etudes et Programmes d'Enseignement dans les Lycées et Collèges de Garçons* supplanted the *revanchard* patriotic patterns laid down by Paul Bert, and this was followed in 1909 by similar programs for the Ecoles Supérieures de Garçons and the Ecoles Normales Primaires. This led to the popularization of texts like those of Aulard and Debidour, Seignobos and Langlois, Jallifier and Vast, and to protests like George Duruy's in his book *Ecole et Patrie* and André Tardieu's in "La Campagne contre la Patrie" (*Revue des Deux Mondes*, July, 1913). Other reactions have been discussed in the body of the work. It is true that, by the time Tardieu wrote, patriotism was reappearing in the textbooks of men like Albert Malet, but only slowly; and with striking exceptions the lower and the higher echelons of the teaching profession were occupied by veterans of the Dreyfus Affair, many of them good patriots, but nearly all antinationalistic.

This telescoping of patriotic manifestations before 1905 and after 1911, which somewhat mars the work of J. F. Scott, is a mistake made by many students of the period. Thus, F. L. Schuman, on page 353 of *War and Diplomacy in the French Republic*, sees the striking unanimity of French opinion in August, 1914, as revealing the ease with which patriotic sentiment can be mobilized by the government for a resort to arms. O. J. Hale, *Germany and the Diplomatic Revolution*, makes no such mistake, and his book provides a thorough and detailed study of the interaction between international politics and public opinion, with the press as the lever by which each side exerts pressure on the other. The press also provides the most interesting evidence in E. M. Carroll's important *French Public Opinion and Foreign Affairs, 1870–1914*, whose later chapters deal almost directly with movement and manipulation of opinion. The book, emphasizing the influence of foreign affairs on political activity, provides a solid counterpart to more recent theses describing French foreign policy as dominated by internal issues with which public opinion is almost exclusively concerned: Miss B. R. Leaman, *The Influence of Domestic Politics on Foreign Affairs in France, 1898–1905* (*J.M.H.*, December, 1942); Mr. J. R. Cairns, *Politics and Foreign Policy: The French Parliament, 1911–14* (*Canadian Historical Review*, September, 1953).

Mr. Carroll limits the "nationalist revival" to the years 1911–1914, and sees it largely as a tool or manufacture of politicians eager to secure military preparedness, the solidity of the alliance network, or merely a point in negotiations, and who use or encourage nationalist propaganda to achieve this purpose. He describes the employment of calculated press leaks to create a turmoil to be used as a countermeasure at the conference table; the use of suspense to inflame public opinion; and the use of money to improve the education of a necessary press. On this last point his discussion shows conclusively how little real influence press subsidies exerted. For the same period E. N. Anderson, *The First Moroccan Crisis*, and Harold Nicolson's biography of his father, *Lord Carnock*, provide details of international operations that had a distinct, though indirect, influence on the movement of opinion in France.

Evidence of such a movement of opinion is also available from certain foreign sources, collections of documents apart, like the memoirs of the German ambassador in Paris, Freiherr von Schoen, a moderate man who meant well; Stieve's study of Izvolsky's activities, based on published Russian documents and showing a man certainly not devoid of duplicity; and the letters written by the Princess Radziwill to her friend, the Italian General de Robilant, interesting letters that owe their importance to the connection of the Princess, *née* Blanc, with French society, aristocratic and *haut-bourgeois*.

Concerning the role of this latter social group, I cannot omit mentioning the extremely suggestive thesis put forward by E. Beau de Loménie in his *Responsabilités des Dynasties Bourgeoises*, whose second volume, tracing the close relationship between personalities and political and economic affairs curiously illuminates certain political activities. Like all books built round a theory, it is spoiled by exaggeration, but well worth reading. A. Hamon's *Les Maîtres de la France* traces in three laborious volumes the intricate personal connections between members of the ruling minority and the interests they so often share. Although the book is chiefly concerned with the realities of a later period, it provides a useful and heavily-documented comment on the generalizations of Loménie. The two make a prejudiced but interesting pair.

The best account of contemporary Catholic activities is Dansette's *Histoire Religieuse de la France Contemporaine*, vol. II. Earlier historians, especially Lecanuet and Debidour, have little to say to our purpose about the period after the separation; Bodley is interesting but insufficient, his essay, *The Church in France*, written too soon to be much help with developments after 1905; Brugerette sometimes quotes Lecanuet and is of little help otherwise; Briand's report tells us more about Briand than about the results of his work. Dansette, on the other hand, covers the years after the separation and especially the relationship between the Church and the Action française.

Useful on this aspect, as on other issues of the period, is M. Petit's monumental *Histoire de la France Contemporaine, 1871–1913*, published by Larousse in 1916 but obviously written before the outbreak of war. In this sense, it is itself evidence of contemporary opinion on contemporary events, while the next edition published in the 'twenties carries on the story to 1914. The general historical background may also be sought conveniently in Seignobos' *Evolution de la Troisième République*. For the wider scene and accounts of those world affairs affecting the politics of France, the works of Pierre Renouvin and Jules Isaac on the one hand, of S. B. Fay and Bernadotte Schmitt on the other, provide documented pictures of the prewar years inevitably colored by some prejudice. However, they trespass only little into the events herein covered and do not appear authoritative, any more than the extremely suggestive but far too one-sided works of George Michon.

It is a risky thing to say, but I think that, of all the evidence at my disposal, contemporary literature has helped me most to understand the problems, attitudes, and live of the times. Barrès, du Gard, Psichari, Péguy, Paul Acker, are witnesses of the first importance. More than many official documents, speeches, and statistics, their true and to a great degree unself-conscious descriptions allowed me to comprehend the ideas and the circumstances of those for whom they were writing.

The same may be said of the works of Paul Bourget, which mirror the fears and perplexities of a "respectable" middle class whose reactions are an important factor of the phenomenon of the nationalist revival. *Le Disciple, Le Divorce*, above all *La Barricade*, read and discussed as novels, seen and discussed as plays, are perfect illustrations of contemporary social problems.

Romain Rolland's *Jean Cristophe* was considered at the time of its publication to be a faithful picture of the enthusiasms and the hopes of the younger generation. Besides its general psychological interest, its last volume carries echoes of the new temper and anxieties of 1911–1912. Proust's *A la Recherche du Temps Perdu* deals more with social than political realities and, concerning the latter, treats rather of the time and aftermath of the Dreyfus Affair than of our own. Roger Martin du Gard's *Jean Barois* is an interesting document whose value is enhanced by the date of publication (1913), but his *Les Thibault*, though a postwar work, gives what seems to be an excellent account of the life and inclinations of an upper-middle-class family. Similarly, the great work of Jules Romains, though the first volume did not appear until 1927, appears as a most detailed presentation of the prewar atmosphere. I should point out that references to this and to other works that are not contemporary have been made only to illustrate certain points and not to substantiate them.

Where no place of publication is given, the book was published in Paris. Dates of publication refer to the edition actually used.

COLLECTIONS OF DOCUMENTS

L'Abominable Vénalité de la Presse, d'après les documents des archives russes, 1897–1917. Edited by Arthur Raffalovitch. Paris: 1931.

Amtliche Aktenstücke zur Geschichte der Europäischen Politik, 1885–1914. (Belgische Weltkriege). Berlin: 1925. 9 vols.

British Documents on the Origin of the 1914 War, 1898–1914. Edited by Gooch and Temperley. London: 1926–1938.

Documents diplomatiques français, 1871–1914. 1e série, 1871–1900; 2e série, 1901–1911; 3e série, 1911–1914. Paris: 1929–1940.

Die Grosse Politik der Europäischen Kabinette, 1871–1914. Berlin: 1922–1927. 39 vols.

Journal Officiel de la République française. Debats, Chambre. Paris: 1900—.

Journal Officiel de la République française. Debats, Sénat. Paris: 1900—.

Un Livre Noir: Diplomatie d'avant-guerre d'après les documents des archives russes, 1910–1917. Paris: 1922–1934. 3 vols.

Oesterreich-Ungarns Aussenpolitik von der Bosnischen Krise 1908 bis zum Kriegsausbruch 1914. Vienna: 1930. 9 vols.

MISCELLANEOUS

Lachapelle, George. *Les élections législatives,* 1910. Paris: 1914.

Les Ministères français, 1789–1911. Société d'Histoire Moderne. Serie des Instruments de Travail. Paris: 1911. Vol. II. *Supplément,* 1912–1922. Paris: 1922. *Bulletin* of the Société d'Histoire Moderne, Feb. 2, 1921.

Samuel, Robert, and G. Bonnet-Maury. *Annuaire du Parlement.*

DAILY NEWSPAPERS, 1905–1914

L'Action française
L'Aurore
La Dépêche de Toulouse
L'Echo de Paris
L'Eclair
Le Figaro
Le Gaulois
L'Homme Libre
L'Humanité

La Lanterne
La Libre Parole
Le Matin
Le Petit Parisien
Le Progrès de Lyon
Le Radical
Le Rappel
Le Temps

CONSULTED

French
La Croix
La Liberté
Le Lyon Republicain
La Patrie

Foreign
Daily Telegraph
Paris Daily Mail
Times (London)

REVIEWS AND MAGAZINES

L'Action française
L'Illustration

CONSULTED

L'Argus de la presse	*La Revue des Deux Mondes*	*John Bull*
Espoir du Monde	*La Revue Hebdomadaire*	*The Nation*
La Guerre Sociale	*La Revue de Paris*	*National Review*
L'Opinion	*La Revue des Revues*	*Westminster Gazette*

FOR THE CHARLES ANDLER CONTROVERSY

L'Action Nationale, January–June, 1913
Les Temps Nouveaux, May 17, 1913
La Vie Ouvrière, February–April, 1913

CONTEMPORARY SOURCES

Agathon. *L'Esprit de la nouvelle Sorbonne*, 1910.

——. *Les jeunes gens d'aujourd'hui*, 1913.

Albin, Pierre. *Le coup d'Agadir*, 1912.

——. *L'Allemagne et la France en Europe*, 1913.

Andler, Charles. *Le socialisme impérialiste dans l'Allemagne contemporaine; dossier d'une polémique avec Jaurès*, 1918.

Anonymous. *Le nationalisme intégral*, Cahiers Lugdunum, n.d.

Bainville, Jacques. *Le coup d'Agadir et la guerre d'Orient*, 1913.

Barrès, Maurice. *Scènes et doctrines du nationalisme*, 2 vols., 1925.

——. *Dans le cloaque—Commission parlementaire sur l'affaire Rochette*, 1914.

——. *La Grande pitié des églises de France*, 1914.

Benda, Julien. *Le Bergsonisme*, 1912.

Bergson, Henri. *Essai sur les données immédiates de la conscience*, 1889.

——. *L'évolution créatrice*, 1907.

——. *La pensée et la mouvant*, 1946.

Bocquillon, Emile. *La crise du patriotisme à l'école*, 1905.

——. *Pour la patrie*, 1907.

Bourdon, G. *L'énigme allemande*, 1913.

Briand, Aristide. *La séparation*, 2 vols., 1908–1909.

Bruneau, Louis. *L'Allemagne en France*, 1915.

Capus, Alfred. *Les Moeurs du temps*, 1912.

Challaye, Félicien. *Le Congo français*, 1906 (introduction by C. Péguy).

Chambure, A. de. *A travers la presse*, 1914.

——. *Guides à l'opinion*, 1914–1918.

Chenu (Batonnier). *La Ligue des Patriotes*, n.d.

Chéradame, André. *La crise française*, 1912.

Clouard, Henri. *La "Cocarde" de Barrès*, 1910.

——. *Les disciplines*, 1913.

Daudet, Léon. *Une campagne d'Action française*, 1912.

——. *L'avant-guerre*, 1915.

Delahache, Georges. *Alsace-Lorraine*, 1st ed., 1909, 4th ed. 1911.

Delaisi, Francis. *Contre la loi Millerand*, 1912.

——. *La guerre qui vient*, 1911.

———. *La démocratie et les financiers* (published in 1911, I have been unable to find any copies of the original work in public libraries. It has, however, been reprinted in Crapouillot, Nov., 1936).

Delassus, R. P. Henri. *La démocratie chrétienne, parti et école,* 1911.

Destrem, L. *Les conditions économiques de la presse,* 1902.

Dimnet, Ernest. *France Herself Again,* London, 1914.

Dumont-Wilden, L., and L. Sougenet. *La victoire des vaincus,* 1911.

Faguet, Émile. *L'anticléricalisme,* 1906.

———. *Le pacifisme,* 1908.

———. *Discussions politiques,* 1909.

———. *La démission de la morale,* 1910.

———. *Le culte de l'incompétence et l'horreur des responsabilités,* 2 vols., 1910–1911.

———. *Les préjugés nécessaires,* 1911.

———. *De l'idée de patrie* (prize-giving speech, Lycée Janson de Sailly, July 12, 1913).

Fatoux, Léon. *Les coulisses du nationalisme,* 1903.

Fleury, C. *La République Juive,* 1910.

Flourens, Émile. *La France conquise, Edouard VII et Clemenceau,* 1906.

François-Poncet, André. *Ce que pense la jeunesse allemande,* 1913.

Giraud, Victor. *Le miracle français,* 1914.

Grosjean, Georges. *L'École et la Patrie,* 1906.

Guérin, Louis. *Avis aux nationalistes,* n.d.

Guignier, F. *L'homme qui se cite: Charles Maurras,* 1912.

Guy-Grand, Georges. *La philosophie nationaliste,* 1911.

———. *Le procès de la démocratie,* 1911.

Halévy, Daniel. *Visites aux paysans du Centre.* 1935.

Hanotaux, Gabriel. *La politique de l'équilibre,* 1914.

———. *La guerre des Balkans et l'Europe, 1912–1913,* 1914.

Henriot, Emile. *A quoi rêvent les jeunes gens,* 1913.

Hervé, Gustave. *L'Alsace-Lorraine,* 1913.

———. *La Patrie en danger,* 1915.

Jaurès, Jean. *L'Armée nouvelle,* 1915.

———. *Oeuvres,* ed. Bonnafous, 1931.

Jouvenel, Robert de. *La République des Camarades,* 1914.

Lacotte, E. *Nos seigneurs républicains,* 1909.

Lantivy, Comte de. *Nationalisme et Religion,* 1903.

Laurent, M., Norard, and Mercereau. *La paix armée et le problème d'Alsace dans l'opinion des nouvelles générations françaises,* 1914.

Lemaître, Jules. *Lettres à mon ami,* 1909.

Leroy, Maxime. *L'Alsace-Lorraine,* 1914.

Maignen, C. *Nationalisme, catholicisme et révolution,* 1901.

Maurras, Charles. *Le dilemme de Marc Sangnier,* 1907.

———. *Kiel et Tanger,* 1910 and 1928.

———. *Enquête sur la Monarchie,* 1899.

———. *La politique religieuse,* 1914.

Mermeix. *Chronique de l'an 1911,* 1912.

Millerand, Alexandre. *Pour la défense nationale: une année au ministère de la guerre,* 1913.

Mollin, Jules Henri. *La vérité sur l'affaire des fiches,* n.d.

Montesquiou, Léon de. *Les raisons du nationalisme,* 1905.

Mun, Albert de. *Ma vocation sociale,* 1908.

Munier, Commandant. *Nation, Armée, et Guerre*, 1907.

Mouthon, F. *Du bluff au chantage: les grandes campagnes du Matin*, 1908.

Orry, A. *Les socialistes indépendants*, 1911.

Péguy, Charles. *Oeuvres Complètes*, 1947.

———. *Par ce demi-clair matin*, 1952.

Picquart, Général G. *De la situation faite à la défense militaire de la France*, 1906.

Pilaut, P. *Le patriotisme en France et à l'étranger*, 1912.

———. *Le péril allemand*, 1913.

Pinon, René. *France et Allemagne*, 1913.

Rey, Etienne. *La renaissance de l'orgueil français*, 1912.

Riou, Gaston. *Lettre aux Jeunes France*, Nancy, 1912.

———. *La mission nationale du protestantisme*, 1913.

———. *Aux Ecoutes de la France qui Vient*, 1913.

Rocafort, Jacques. *Mes campagnes catholiques*, 1910.

Sangnier, Marc. *Cinq années d'action, Le Sillon*, March 10, 1907.

———. *L'histoire et les idées du Sillon*, 1907.

———. *Discours, 1910–1913*, 1914.

Séailles, Gabriel Paix. *La diplomatie secrète sous la 3e République, 1910–1911*, 1912.

Sembat, Marcel. *Faites un Roi, sinon faites la Paix*, 1913.

Sorel, Georges. *La révolution Dreyfusienne*, 1911.

Stefanov, S. *La question nationaliste et le socialisme*, 1906.

Thomas, Albert. *La politique socialiste*, 1913.

Tour du Pin, Marquis R. de la. *Vers un ordre social chrétien, 1882–1907*, 1907.

———. *La Monarchie française*, 1908.

Valerie, G. *Notes sur le nationalisme français*, 1901.

Valois, Georges. *L'homme qui vient*, 1906.

Vaugeois, Henri. *Notre pays*, 1916.

———. *La fin de l'erreur française*, 1928.

Vialatte and Caudel. *La vie politique dans les Deux Mondes, 1906–1918*, 9 vols., 1908–1922.

CORRESPONDENCE AND DIARIES

Barrès, Maurice. *Mes Cahiers*, 1929.

Cambon, Paul. *Correspondance*, 3 vols., 1940–1946.

Desbois and Descolas. *Correspondance, Corresp. de l'Union pour la Vérité*, 1921.

Fournier, Alain, and Jacques Rivière. *Correspondance, 1905–1914*, 2 vols., 1948.

Franck, Henri. *Lettres à quelques amis*, 1926.

Gide, André. *Journal, 1889–1939*, 1948.

Kérallain, R. de. *Correspondance, 1829–1926*, 2 vols., Quimper, 1933–1935.

Lacombe, Charles de. *Journal politique*, 1907–1908.

Louis, Georges. *Carnets*, 2 vols., 1926.

Paléologue, Maurice. *Un grand tournant de la politique mondiale, 1904–1906*, 1934.

———. *Journal, 1913–1914*, 1947.

Psichari, Ernest. *Lettres du Centurion*, 1947.

Radziwill, Marie Dorothea Elisabeth (de Castellane). *Lettres de la Princesse Radziwill*, 4 vols., Bologna, 1934.

Renard, Jules. *Correspondance, 1864–1910*, 1928.

———. *Journal, 1887–1910*, 1935.

Ribot, Alexandre. *Journal, 1914–1922*. 1936.

Wilhelm II. *Briefe an den Zaren*, Berlin, 1920.

MEMOIRS

Barrère, Camille. *Mémoires*, n.d.

———. On Delcassé's fall, cf. *Revue des Deux Mondes*, Aug. 1, 1932, and Jan. 15, 1933.

Benoist, Charles. *Souvenirs*, especially vol. III, 1934.

Bertaut, Jules. *Figures contemporaines*, 1906.

———. *Paris, 1870–1935*, 1936.

Brulôt, Fernand. *Souvenirs*, 1912.

Caillaux, Joseph. *Agadir*, 1919.

———. *Mes Prisons*, 1921.

———. *Mémoires*, 3 vols., 1942–1947.

Castellane, Boni de. *L'art d'être pauvre*, 1925.

Chichet, Etienne. *Quarante ans de journalisme*, 1935.

Corpechot, Lucien. *Souvenirs d'un journaliste*, 1936.

Daudet, Léon. *Panorama de la 3ᵉ République*, 1925.

———. *Etudes et milieux littéraires*, 1927.

———. *Charles Maurras et son temps*, 1927.

———. *Paris vécu*, 1930.

———. *Vers le Roi (Souvenirs)*, 1936.

Dell, Robert. *My Second Country, France*, London, 1920.

Delourme, P. *Trente-cinq ans de politique religieuse*, 1936.

Dimier, Louis. *Souvenirs d'action publique et universitaire*, 1920.

———. *Vingt ans d'Action française*, 1926.

Drault, Jean. *Drumont, la France Juive, et la Libre Parole*, 1935.

Fonsegrive, George. *Regards en arrière*, 1908.

Hanotaux, Gabriel. *Mon temps*, 1933.

Herriot, Edouard. *Jadis*, vol. I, 1948.

Iswolsky, Alexander Petrovich. *Mémoires*, 1923.

Joffre, Joseph Jacques. *Mémoires*, 2 vols., 1932.

Judet, Ernest. *Ma politique, 1905–1917*, 1918.

Lancken, von der. *Meine 30 Dienstjahre*, Berlin, 1931.

Las Cases, E. de. *Deux ans au Sénat, 1903–1905*, n.d.

———. *Au Sénat, 1906–1919*, n.d.

Maurras, Charles. *Au signe de Flore*, 1931.

———. *Quand les français ne s'aimaient pas*, 1926.

Massis, Henri. *Evocations, Souvenirs*, 1931.

Messimy, Adolphe. *Mes Souvenirs*, 1937.

Meyer, Arthur. *Ce que mes yeux ont vu*, 1911.

———. *Ce que je peux dire*, 1912.

Noulens, Joseph. *Le gouvernment français à la veille de la guerre*.

———. *Revue des Deux Mondes*, Feb. 1, 1931.

Pariset, C. *Plus d'un demi-siècle d'administration au temps*, Macon, 1932.

Paul-Boncour, Joseph. *Entre Deux Guerres*, vol. I, 1945.

Piou, Jacques. *Le Ralliement; son histoire*, 1928.

Poincaré, Raymond. *Au service de la France: neuf années de souvenirs*, 1926—.

Schoen, Wilhelm Edouard von. *Mémoires*, 1922.

Steed, Henry Wickham. *Through Thirty Years, 1892–1922*, 2 vols., London, 1924.

Tavernier, Eugène. *Cinquante ans de politique*, 1925.

Tharaud, Jérome and Jean. *Mes années chez Barrès*, 1928.

Valois, Georges. *D'un siècle à l'autre, chronique d'une génération*, 1924.

Viau, Raphael. *Vingt ans d'antisémitisme*, 1910.

Secondary Sources

Bainville, Jacques. *Au seuil du siècle*, 1927.
————. *Chroniques*, 1938.
————. *Doit-on le dire?* 1939.
————. *Esquisses et portraits*, 1946.
Maurras, Charles. *Dictionnaire politique et critique*, 1931.
————. *La contre-révolution spontannée*, 1943.
————. *Principes*, 1931.
————. *Pour un jeune français*, 1949.
Massis, Henri. *Débats*, 1931.
————. *L'Honneur de servir*, 1937.
————. *La guerre de trente ans*, 1940.
————. *Jugements*, 1924.
————. *En marge des jugements*, 1927.
————. *Maurras et notre temps*, 2 vols., 1951.
Valois, Georges. *La Monarchie et la classe ouvrière*, 1924.
Varillon, Pierre, and Henri Rambaud. *Enquête sur la jeune littérature*, 1924.
Variot, Jean. *Propos de Georges Sorel*, 1935.
Vaussart, Maurice. *Enquête sur le nationalisme*, 1924.

Secondary Historical Works

Anderson, Eugene N. *The First Moroccan Crisis, 1904–1906*, Chicago, 1930.
Andler, Charles. *Vie de Lucien Herr*, 1932.
Anonymous. *La France et la Révanche*, Berlin, 1918.
Bainville, Jacques. *Histoire de trois générations*, 1934.
————. *La 3e République*, 1934.
Balfour, Reginald E. "The Action française movement," *Cambridge Historical Journal*, III (1930), 2.
Bodley, John Edward Courtenay. *The Church in France*, London, 1906.
————. *Cardinal Manning and Other Essays*, London, 1912.
Bourgin, Herbert. *De Jaurès à Léon Blum*, 1938.
Buell, Raymond Leslie. *Contemporary French Politics*, New York, 1920.
Buthman, William Cuthbert. *The Rise of Integral Nationalism in France*, New York, 1939.
Byrnes, Robert Francis. *Anti-Semitism in Modern France*, Rutgers, 1951.
Cairns, John C. "International politics and the military mind," *Journal of Modern History* (Sept., 1953).
Carroll, Eber Malcolm. *French Public Opinion and Foreign Affairs, 1870–1914*, New York, 1931.
Charpentier, Armand. *Le parti radical et radical-socialiste à travers ses congrès, 1901–1911*, n.d.
Chevallier, Louis. "Les fondements économiques et sociaux de l'histoire politique de la région parisienne," *Thèse de Lettres*, 1950.
Clérmont, Louis. *Emile Clérmont, sa vie, son oeuvre*, 1919.
Compère-Morel, Jacques. *Jules Guesde*, 1937.
Cornilleau, R. *De Waldeck-Rousseau à Poincaré*, 1926.
————. *Le Ralliement a-t-il échoué?* 1927.
————. *L'abbé Naudet*, 1935.
Coudekerque-Lambrecht, Mme de. *Léon de Montesquiou*, 1925.
Cousin, L. *Vie et doctrine du Sillon*, 1928.

Curtius, Ernst Robert. *Barrès und die Geistigen Grundlagen des Französischen Nationalismus*, Bonn, 1921.

Dansette, Albert. *Le Boulangisme*, 1946.

——. *Histoire religieuse de la France contemporaine*, 2 vols., 1948–1951.

Demaison, André. *La presse de province au vingtième siècle*, 1932.

Ducray, Camille. *Henri Rochefort*, 1913.

Feuillerat, Albert. *Paul Bourget*, 1937.

Fleurieu, Roger de. *Caillaux à travers les ans*, 1951.

Franck, Walter. *Nationalismus und Demokratie im Frankreich der Dritten Republik, 1871–1918*, Hamburg, 1933.

George, Pierre. *Études sur la banlieue de Paris*, 1950.

Gérin-Richard, Lazare de, and Louis Truc. *Histoire de l'Action française*, 1945.

Goguel, François. *La politique des partis sous la 3e République*, 1947.

——. *Géographie des élections françaises, 1871–1951*, 1951.

Goichon, E. *A la mémoire d'Ernest Psichari*, 1946.

Gooch, George Peabody. *Franco-German Relations, 1871–1914*, London, 1923.

——. *Recent Revelations of European Diplomacy*, London, 1940.

Gouttenoire de Toury, Ferdinand. *Poincaré a-t-il voulu la guerre?* 1920.

——. *Jaurès et le parti de la guerre*, 1922.

Hale, Oron James. *Publicity and Diplomacy, England and Germany 1890–1914*, New York, 1940.

——. *Germany and the Diplomatic Revolution*, Philadelphia, 1931.

Halévy, Daniel. *Péguy et les Cahiers de la Quinzaine*, 1943.

——. *La décadence de la liberté*, 1931.

——. *Pour l'étude de la 3e République*, 1937.

——. "Hommage à Charles Maurras," *Revue Universelle*, Jan. 1, 1937.

Hamburger, Maurice. *Léon Bourgeois*, 1932.

Hamon, Augustin. *Les maîtres de la France*, 3 vols., 1936–1938.

Hanotaux, Gabriel. *Sur les chemins de l'histoire*, 2 vols., 1924.

Headings, Mildred J. *French Freemasonry under the Third Republic*, Baltimore, 1949.

Hertz, Friedrich Otto. *Nationality in History and Politics*, London, 1944.

Isaac, Jules. *Un débat historique—1914*, 1933.

Jäckh, Ernst. *Kiderlen-Waechter intime*, 1928.

Jacques, Léon Ernest. *Les partis politiques*, 1913.

Judet, E. *Georges Louis*, 1925.

Justin. *Jaurès patriote*, 1920.

Kohn, Hans. *The Idea of Nationalism*, New York, 1944.

Krehbiel, Edward. *Nationalism, War, and Socialism*, New York, 1916.

Lachapelle, Georges. *Le ministère Méline*, 1928.

Lanessan, Jean de. *Histoire de l'Entente Cordiale*, 1916.

Lasserre, Pierre. *Georges Sorel*, 1926

——. *Mise au point*, 1931.

Lecanuet, R. P. *L'Eglise de France sous la 3e République*, 4 vols., 1930–1931.

Loménie, Eugène Beau de. *Les responsabilités des dynasties bourgeoises*, 3 vols., 1947–1954.

Martin, Gaston. *Joseph Caillaux*, 1931.

Massis, Henri. *Notre ami Psichari*, 1919.

Mermeix. *Le Ralliement et l'Action française*, 1927.

Michon, Georges. *Clemenceau*, 1931.

——. *L'Alliance franco-russe, 1891–1917*, 1931.

——. *La préparation à la guerre: la loi de trois ans*, 1935.

Muret, Charlotte. *French Royalist Doctrines since the Revolution*, New York, 1933.

Muret, Pierre. "La politique personelle de Rouvier et la chute de Delcassé," *Rev. Hist. Guerre Mondiale*, July and Oct., 1939.

Nicolson, Harold. *Lord Carnock: Portrait of a Diplomatist*, London, 1930.

Noel-Baker, Philip. *The Private Manufacture of Armaments*, vol. I, London, 1936.

Nolde, Boris Emmanuilovich. *L'Alliance franco-russe*, 1936.

Orwell, George. "Notes on Nationalism," *Such, Such Were the Joys*, New York, 1953.

Persil, Raoul. *Alexandre Millerand*, 1951.

Piou, Jacques. *Albert de Mun*, 1925.

Playne, Caroline Elizabeth. *The Neuroses of the Nations: the Neuroses of France and Germany before the War*, 1925.

Prélot, Marcel. *Evolution politique du socialisme français*, 1939.

Pressac, Pierre de. *Les forces historiques de la France: la tradition dans l'orientation des provinces*, 1928.

Reisner, Edward Hartmann. *Nationalism in Education since 1789*, New York, 1922.

Renouvin, Pierre. "The part played in international relations by the conversations between the general staffs on the eve of the World War," A. Coville and H. Temperley, eds., *Studies in Anglo-French History*, Cambridge, 1935.

Roux, Marquis de. *Charles Maurras et le nationalisme d'Action française*, 1927.

Sait, Edward M. Chesney. *Government and Politics of France*, Yonkers, 1920.

Schuman, Frederick Lewis. *War and Diplomacy in the French Republic*, Chicago, 1931.

Schwertfeger, Bernhard. *Zur Europäischen Politik, 1871–1914*, Berlin, 1919.

Secrétain, Roger. *Péguy*, Marseille, 1941; Paris, 1943.

Sée, Henri Eugène. *Histoire de la Ligue des Droits de l'Homme*, 1927.

Seignobos, Charles. *Etudes de politique et d'histoire*, 1934.

Siegfried, André. *Tableau politique de la France de l'Ouest sous la 3ᵉ République*, 1913.

——. *Tableau des partis en France*, 1930.

——. *Le problème français*, 1939.

——. *Mes souvenirs de la 3ᵉ République*, 1946.

——. *Géographie électorale de l'Ardèche sous la 3ᵉ République*, 1948.

Soulier, Auguste. *L'instabilité ministérielle sous la 3ᵉ République*, 1939.

Stieve, Friedrich. *Izvolsky and the World War*, London, 1926.

——. *L'Allemagne et la politique européenne*, 1929.

Suarez, Georges. *La vie orgueilleuse de Clemenceau*, 1930.

Tarde, Alfred de. *Le Maroc*, 1929.

Tardieu, Alfred. *La France et les Alliances*, 1909.

——. *La conférence d'Algeçiras*, 1909.

——. *Le mystère d'Agadir*, 1912.

Tharaud, Jérome, and Jean. *Vie et mort de Paul Déroulède*, 1914.

——. *Notre cher Péguy*, 1926.

——. *Pour les fidèles de Péguy*, 1949.

Thibaudet, Albert. *Trente ans de vie française*, 3 vols., 1920–1939.

——. *Les princes lorrains*, 1924.

——. *La république des professeurs*, 1927.

——. *Les idées politiques de la France*, 1932.

Times, The. *A History of the Times*, vols. III–IV, London, 1947–1952.

Tony-Revillon. *Camille Pelletan, 1846–1915*, 1930.

Weinstein, Harold R. *Jean Jaurès; A Study of Patriotism in the French Socialist Movement*, New York, 1936.

Wright, Gordon. *Raymond Poincaré and the Presidency*, Stanford, 1942.

Fiction

Acker, Paul. *Le soldat Bernard*, 1910.
———. *La Classe*, n.d.
Barrès, Maurice. *Les Déracinés*, 2 vols., 1947.
———. *L'Appel au Soldat*, 2 vols., 1926.
———. *Leurs figures*, 1932.
———. *Au service de l'Allemagne*, 1916.
———. *Colette Baudoche*, 1938.
———. *Les amités françaises*, 1931.
Bourget, Paul. *Le disciple*, 1889.
———. *L'Etape*, 1902.
———. *Un divorce*, 1908.
———. *La barricade, chronique de 1910*, 1910.
———. *La crise*, 1912.
France, Anatole. *Histoire Contemporaine*, 1948.
Martin du Gard, Roger. *Jean Barois*, 1913.
———. *Les Thibault*, 9 vols., 1941.
Proust, Marcel. *A la recherche du temps perdu*, 10 vols., 1929–1936.
Psichari, Ernest. *Oeuvres Complètes*, 3 vols., 1948.
———. *Le Voyage du Centurion*, 1947.
———. *L'Appel des Armes*, 1945.
Romains, Jules. *Les Hommes de Bonne Volonté*, vols. 1–14, 1932—.
Rolland, Romain. *Jean Cristophe*, 10 vols., 1905–1912.

Works Providing the General Background

Brogan, Dennis. *The Development of Modern France*, London, 1947.
Chastenet, Jacques. *La France de M. Fallières*, 1949.
Madaule, Jacques. *Histoire de France*, vol. II, 1945.
Petit, M. *Histoire de la France Contemporaine de 1871 à 1914*, 1916.
———. *Histoire de la 3ᵉ République*, 2 vols., 1936.
Seignobos, Charles. *L'Evolution de la 3ᵉ République, 1875–1914*, 1921.
Thomson, David. *Democracy in France*, London, 1953.

References

Muel, Léon. *Tableau synoptique de tous les ministères de la 3ᵉ République, 1870–1915*.
Pinson, Koppel S. *A Bibliographical Introduction to Nationalism*, New York, 1935.
Samuel, Robert, and G. Bonnet-Maury. *Les parlementaires français* (annual) 1900–1914.
Winnacker, R. A. "Bibliography of the Third Republic, 1870–1914," *Journal of Modern History*, X (1938), 372.

BIOGRAPHICAL NOTES

BIOGRAPHICAL NOTES

ADAM, PAUL: (1862–1920) Paris-born novelist, symbolist, author of *Le mystère des foules* (1895) dealing with the Boulangist adventure in which he had taken an active part.

AGATHON: pseudonym of Henri Massis and Alfred de Tarde. The original Agathon (c. 448–400 B.C.) was an Athenian tragic poet, friend of Euripides and Plato, mocked by Aristophanes.

ALAIN: pseudonym of Emile Chartier (1868–1954), essayist and philosopher, born Mortagne, Normandy. Normalien, great teacher at the Lycées of Lorient, Rouen, and Henry IV (A. Maurois, H. Massis, and J. Prévost among his students); author of the *Propos*, which appeared in the *Dépêche de Rouen* (1906–1914), *Libres Propos* (1921–1924), and many other publications.

ALAIN-FOURNIER: pseudonym of Henri Fournier (1886–1914), born LaChapelle d'Angillon, near Bourges, Cher, where both parents were schoolteachers. Educated at Brest and Lycée Lakanal, Paris, where he met Jacques Rivière, later to become his brother-in-law. Their correspondence, besides its literary value, provides a fascinating document of their times. Fournier himself is best known for his curious novel, *Le Grand Meaulnes* (1913). Killed in action, September, 1914.

ANDRÈ, LOUIS JOSEPH NICOLAS, general: (1838–1913) born Nuits-Saint-Georges (Côte d'Or); drawn from obscurity when appointed minister of war by Waldeck-Rousseau (1900), resigned from Combes cabinet after being denounced for communicating officers' personal record files to the *Grand-Orient* (1904). Author of *De la navigation aérienne et de l'aviation* (1865) which concluded, quite rightly, that flight by engines heavier than air was impossible for the moment.

AUGAGNEUR, JEAN VICTOR: (1855–1931) doctor and politician, born Lyon. Professor on the medical faculty, Lyon; mayor 1900–1905; Republican-Socialist deputy 1904; governor of Madagascar 1905–1910; minister of public works under Caillaux 1911–1912; minister of education under Viviani, 1914.

AULARD, FRANÇOIS VICTOR ALPHONSE: (1849–1928) born Montbron, Charente. Historian of the French Revolution; influential professor at the Sorbonne.

BAINVILLE, JACQUES: (1879–1936) historian and journalist, born Vincennes, Seine. Precise, lucid, pessimistic, his work makes agreeable reading and brilliant history. Came early under influence of Maurras, and became one of the editors of the *Action française* in its original monthly form. A constant contributor to the paper during our period, he later founded the *Revue Universelle* (1920) with Massis. Under his pen, the dogma of Maurrasian royalism is modified and made palatable by good style and good sense. Elected to the Académie française in 1935.

BARRÈS, MAURICE: (1862–1923) writer and politician, born Charmes, Vosges. Lorrainer by birth and profession, excellent writer, reached popularity early with *Huit jours chez M. Renan* (1888) and his election to the Chamber as Boulangist deputy of Nancy (1889). Graduated from *Le Culte du Moi* (1888–1891) to *Le Roman de l'énergie nationale* (1897–1903), this latter an excellent portrayal of people and events in the decade preceding the Dreyfus Affair. Deeply involved in the Affair, he emerged a vehement nationalist. *Au Service de l'Allemagne* (1905) and *Colette Baudoche* (1909), read more after 1914 than before, were propagandistic novels about the plight of Alsatians and Lorrainers under German occupation. Occasionally influential in the Chamber, excellent and widely read as a journalist, he was the most respected of the leaders of patriotic movements. His *Cahiers, 1896–1918* (11 vols., Paris 1928–1938) must be read for a full understanding of his life and work, and of the contemporary political and literary world of France.

BARTHOU, JEAN LOUIS: (1862–1934) born Oloron-Sainte-Marie, lawyer in Pau; deputy 1889; minister of public works 1894 under Dupuy; of interior 1896 under Méline; of public works 1906 under Sarrien. Keeper of the seals and minister of justice, graduated to premier and minister of education, 1913; essayist and bibliophile; murdered at Marseille in 1934.

BAZIRE, HENRI: (1873–1919) lawyer and politician, born Fontenay-le-Comte; leader of the Association catholique de la jeunesse française (A.C.J.F.); inspired by de Mun, carried his organization into the field of social action, but gave up its presidency (1904) to devote himself more fully to Catholic action in the courts and the press. Chief editor of *La Libre Parole* after Drumont, fought by both government and *Action française*, he was elected deputy in 1914 only to be cheated and deposed in favor of his Radical opponent by a government commission abetted by his royalist enemies. Gassed in 1917, died of effects 1919.

BEAUREGARD, PAUL: (1853–1919) economist and politician, born le Havre. Professor in the Universities of Douai and Paris, founded *Le Monde économique* (1891), *La France économique et financière* (1902), to preach free trade and defend private enterprise. Deputy 1898–1919; member of the Académie des sciences morales et politiques (1905).

BERNANOS, GEORGES: (1888–1948) novelist and political writer, born Paris. Catholic, monarchist, militant of the *Action française* who left it in 1926, powerful polemicist, burdened by an intransigent conscience.

BILLOT, JEAN BAPTISTE, general: (1828–1907) deputy 1871, he helped reorganize the army of the new Republic. Senator 1875, minister of war 1882–1883 and 1886, bitterly opposed introduction of two-year military service in 1905.

BOULANGER, GEORGES ERNEST JEAN MARIE: (1837–1891) born Rennes. Smart soldier, rose rapidly to become brigadier-general 1880, director of infantry at the war office 1882, G.O.C. Tunis 1884, minister of war 1886 under Freycinet. Ambitious, reforming, he sought and won great popularity as hero of *revanche*. Abandoned as too dangerous by Republican politicians, regarded in certain circles as a potential Monck, became center of Boulangist movement that during 1888 and early 1889 dominated the French political scene, and threatened the Republic with overthrow. Fearing prosecution, he fled to Brussels, was tried and found guilty of treason *in absentia* (Oct., 1889); committed suicide soon after on the tomb of his mistress.

BOURGEOIS, LÉON VICTOR AUGUSTE: (1851–1925) statesman and legist, born Paris. One of the first of his time to suggest a league of nations. Prefect of police, 1887; Radical deputy 1888, defeated Boulanger in the Marne; member of many cabinets; premier 1895; foreign minister 1906 under Sarrien, and responsible for French policy at Algeçiras; foreign minister in short-lived Ribot cabinet of June, 1914; Nobel Peace Prize, 1920.

BOURGET, PAUL CHARLES JOSEPH: (1852–1935) born Amiens. Popular novelist, critic, and playwright, the lightness of his work soon gave way to a graver attitude. *Le Disciple* (1889) led on to the plays *La Barricade* (1910) and *Le Tribun* (1911), "chronicles" of the years 1910–1911 concerned with the sociopolitical history of the time. He was hailed as a recruit by the forces of the Right, who appreciated his calls for stricter morality, national unity, hierarchical order, and social discipline.

BRIAND, ARISTIDE: (1862–1932) lawyer and politician, born Nantes. Entered public life as journalist and labor leader. Socialist deputy 1902; *rapporteur* and chief figure in the separation of Church and state; left Socialist party and accepted min. of education and public worship, 1906 under Sarrien and Clemenceau. Minister of justice, 1908; premier 1909–1911; minister of justice 1912 under Poincaré; premier again in 1913 for a short while; did not hold office again until war. A great liberal parliamentarian, one of the school of brilliant former-Socialist statesmen; incidentally, with François Pelloutier, one of the earliest Syndicalist theorists.

BRISSON, EUGÈNE HENRI: (1835–1912) born Bourges; deputy of extreme Left 1871; proposed amnesty for condemned Communards but was voted down; anticlerical and strong supporter of obligatory primary education; president of Chamber, 1881–1885, 1894–1898, 1906–1912; premier 1885 and 1898; active supporter of Waldeck-Rousseau and Combes, especially in their anticlerical policies.

BROGLIE, JACQUES VICTOR ALBERT, Duc de: (1821–1901) born Paris. Diplomat and writer of extreme conservative views, succeeded to title 1870, came out of retirement to be elected deputy 1871, and was sent to London as ambassador. Resigning this post 1872, he became leader of the monarchist anti-Thiers faction in Assembly; premier 1873–1874, under MacMahon, and again on occasion of May 16, 1877. Defeated on that occasion, failing to secure reëlection both in 1877 and 1885, he abandoned politics for the study of history.

BRUNETIÈRE, FERDINAND: (1849–1906) critic and writer, born Toulon. His name is connected with the *Revue des Deux Mondes*, which he edited from 1893 until his death. Professor of French language and literature at the École Normale, 1886; elected to the Académie française in 1893; orthodox Catholic, reactionary in his politics, logical, erudite, and unafraid in his thinking.

BÜLOW, BERNHARD, Prinz von: (1849–1929) German diplomat and statesman, born Flottbeck, on Lower Elbe, of Holsteiner stock. Ambassador in Rome 1894; head of foreign office, Berlin, 1897; imperial chancellor 1900; resigned 1909; brilliant parliamentarian, polished, urbane, inspired but dwarfed by the august shade of his predecessor.

CABRIÈRES, FRANÇOIS MARIE ANATOLE DE ROVÉRIE DE: (1830–1922) born Beaucaire, Gard. Bishop of Montpellier 1873, made cardinal by Pius X, an independent and influential *grand seigneur*.

CAILLAUX, JOSEPH MARIE AUGUSTE: (1863–1944) born Le Mans. Brilliant descendant of a bourgeois dynasty. Inspecteur des Finances 1888; elected deputy for Mamers, Sarthe, in 1898, he held the seat until 1917; minister of finance 1899, under Waldeck-Rousseau and again, 1906, under Clemenceau when he tried to introduce an income tax. Premier 1911–1912, he conducted the greater part of the negotiations after the Agadir crisis. Minister of finance under Doumergue 1913, he resigned when his second wife shot Calmette, editor of *Le Figaro*, for publishing intimate and damaging letters.

CAIN, JULIEN: (1887—) historian and scholar, born Montmorency; general administrator of the Bibliothèque nationale since 1930.

CAMBON, JULES MARTIN: (1845–1935) Paul's younger brother; prefect in Nord 1882; Rhône 1887; governor-general of Algeria 1891; ambassador in Washington 1897, where he helped to negotiate preliminaries of peace after Spanish-American War. Ambassador in Madrid 1902; Berlin 1907–1914.

CAMBON, PIERRE PAUL: (1843–1924) private secretary to Ferry during Commune; was then appointed prefect of Lille; resident in Tunis 1882; ambassador in Madrid 1886, Constantinople 1890, London 1898–1920. Largely responsible for improving relations between Britain and France; signed the Anglo-French agreement with Lansdowne 1904; promoted Anglo-Russian agreement 1907; achieved Grey-Cambon exchange of letters regarding naval and military coöperation between Britain and France in the event of war, November, 1912.

CARNOCK, ARTHUR NICOLSON, first baron: (1849–1928) British diplomatist, born London, son of an admiral, educated at Rugby and Brasenose, entered foreign office 1870, held posts in Berlin, Teheran, Constantinople, Sofia, and Morocco; ambassador in St. Petersburg 1906; under-secretary for foreign affairs 1910–1916.

CHARMES, FRANCIS: (1848–1916) journalist and politician, born Aurillac, Cantal. Editor, *Journal des Débats* (1872–1880 and 1889–1907); *Revue des Deux Mondes* (1907–1916); deputy 1881–1885 and 1889–1898: senator 1900.

CHARMES, FRANÇOIS MARIE XAVIER: (1849–1919) his brother, born Aurillac, director in the minister of education, member of the Académie des sciences morales et politiques.

CLAUDEL, PAUL: (1868–1956) poet, dramatist, diplomat, born Villeneuve-sur-Fère en Tardenois, entered consular service 1892, served as consul in the United States, China, Germany, and Italy; minister in Rio de Janeiro; ambassador in Tokyo 1921, Washington 1927, and Brussels. Converted on Christmas Night 1886 during midnight Mass in Notre Dame, all his work is inspired by his Christian and Catholic elation. Many of his writings seem to be hopeless fairy stories without fairies (*Le soulier de satin, L'Otage, Partage de Midi*), but full of power and not devoid of beauty.

CLEMENCEAU, GEORGES: (1841–1929) born Mouilleron-en-Pareds, Vendée; trained to be a doctor, he spent 1866–1869 in the United States teaching French and writing articles for *Le Temps*. Mayor of Montmartre 1870; Radical deputy 1871, ran into trouble at time of Commune, resigned. Reëlected 1876, soon became leader of the Radical opposition and forged a reputation as destroyer of ministries. Upset Ferry, made and unmade Boulanger, exposed Wilson scandal, and helped upset Grévy. Defeated 1893, played important part in the Dreyfus Affair, founded *L'Aurore*, was elected to the Senate in 1902; minister of interior and premier 1906–1909; founded *L'Homme Libre* (1913) which, under war censorship, became *L'Homme Enchaîné;* immortalized as *Le Père de la Victoire.*

CLERMONT, EMILE: (1880–1916) born Auvergne, student École Normale, collaborated with Emile Bourgeois in the publication of a historical study, *Rome et Napoléon* (1907), then published two novels of his own. Pessimistic, troubled, he died in the trenches.

COMBES, EMILE: (1835–1921) Radical politician, born Roquecourbe, Tarn; doctor by profession; senator 1885; minister of education 1895 under Bourgeois; premier and minister of interior 1903; his reign was that of the *bloc républicain* formed to carry out a mainly anticlerical program. Passed bill on congregations 1904, and took first steps toward separation of Church and state. Resigned 1905, after Socialists left the bloc and Radical support wavered following the *affaire des fiches.*

COCTEAU, JEAN: (1891–) poet, dramatist, novelist, eccentric; sophisticated and tormented; retired to the Académie française in 1956.

COPPÉE, FRANÇOIS: (1842–1908) poet and novelist, born Paris. Archivist of the Comédie française (1878–84); became known as *poète des humbles;* Académie française 1884; agnostic to begin with, illness returned him to the Church; published *La Bonne Souffrance,* 1898, which made him popular with *bien-pensants;* became violent nationalist, took a leading part against Dreyfus, and was one of the founders of the Ligue de la Patrie Française.

DAUDET, LÉON: (1867–1942) novelist, critic, journalist, born Paris; son of Alphonse Daudet, married a granddaughter of Victor Hugo, whom he subsequently divorced.

Violent, vulgar, forceful polemist, he wrote for the press of the irreconcilable Right, came under the spell of Maurras and became one of leaders of the Action française.

DELCASSÉ, THÉOPHILE: (1852–1924) statesman and diplomat, born Pamiers, Ariège. Entered politics from the bottom, eventually (1889) succeeded both to the widow and to the seat in the Chamber of his *patron*. Under-secretary, then minister of colonies 1893–1895; foreign secretary 1898–1905; minister of marine 1911–1913; ambassador in St. Petersburg 1913–1914; minister of war in Ribot cabinet of June, 1914; his daughter Suzanne married general Noguès.

DEMANGE, CHARLES GABRIEL EDGAR: (1841–1925) great lawyer, born Versailles, pleaded for Pierre Bonaparte, killer of Victor Noir, and in other great cases: Wilson, Panama, Dreyfus, after the war—Caillaux.

DENAIS, JOSPEH: (1877–1956) lawyer and politician, born Savenay, Loire-Inférieure. Codirector of the *Libre Parole* with Bazire, lieutenant of Jacques Piou in the *Action Libérale Populaire*, deputy of Batignolles since 1911.

DÉROULÈDE, PAUL: (1846–1914) author and politician, enthusiastic soldier 1870–1871, poet (*Chants du soldat*, and others), patriot, born Paris. Founded *revanchard* Ligue des patriotes, 1882; worked for Franco-Russian alliance, Boulanger, overthrow of the Republic. Deputy 1889, expelled 1890, reelected 1898, acquitted of treason charge 1899, sentenced to ten years' banishment for conspiracy against the Republic 1900; retired to San Sebastian; amnestied, he returned to France in 1905.

DESCHANEL, PAUL EUGÈNE LOUIS: (1856–1922) politician and orator, born Brussels. Secretary to Jules Simon 1876–1877; progressive Republican deputy 1885; supported law on separation of Church and state; president of commission on foreign and colonial affairs (1905–1909); elected president of the Republic in 1920 being "safer" than Clemenceau; he resigned the same year and died soon after.

DOUMER, PAUL: (1857–1932) politician and financier, born Aurillac. Deputy 1888; minister of finance 1895, under Bourgeois, tried but failed to introduce income tax. Governor of Indochina 1897–1902; on return, contributed to fall of Combes; president of Chamber 1905–1907; lost presidential election of 1906 to Fallières: senator 1912; president of Senate 1927; president of Republic 1931; murdered 1932.

DOUMERGUE, GASTON: (1863–1934) barrister, magistrate, politician of dependable mediocrity, born Aigues-Vives. Deputy 1893; minister of colonies under Combes, 1902–1905; minister of commerce under Sarrien and Clemenceau, 1906–1909; minister of education under Briand, 1909–1910; senator 1910, and strong advocate of Three-Year Law. Premier 1913–1914; president of the Republic, 1924–1931.

DRIANT, EMILE AUGUSTE CYPRIEN: (1855–1916) officer and military writer, born Neuchatel, Aisne; served as one of Boulanger's aides, married one of his daughters. Protested violently at the time of the *affaire des fiches;* retired from army, 1905; deputy 1910; killed at Verdun, 1916.

DRUMONT, EDOUARD ADOLPHE: (1844–1917) politician and writer, born Paris. Obsessed by anti-Semitism, he founded *La Libre Parole*, 1882; deputy of Algiers, 1898–1902.

DUBOST, HENRI ANTOINE (Antonin): (1844–1921) politician, born L'Arbresle, Rhône. Opponent of the Empire, he became general secretary of the Préfécture de Police when the Empire fell, left Paris by balloon for Tours 1870; was appointed prefect of Orne, 1871; conseiller d'Etat, 1879; deputy 1880–1897; minister of justice under Casimir-Périer, 1893–1894; senator 1897; president of Senate 1906–1920.

DUPUY, CHARLES ALEXANDRE: (1851–1923) politican, born LePuy, Haute-Loire. Opportunist Radical deputy 1885; minister of education under Ribot, 1892; premier,

1893; president of Chamber at the time of Vaillant's anarchistic bombing, 1893; he was premier 1894–1895, when Dreyfus was arrested and condemned, and at the time of the first Dreyfus court martial; when this verdict seemed endangered he formed a cabinet of Republican concentration (1898–1899); senator 1900.

DUVAL, EDGAR RAOUL: (1832–1887) magistrate and politician, born Laon. Deputy 1871, he became one of the Bonapartist party leaders, founded *La Nation*, abstained on May 16, returned to the Chamber in 1884, and rallied to the moderate Republic.

ESTOURNELLES DE CONSTANT, PAUL HENRI BENJAMIN BALLUAT D', Baron de Constant de Rebecque: (1852–1924) diplomat and politician, apostle of international conciliation, born Créans, Sarthe. Deputy 1895; senator 1904; delegate to the Hague Conference 1907; Nobel Peace Prize 1909.

ETIENNE, EUGÈNE: (1844–1921) politician and industrialist, born Oran. Republican deputy of Oran 1881; Subsecretary of state to the minister of marine and colonies, 1887–1892; vice-president of Chamber 1894, 1895, 1902–1904; minister of interior, then war, under Rouvier and Sarrien, 1905–1906; and again minister of war under Briand and Barthou, 1913.

FAGUET, EMILE: (1847–1916) critic and teacher, born La Roche-sur-Yon, professor at La Rochelle, Bordeaux, Sorbonne; Académie française 1900; wrote for *Revue Bleue* from 1892, *Journal des Débats* from 1896, as well as producing some of the most attractive and lucid critical essays of his time.

FALLIÈRES, CLÉMENT ARMAND: (1841–1931) lawyer and politician, born Mézin, Lot-et-Garonne. Deputy of the Republican Left in 1876, he held many ministerial offices, including the premiership for a month in 1883. Senator 1890; president of Senate 1899–1906; president of the Republic, 1906–1913.

FAURE, FRANÇOIS FÉLIX: (1841–1899) merchant and politician, born Paris. Deputy of the Republican Left in 1881; held several ministerial posts before being elected president of the Republic unexpectedly, on the resignation of Casimir-Périer. Involved in Dreyfus Affair, which he wanted to regard as *chose jugée*; died of apoplexy in the company of his mistress.

FAVRE, GABRIEL CLAUDE JULES: (1809–1890) lawyer and politician, born Lyon. Ardent Republican, held office under Second Republic, opposed Empire; defended Orsini 1858; deputy 1863; Académie Française 1868; vice-president of the government of national defense, and foreign minister 1871; negotiated treaty of Frankfurt; senator 1876.

FERRY, JULES FRANÇOIS CAMILLE: (1832–1893) lawyer and statesman, born Saint-Dié, Vosges. Deputy 1869; prefect of Seine for the government of national defense, 1870; he resigned after the Commune. Minister in Athens 1872–1873; deputy 1873, and one of leaders of the Republican party. In office with short interruptions 1879–1885, premier 1880–1881 and 1883–1885, he began the colonial expansion of the Republic, and encouraged the secular organization of French public education. Center of violent polemics, died of effects of a madman's shots.

FOCH, FERDINAND: (1851–1929) soldier, born Tarbes, educated at seminary of Polignan, Jesuit College of St. Etienne, École Polytechnique. Made his reputation teaching in, then commanding, École Supérieure de Guerre; C.G.S. 1917; Chief of Allied Armies fighting in France 1918; marshal of France; British field marshal; Académie Française 1919.

FRANCE, ANATOLE: pseudonym of Jacques Anatole Thibault (1844–1924), novelist, critic, and historian, born Paris. Tremendous reader, writer, ironist, social historian of his time; friend of Jaurès, supporter of socialism, he took sides in all current political issues against intolerance, injustice, demagogy, for freedom of thought and social reform, a possible clash between the two not having at that time been revealed.

GALLIFFET, GASTON ALEXANDRE AUGUSTE, Marquis de, Prince de Martignes: (1830–1909) general, born Paris. Served Crimea 1855; Italy 1859; Algeria 1860; Mexico 1863; France 1870–1871; distinguished himself at Sedan, and in a different manner against the Commune. Retired in 1894, he served as minister of war under Waldeck-Rousseau, 1899–1900.

GAMBETTA, LÉON: (1838–1882) lawyer and politician, born Cahors; opponent of Empire; deputy 1869; minister of interior in government of National Defense, 1870, he led resistance in the provinces, resigned 1871. Reëlected, he became chief leader and orator of the Republican party, president of Chamber 1879, head of an unsuccessful cabinet 1882.

GOBLET, RENÉ: (1828–1905) born Aire-sur-la-Lys, Pas-de-Calais. Contentious politician of the extreme Left. Held a series of ministerial posts throughout the 'eighties, under Brisson, Freycinet, Floquet. Premier 1886–1887, with Boulanger as his minister of war. Senator 1891–1893; deputy 1893–1905.

GOHIER, URBAIN: (1862–1952) journalist and political writer, born Versailles. Started by writing in the conservative press, *Le Soleil*, *Le Figaro;* took the Dreyfus side, wrote for *L'Aurore*, directed *Cri de Paris*, 1905–1906, and *L'Oeuvre*, 1906–1908; broke violently with his *Dreyfusard* friends and became bitter anti-Semite and revolutionary.

GRÉVY, FRANÇOIS PAUL JULES: (1813–1891) lawyer and politician, born Mont-sous-Vaudrey, Jura; deputy 1848; his opposition to Louis-Napoleon kept him out of public affairs until 1868, when he came into his own in the Republican party. President of the National Assembly 1871–1873; of the Chamber 1876–1879; of the Republic 1879; reëlected 1885, had to resign after a scandal, 1887.

GUESDE, JULES: (1845–1922) socialist politician and writer, born Paris. Defended Commune, preached Marxian collectivism, and stood throughout his life for the orthodox doctrine against possibilists, gradualists, and so on. Deputy 1893–1902, 1906–1922.

HABERT, HENRI ERNEST MARCEL: (1862–) lawyer and politician, born Montfort l'Amaury; Boulangist; deputy 1893 and 1912–1924; one of the leaders of the Ligue des Patriotes, shared fate of Déroulèdes whom he joined at St. Sebastian. Delegate-general of the Ligue after his return.

HALÉVY, DANIEL: (1872–) born Paris; son of Ludovic, brother of Elie Halévy; himself an interesting writer and social historian, collaborator and friend of Péguy.

HANOTAUX, ALBERT AUGUSTE GABRIEL: (1853–1944) politician and historian, born Beaurevoir, Aisne; *Maître de conférences* in the Ecole d'Hautes Etudes; Académie française 1897; foreign minister 1894–1898.

HERRIOT, EDOUARD: (1872–1957) politician and scholar, born Troyes, Champagne. Mayor of Lyon, 1910; senator 1912.

HERVÉ, GUSTAVE: (1871–) politician and agitator, born Brest. Progressed from calling for *le drapeau sur le fumier* and being a member of the S.F.I.O. and leader of its antipatriotic and antimilitarist campaigns, to patriotic socialism in 1914, and to *C'est Pétain qu'il nous faut* in 1934.

HUYSMANS, CHARLES MARIE GEORGES: (1848–1907) symbolist novelist and critic, born Paris, converted to Catholicism after 1892.

IZVOLSKY, ALEXANDER PETROVICH: (1856–1919) Russian politician and diplomat, born Moscow. Minister in Belgrade, Munich, Tokyo, Copenhagen; minister of foreign affairs 1906–1910; ambassador in Paris 1910–1917. Owed much to the friendship be-tween his wife and Dowager Empress Maria Feodorovna, but was quite a clever diplo-mat himself. Liquidated the war against Japan; concluded the Anglo-Russian agree-ment but was fooled by Aehrenthal over Bosnia-Herzegovina.

JAMMES, FRANCIS: (1868–1938) poet and novelist, born Tournay, Hautes-Pyrénées. Much of his work is profoundly religious and Catholic.

JAURÈS, AUGUST MARIE JOSEPH JEAN: (1859–1914) Socialist leader and historian, born Castres, Tarn. Brilliant student, teacher, and university lecturer; elected to the Chamber in 1885; he joined the Socialist party in 1890; founded *L'Humanité* with Briand in 1904; became leader of the newly-united S.F.I.O. in 1905; was murdered on July 31, 1914.

JOUVENEL, HENRI DE: (1876–1935) politician, born Paris. Secretary of the com-mittee of Democratic Conferences 1900; chief correspondent of *Le Matin*, deputy 1906; senator 1921.

JOUVENEL, ROBERT DE: (1881–1924) his brother; journalist, editor of *L'Oeuvre*.

LAFARGUE, PAUL: (1842–1911) politician and socialist writer, born Santiago de Cuba; married daughter of Karl Marx; active member of Socialist International, he was forced to live abroad after Commune but returned 1880; friend of Guesde, oppo-nent of Jaurès and reformist Socialists. He and his wife committed suicide by poison.

LAMARZELLE, GUSTAVE LOUIS EDOUARD DE: (1852–1929) politician. Professor of law at the Institut Catholique de Paris; deputy 1885–1893; senator 1894–1923; elo-quent orator of the Catholic Right.

LAVISSE, ERNEST: (1842–1922) historian, born Nouvion-en-Thiérache, Aisne. Pri-vate secretary to Victor Duruy, succeeded Fustel de Coulanges as *maître de conférences* at the École Normale; professor of modern history at the Sorbonne 1883; director of the École Normale, 1904–1919; Académie française 1892; editor of the *Revue de Paris*, 1894. Great teacher, organizer, and academic politician.

LEBLOND, M., *and* A.: pseudonym of Georges Athenas, born Réunion (1877) and Aimé Merlo, born Réunion (1880). Marius and Ary, writers and journalists chiefly interested in colonial and social questions.

LEBRUN, ALBERT: (1871–1950) engineer and politician, born Mercy-le-Haut, Meurthe-et-Moselle; deputy 1900–1920; senator 1920–1932; minister of colonies under Caillaux, Poincaré, and Doumergue, 1911–1914; with a spell as minister of war after Millerand's resignation, 1913. President of the Republic 1932, until he stepped down in 1940 and off the French political scene.

LEMAÎTRE, JULES: (1853–1914) critic and dramatist, born Vennecy, Loiret. Dra-matic critic in *Journal des Débats* and *Revue des Deux Mondes;* Académie française 1896; politically on the Right, his views are given in a volume of lectures, *La Cam-pagne nationaliste* (1902) and in his articles in *L'Echo de Paris*. President of the Ligue de la Patrie Française, he resigned in 1904.

LESSEPS, FERDINAND DE: (1805–1894) diplomat, builder of the Suez Canal, born Versailles. Undertook project of a Panama Canal in 1879, but the company headed by him and his son crashed in great political and financial scandal, 1892.

LIEBKNECHT, KARL: (1871–1919) German socialist, born Leipzig; leader of Left Wing of the Social Democratic party, elected to Prussian Chamber 1908, to Reichs-tag 1912. Refused to vote war credits, violently opposed war, was imprisoned, even-tually murdered together with Rosa Luxemburg after failure of Spartacist rising in postwar Berlin.

LUR-SALUCES, EUGÈNE HENRI MARIE DE: (1852–1922) born Sauternes. Brilliant cavalry officer 1870; resigned 1894 to enter politics in the royalist cause in the southwest. Implicated in a plot, condemned *in absentia* in 1900, to 10 years' banishment, he returned to France 1901, was arrested, tried, banished again; returned under amnesty of 1905 to take up once more his anti-Semitic, royalist, and nationalist political work.

LYAUTEY, LOUIS HUBERT GONZALVE: (1854–1934) marshal of France, born Nancy, Meurthe-et-Moselle; served under Galliéni; pacificator and administrator of Morocco from 1912.

MARITAIN, JACQUES: (1882—) philosopher and theologian, born Paris of a Protestant family; grandson of Jules Favre; married Raïssa Oumançoff 1904; both baptized in Catholic Church 1906; strongly influenced by Bergson, Péguy, Bloy, concentrated his studies on Thomas Aquinas; taught first at the Collège Stanislas and the Institut Catholique de Paris.

MASSIS, HENRI: (1886—) critic and essayist, born Paris. Influenced in turn by Alain, Barrès, Maurras, he collaborated with Alfred de Tarde to produce a sensational series of articles, attacks on a Sorbonne given over to German admirations and German methods (1911); their success was repeated in an influential though restricted inquiry on opinion among the young (1913).

MAUCLAIR, CAMILLE FAUST: (1872—) writer, born Paris. Poet, novelist, critic, art historian, influenced by Mallarmé, Barrès, Maeterlinck. With Lugné Poe, founded the Théâtre de l'Oeuvre, 1893.

MAURRAS, CHARLES: (1868–1952) journalist, critic, deaf and authoritarian leader of the Action française, born Martigues, Provence. Fought through the Dreyfus Affair, converted most of his friends to royalism, set himself to sap the foundations of the Republic by proving it hopeless and absurd.

MÉLINE, FÉLIX JULES: (1838–1925) politician, born Remiremont. Deputy 1872; apostle of protection, both for industry and agriculture, played great part in protectionist legislation of 1890–1902. Minister of agriculture 1883–1885; president of Chamber 1888–1889; premier and minister of agriculture 1896–1898; senator 1903.

MERCIER, AUGUSTE: (1833–1921) general, born Arras; served in Mexico and at Metz. Minister of war under Casimir-Périer and Dupuy, 1893–1895, he was responsible for the trial of Dreyfus in 1894, and always affirmed his guilt; nationalist senator 1900.

MESSIMY, ADOLPHE: (1869–1935) politician, born Lyon. Minister of colonies under Monis 1911; of war under Caillaux 1911, and Viviani 1914; resigned to serve in the war as general of the Reserve.

MICHEL, HENRI: (1857–1904) professor and writer, born Metz; educated Ecole Normale; wrote for *Le Temps;* taught at the Sorbonne.

MILLERAND, ALEXANDRE: (1859–1943) lawyer and politician, born Paris. Radical-Socialist deputy 1885; leader of the Socialist Left and (until 1896) editor of *La Petite République;* minister of commerce under Waldeck-Rousseau; opposed the anticlericalism of Combes; minister of public works under Briand 1909; minister of war under Poincaré 1912; president of the Republic 1920; resigned 1924.

MONIS, ALEXANDRE EMMANUEL ERNEST: (1846–1929) politician, born Chateauneuf, Charente. Moderate Republican deputy 1885–1889, senator 1891–1920; minister of justice under Waldeck-Rousseau 1899; premier 1911; minister of marine 1913.

MUN, ADRIEN ALBERT MARIE, Comte de: (1841–1914), born Lumigny, Seine-et-Marne. Resigned his commission in the army to work for a paternalistic Christian socialism that he preached with great eloquence. Royalist Catholic deputy 1876–1910; he supported Boulanger, rallied to the Republic after the encyclical of 1892 while remaining on the extreme Right. Académie française 1897.

NOAILLES, ANNA ELISABETH DE BRÂNCOVAN, Comtesse de: (1876–1933) French poet, born Paris, of Rumanian father and Greek mother; m. Henri de Noailles 1897. Received much literary recognition during her lifetime; sensuous poetry and reminders of her Byzantine and Rumanian origins make way at times for her great and constant French patriotism.

ORLEANS, LOUIS PHILIPPE ROBERT, Duc d': (1869–1926) eldest son of the Comte de Paris, born Twickenham, educated in France and at Sandhurst. On death of the Comte de Chambord, his father became head of the Bourbons, and pretender to the French throne. Exiled under law of 1886, Philippe tried to perform his military service 1890; was arrested, sentenced, but liberated, having reminded Frenchmen of his existence. Became head of the House 1894; married Archduchess Maria Dorothea Amalia of Austria 1896, with no issue; interested himself in travel and exploration.

PAINLEVÉ, PAUL: (1863–1933) mathematician and politician, born Paris. Professor at Sorbonne; member of Académie des Sciences; entered politics at time of Dreyfus Affair. Elected to the Chamber in 1906 as an Independent Socialist, he took special interest in military and naval questions.

PALÉOLOGUE, MAURICE GEORGES: (1859–1944) diplomat and writer, born Paris. Deputy-director of affairs in the foreign office 1909; director 1911; ambassador to St. Petersburg 1914.

PAU, PAUL MARIE CÉSAR GÉRALD: (1844–1932) general, born Montélimar; lost right hand at Froeschwiller, 1870; good instructor and organizer, he joined the Superior War Council in 1909, and took great part in preparing and putting through the Three-Year Law.

PAUL-BONCOUR, JOSEPH: (1873–) politician, born St. Aignan. Taught in the University, practised at the Paris bar; Independent Socialist deputy 1906; minister of labor under Monis, 1911.

PARIS, LOUIS PHILIPPE ALBERT D'ORLÉANS, Comte de: (1838–1894) son of the Duc d'Orléans, eldest son of king Louis Philippe, born of a Protestant mother. Waived his claims to the throne in favor of the Comte de Chambord, 1873; on the latter's death became undisputed head of the House of Bourbon, 1883. Living mostly in England, he backed Boulanger, but devoted most of his leisure to study.

PÉGUY, CHARLES: (1873–1914) author and poet, born Orléans. Proud of his peasant origins, great lover of France, strong socialist à sa façon, he cut across all party lines in his determination to speak his mind. Founded Les Cahiers de la Quinzaine (1900).

PELLETAN, CHARLES CAMILLE: (1846–1915) writer and politician, born Paris. Son of a republican politician and publicist, member of the government of national defense. Himself trained as archivist and paleographer, became journalist, collaborated with Clemenceau on *La Justice;* Radical Socialist deputy 1881; violently criticized for his work as minister of marine under Combes, 1902–1905; a man of legendary untidiness and enthusiastic prophet of social reform.

PEYTRAL, PAUL LOUIS: (1842–1919) politician, born Marseilles; deputy 1881; senator 1894; specialized in financial questions; minister of finance 1888, 1893, 1898, and 1899.

POINCARÉ, RAYMOND: (1862–1934) born Bar-le-Duc. Successful lawyer in Paris; deputy 1887, made his reputation as financial expert; minister of education 1893; minister of finance under Dupuy, 1894–1895; minister of education under Ribot 1895; vice-president of the Chamber 1895–1897. Minister of finance under Sarrien 1906; Académie française 1909; premier and foreign minister 1912–1913; president of the Republic, 1913–1920.

PRÉVOST, MARCEL: (1862–1941) novelist, born Paris; educated in Jesuit schools and at the École Polytechnique; made his reputation by providing a mixture of morality and sensuality (*Les Demi-Vierges*, 1894); Académie française 1909.

REINACH, JOSEPH (1856–1921) lawyer, author and politician, born Paris. Secretary to Gambetta, harsh opponent of Boulanger; deputy 1889–1898 and again 1906–1914, he championed Dreyfus, later wrote a history of the case.

RENARD, JULES: (1864–1910) novelist, playwright, and essayist, born Chalons, Mayenne. Helped launch the *Mercure de France* (1890); best remembered for his play *Poil de Carotte* (1900); his *Journal* and his letters are important documents for the understanding of his time. Sincere republican and socialist sympathizer, he took part in Nivernais politics, was mayor of Chitry, 1904–1910.

RIBOT, ALEXANDRE FÉLIX JOSEPH: (1842–1923) lawyer and politician, born St. Omer. Deputy 1878–1885, reëlected in 1887; he was the leading moderate Republican opponent of the Radicals and as such fought both Gambetta and Ferry. Foreign minister under Freycinet and Loubet 1890–1892; premier and foreign minister 1892–1893; premier and minister of finance 1895. True to his conservatism, he opposed both Waldeck-Rousseau and Combes on the religious issue. His "cabinets of conciliation" failed, both in 1898 and 1914. Member of the Académie française and the Académie des sciences politiques et morales.

RICHEPIN, JEAN: (1849–1930) poet, novelist, dramatist, born Médéa, Algeria. Bohemian (*La Chanson des gueux*, 1876), notorious in his youth, domesticated into the Académie française 1908; produced skilful, often hollow, rhetoric.

RIVIÈRE, JACQUES: (1886–1925) critic and editor, born Bordeaux; married Alain-Fournier's sister Isabelle 1909, and gave up academic career to bring out, together with Gide, the *Nouvelle Revue Française;* prisoner of war 1914–1918; editor of N.R.F. 1919; died of typhoid fever.

ROUVIER, MAURICE: (1842–1911) born Aix. Gambettist opponent of the Empire; deputy 1871; authority on financial matters. Minister of commerce and colonies under Gambetta 1881; and Ferry 1883–1885; premier and minister of finance 1887; his cabinet fell over Wilson scandal. Minister of finance several times between 1889–1893, driven out of office by Panama scandal, he served again under Combes 1902–1905; and was premier 1905–1906 at the time of Tangier crisis.

SARRAUT, ALBERT PIERRE: (1872–) journalist and politician, born Bordeaux. Took part in local politics as Radical Socialist, and collaborated with his brother Maurice on the *Dépêche de Toulouse*. Undersecretary of state for the interior under Clemenceau, he resigned because he was unwilling to countenance the premier's policy against his wine-growing constituents of Narbonne. Served again as undersecretary of war under Briand; governor-general of Indochina 1911–1914.

SARRIEN, JEAN MARIE FERDINAND: (1840–1915) lawyer and politician, born Bourbon-Lancy. Deputy 1876; held the post office under Brisson 1885; minister of interior under Freycinet 1886; minister of justice under Goblet 1887; minister of interior under Tirard 1887–1888; minister of justice under Brisson 1888; premier 1906, resigned for "reasons of health" to make way for Clemenceau. Senator 1908.

SCHEURER-KESTNER, AUGUSTE: (1833–1899) French-Alsatian politician, born Mulhouse. Alsatian industrialist, he opposed Empire; deputy 1871, he opposed cession of Alsace and Lorraine, resigned, was reëlected, became senator 1875; vice-president of Senate 1896; took initiative of Dreyfus revision. President of the Société chimique de Paris and author of several technical works.

SCHOEN, WILHELM, Freiherr von: German diplomat, born Worms, 1851, died Berchtesgaden 1933. Resigned his commission in the army to enter diplomatic service 1877; minister in Copenhagen 1900; ambassador to St. Petersburg 1906; secretary of state for foreign affairs 1907–1909; ambassador to Paris 1910–1914.

SELVES, JUSTIN GERMAIN CASIMIR DE: (1848–1934) public servant and politician, born Toulouse. Practiced law in Montauban; prefect of Tarn-et-Garonne 1880; of the Oise 1882; Meurthe-et-Moselle 1885; Gironde 1885; director-general of the postal services 1890; succeeded Poubelle as prefect of the Seine 1896–1911; senator 1909; minister of foreign affairs under Caillaux 1911–1912; president of Senate, 1924–1927.

SEMBAT, MARCEL: (1862–1922) born Bonnières, Seine-et-Oise. Socialist deputy 1893; sided first with Blanquist faction led by Vaillant, became one of the party's most popular speakers and leaders.

SYVETON, GABRIEL: (1864–1904) born Boen-sur-Lignon, Loire. Taught history in the provinces, entered politics, founded Ligue de la Patrie française, with Lemaître and Coppée; fiery nationalist deputy of Paris, he provoked several incidents in the Chamber, finally struck the minister of war, General André, during debate on the *affaire des fiches*. On the eve of his trial in connection with this incident, he was found gassed in his study, probably having committed suicide.

TARDIEU, ANDRÉ PIERRE GABRIEL AMÉDÉE: (1876–1945) politician and writer, born Paris. Chef-de-cabinet to Waldeck-Rousseau, 1899–1902; lecturer at the École des Sciences Politiques and the École Supérieure de Guerre; foreign news editor of *Le Temps*, 1902–1914.

THOMAS, ALBERT: (1878–1932) statesman and socialist, born Champigny-sur-Marne, near Paris; assistant editor of *L'Humanité*, 1904; Right-Wing leader in the Conféderation Générale du Travail (C.G.T.); deputy 1910; organizer of munitions production during the war; director of International Labor Office (I.L.O.) after the war.

THOMSON, GASTON ARNOLD MARIE: (1848–1932) politician and industrialist, born Oran; friend of Gambetta; deputy 1877; supporter of Ferry; minister of marine under Rouvier, Sarrien, and Clemenceau, 1905–1909.

TIRPITZ, ALFRED VON: (1849–1930) German admiral, born Kustrin. Secretary of state for naval affairs 1897; admiral 1903; admiral of the fleet 1911; resigned all his offices for political reasons, 1916. He preached and organized the great German naval program before 1914.

VAILLANT, EDOUARD MARIE: (1840–1915) born Vierzon, Cher. Studied science, took part in the socialist opposition to Empire, becoming disciple and friend of Blanqui. Member of Commune, fled to England, became associated with Marx but seceded with a small Blanquist group from First International, 1872. Returned to France under amnesty of 1880, he helped found Socialist Revolutionary party, was elected to the Chamber in 1893. Opposed Boulanger, worked for Socialist unity, became close friend of Jaurès; in 1914 considered that France had been attacked, and came out in favor of national defense.

VANDERVELDE, EMILE: (1866–1938) Belgian socialist politician, born Ixelles, near Brussels. Deputy 1894; leader of the Belgian labor party and political economist.

VERNE, JULES: (1828–1905) immensely popular author, born Nantes. Foresaw the scientific and mechanical developments of the twentieth century. "For the last twenty years," said Marshal Lyautey, "the advance of the peoples is merely living the novels of Jules Verne."

VISCONTI-VENOSTA, EMILIO, Marquis de: (1829–1914) Italian statesman, born Milan; disciple of Mazzini, then of Cavour. Minister of foreign affairs with interruptions 1863–1876, 1896–1898, 1899–1901. Italian delegate to the conference of Algeçiras. A mán of great prudence and prestige.

VIVIANI, RENÉ: (1863–1925) lawyer and politician, born Sidi-bel-Abbès, Algeria. Socialist deputy 1893; first minister of labor under Clemenceau and Briand 1906–1910; minister of education under Doumergue 1913; premier and foreign minister 1914.

WALDECK-ROUSSEAU, PIERRE MARIE RENÉ ERNEST: (1846–1904) lawyer and statesman, born Nantes. Deputy 1879; supporter of Gambetta; minister of interior under Gambetta 1881, and Ferry 1883–1885. Defended de Lesseps 1893; senator 1894; leader of the moderate Republicans. Premier 1899–1902, he quieted the Dreyfus storm, and passed anticlerical measures, especially the bill of 1901 against congregations.

WILSON, SIR HENRY HUGHES: (1864–1922) British soldier, born Edgeworthstown, County Longford, Ireland; educated at Marlborough and Sandhurst. Commandant of the Staff College at Camberley, 1906, he established close relations with the École de Guerre and its commandant, Ferdinand Foch. Director of military operations under the C.I.G.S. 1910; deputy chief of the general staff in France 1914; C.I.G.S. 1918.

ZOLA, ÉMILE EDOUARD CHARLES ANTOINE: (1840–1902) novelist, born Paris. The "naturalistic" style and the subject matter of his work made him a controversial figure. He played an important part in the Dreyfus Affair (*J'Accuse*, 1898; *La Vérité en Marche*, 1899) and his last years were largely taken up with its consequences.

INDEX

INDEX OF PERSONS

(See also Biographical Notes)

Adam, Paul, 42
Agathon (pseudonym of Henri Massis and Alfred de Tarde), 36, 61, 80–81, 107, 108, 109–110, 113, 114, 117
Andler, Charles, 65–66
André, Louis Joseph Nicolas, 23, 27–28, 153
Augagneur, Jean Victor, 141–142
Aulard, François Victor Alphonse, 81, 124, 126

Bainville, Jacques, 56, 89, 105, 127, 135, 138
Barrère, Camille, 27, 34, 85, 88, 101
Barrès, Maurice, 9, 10, 11, 12–13, 22, 25, 55, 61–63, 65, 72, 79, 81, 83, 100, 107, 109, 117, 126–127, 129, 144, 151
Barthélémy, Edmond, 127
Barthou, Jean Louis, 117–118, 125 et seq., 134–135
Bazire, Henri, 76, 82, 83, 96, 105, 106–107, 141
Beauregard, Paul, 100
Benda, Julien, 60, 152
Benjamin, René, 46
Benoist, Charles, 10, 33
Bergeret, Pauline, 150
Bergson, Henri, 80, 160
Bernanos, Georges, 59
Bernstein, Henri, 78
Bert, Paul, 24
Billot, Jean Baptiste, 110
Bocquillon, Emile, 24
Bompard, Maurice, 33
Bonvalot, Gabriel, 113
Boulanger, Georges Ernest Jean Marie, 12–13, 20–21
Bourgeois, Léon Victor Auguste, 140
Bourget, Paul Charles Joseph, 72, 83
Braunschwig, Marcel, 38–39
Briand, Aristide, 46, 55, 100, 112, 115, 125, 144
Brisson, Eugène Henri, 102, 154
Broglie, Jacques Victor Albert de, 19
Brunetière, Ferdinand, 79, 83
Bülow, Bernhard, Prinz von, 26, 33, 41, 85, 86, 88

Cabrières, François Marie Anatole de Rovérie de, 48, 148
Caillaux, Joseph Marie Auguste, 24, 90, 96, 99–100, 112, 127, 129–130, 134–135, 136, 147, 154
Cain, Julien, 37
Cambon, Jules Martin, 96, 101, 115, 123–124, 132, 159
Cambon, Pierre Paul, 26, 32–33, 35–36, 85, 95, 96, 153

Capus, Alfred, 105
Carroll, E. Malcolm, 3, 96
Chamberlain, Joseph, 26
Charmes, Francis, 153
Charmes, François Marie Xavier, 153
Claudel, Paul, 83
Clemenceau, Georges, 26, 30, 48–50, 86, 87, 88, 124, 127, 135, 142
Clermont, Emile, 80
Cocteau, Jean, 25
Combes, Justin Louis Emile, 23, 28, 129, 146
Coppée, François, 83
Cury, Léon, 114

Daudet, Léon, 56, 73
Delcassé, Théophile, 26, 27, 30–31, 33, 34, 85, 94, 98, 140, 144
Demange, Charles Gabriel Edgar, 80
Denais, Joseph, 64, 76, 112
Déroulède, Paul, 5, 33, 61, 86
Deschanel, Paul Eugène Louis, 67, 98, 102, 103, 139
Desjardins, Paul, 98
Deville, Gabriel, 22
Dimier, Louis, 29–30
Doumer, Paul, 36, 39, 41–42, 75, 113, 120, 154
Doumergue, Gaston, 131 et seq.
Dreyfus, Alfred, 22, 62, 66, 68
Dreyfus, Louis, 139
Driant, Emile Auguste Cyprien, 124
Drumont, Edouard Adolphe, 2, 40, 42, 62, 76, 98
Dubost, Henri Antoine (Antonin), 99
Dupuy, Charles Alexandre, 100
Dupuy, Jean, 136
Duval, Edgar Raoul, 20

Estournelles de Constant, Paul Henri Benjamin Balluat d', 31, 41, 124
Etienne, Eugène, 33, 116, 120

Faguet, Emile, 60
Fallières, Clément Armand, 39, 55, 112, 154
Faure, François Félix, 21
Favre, Geneviève, 122
Ferry, Jules François Camille, 12, 15, 19–20
Foch, Ferdinand, 114
Fournier, Henri, 55, 64–65
Fournière, Eugène, 79
France, Anatole (pseudonym of Jacques Anatole Thibault), 41, 72–73
Francois-Ponçet, André, 110

Galli, Henri, 126
Galliffet, Gaston Alexandre Auguste, Marquis de, Prince de Martignes, 24
Gambetta, Léon, 11–12
Gaucher, André, 67–68
Gerard, Auguste, 95
Gide, André, 83, 144
Gillet, Louis, 83
Goblet, René, 27, 29
Goguel, François, 5, 146
Goichon, E., 58–59
Gontard, Paul von, 86
Gooch, G. P., 34
Grévy, François Paul Jules, 19, 20
Grey, Sir Edward, 35, 36
Guasco, J. Raymond, 107
Guesde, Jules, 46, 144

Habert, Henri Ernest Marcel, 81
Halévy, Daniel, 39, 84, 93, 142
Halévy, Elie, 11
Hanotaux, Albert Auguste Gabriel, 26, 127, 135
Hegel, Georg Wilhelm Friedrich, 2
Herriot, Edouard, 109–110, 113, 128
Hervé, Gustave, 38–39, 45–47, 137
House, Colonel Edward Mandell, 143
Hugo, Victor, 154
Huysmans, Charles Marie Georges, 83

Isaac, Jules, 104
Izvolsky, Alexander Petrovich, 88, 112, 132

Jammes, Francis, 83
Jaurès, August Marie Joseph Jean, 22, 38, 45, 47, 48, 77, 89, 94, 104, 115, 124, 130, 138, 139–140, 141, 142, 143–144, 151, 153
Jeanne d'Arc, 69–71
Joffre, Joseph Jacques Césaire, 123
Jouvenel, Henri de, 39
Jouvenel, Robert de, 55, 132, 159
Judet, Ernest, 71, 75, 98, 100, 110, 116, 141–142

Keynes, J. M., 49
Kitchener, Horatio Herbert, 115

Lafargue, Paul, 45
Lamarzelle, Gustave Louis Edouard de, 108
Lamy, Eugène, 132
Lanson, Gustave, 118
Larègle, Comte de, 74
Lauzanne, Stéphane, 85
Lavaud, G. E., 5
Lavisse, Ernest, 36, 41, 97, 117, 132
Leaman, Miss B. R., 8–9
Lebon, André, 15
Lebrun, Albert, 140

Lee, Mrs. Vernon, 98
Lefèvre, André, 147
Lemaître, Jules, 64, 73, 79, 81
Léon, Henri, 154
Liebknecht, Karl, 46
Lippman, Walter, 4
Lotte, Joseph, 80, 83, 122
Louis, Georges, 85, 86
Loyson, Paul-Hyacinthe, 129
Lur-Saluces, Eugène Henri Marie de, 48, 148
Lyautey, Louis Hubert Gonzalve, 94, 108

MacMahon, Marie Edme Patrice Maurice de, Comte, 15
MacMahon, Marquis de, 56
Magallon, Xavier de, 78
Malibran, Ernest de, 59
Maritain, Jacques, 80, 83
Maritain, Raïssa, 80, 83
Martin du Gard, Roger, 117
Massis, Henri, 37, 58, 60–61, 80, 83, 108, 109–110, 122
Mauclair, Camille Faust, 30
Maurras, Charles, 2, 5, 9, 25, 56 *et seq.*, 96, 98, 103, 111–112, 122, 126
Maury, Lucien, 113
Méline, Félix Jules, 12, 21
Mercier, Auguste, 62
Méry, Gaston, 62
Messimy, Adolphe, 97, 141, 142, 154
Mévil, André, 85
Meyer, Albert, 10
Meyer, Arthur, 73–74
Michel, Henri, 86
Michon, Georges, 139
Millerand, Alexandre, 22, 100, 101–102, 110, 111, 120, 121–122, 144, 153
Millevoye, Louis, 100
Monis, Alexandre Emmanuel Ernest, 90, 100
Monod, Gabriel, 1
Mun, Adrien Albert Marie, Comte de, 15–16, 71, 98, 99, 101, 109–110, 111, 133, 138, 140

Nicolson, Sir Arthur, 114
Nintchitch, M., 88
Noel-Baker, Philip, 87

Orleans, Louis Philippe Robert, Duc d', 74
Orsay, Jean d', 36
Orwell, George, 2

Painlevé, Paul, 77
Paléologue, Maurice Georges, 24, 26, 31–32, 104
Passy, Paul, 116–117
Pau, Paul Marie César Gérald, 124
Paul-Boncour, Joseph, 109–110

Péguy, Charles, 31, 64, 80, 83, 121–122, 154
Pelletan, Charles Camille, 22, 47, 49, 51, 90, 98, 125, 130
Peytral, Paul Louis, 140
Pichon, Stephen, 77, 86, 88, 118, 132
Piot, Jean, 136
Piou, Jacques, 8, 134, 139
Poincaré, Raymond, 6, 11, 14, 15–16, 28, 51, 88, 96, 99 *et seq.*, 120, 129, 130, 132, 139, 140, 142, 143, 144
Poncet, Henri, 138–139
Prévost, Marcel, 72–73
Psichari, Ernest, 58–59, 80, 83, 108–109, 110, 122
Pujo, Maurice, 69, 129

Quinton, René, 114

Real del Sarte, Maxime, 69
Reclus, Maurice, 121, 122
Reinach, Joseph, 138
Renan, Joseph Ernest, 83
Renard, Jules, 32, 64
Renouvin, Pierre, 35
Reville, Marc, 77
Revoil, Paul, 32–33, 85
Rey, Etienne, 102
Ribot, Alexandre Félix Joseph, 141, 146
Richepin, Jean, 81
Riou, Gaston, 113
Rivière, Jacques, 64–65, 80
Rochefort, Henri, 22
Rolland, Romain, 5, 110
Romains, Jules, 109–110
Rousseau, Jean Jacques, 109
Rouvier, Maurice, 15, 20, 28, 32–33, 35, 85, 100, 147

Sangnier, Marc, 11
Sarraut, Albert Pierre, 77
Scheurer-Kestner, Auguste, 86
Schiemann, Theodor, 31
Schoen, Wilhelm, Freiherr von, 96, 118
Seignobos, Charles, 15, 22, 25–26, 39
Selves, Justin Germain Casimir de, 96
Sembat, Marcel, 22, 48, 75, 133, 144, 160
Siegfried, André, 5, 13, 21, 100, 105
Simon, Jules, 15
Sonnenburg, Liebermann von, 114
Sorel, Georges, 104, 122
Syveton, Gabriel, 28, 73

Taine, Hippolyte Adolphe, 1
Tarde, Alfred de, 80, 107–108
Tardieu, André Pierre Gabriel Amédée, 35
Téry, Gustave, 136–137
Thalamas, M., 69–71
Thibaudet, Albert, 5
Thomas, Albert, 130
Thomson, David, 38
Thomson, Gaston Arnold Marie, 126
Tirpitz, Alfred von, 35

Vaillant, Edouard Marie, 39, 119
Vandervelde, Emile, 143
Vaugeois, Henri, 25
Visconti-Venosta, Emilio, Marquis de, 35
Viviani, René, 11, 16, 140 *et seq.*
Vogué, Eugène-Melchior de, 56
Vuillaume, Maxime, 102, 133, 142

Waldeck-Rousseau, Pierre Marie René Ernest, 24, 146, 153
Weizsäcker, Conrad von, 93
Wilson, Daniel, 20, 21
Wilson, Sir Henry Hughes, 114

Zola, Emile Edouard Charles Antoine, 63